HEATH
DISCOVERING
FRENCH

PREMIÈRE PARTIE

BLEU

Jean-Paul Valette
Rebecca M. Valette

McDougal Littell
Evanston, Illinois • Boston • Dallas

Teacher Consultants

Sue Arandjelovic, *Dobson High School, Arizona*
Kay Dagg, *Washburn Rural High School, Kansas*
Olga Davis, *G. H. Englesby Junior High School, Massachusetts*
Tina Dietrich, *Washington Junior High School, Ohio*
Rosine Gardner, *Newcomb Central School, New York*
Andrea Henderson, *First Colony Middle School, Texas*
Bill Price, *Day Junior High School, Massachusetts*
T. Jeffrey Richards, *Roosevelt High School, South Dakota*
Margie Ricks, *Dulles High School, Texas*
Valerie Sacks, *Britton Middle School, California*

McDougal Littell wishes to express its heartfelt appreciation to **Gail Smith,** Supervising Editor for *DISCOVERING FRENCH.* Her creativity, organizational skills, determination and sheer hard work have been invaluable in all aspects of the program, including the award winning *DISCOVERING FRENCH* CD-ROM.

Illustrations

Yves Calarnou
Jean-Pierre Foissy
Élisabeth Schlossberg

Printed in the United States of America
International Standard Book Number: 0-618-03500-1

2 3 4 5 6 7 8 9 10 – VHP – 06 05 04 03 02 01 00

Lycée Jean-Baptiste Corot

MERCI

Special thanks to the students and staff of
•**Collège Eugène Delacroix,** *Paris*
•**Lycée Jean-Baptiste Corot,** *Savigny-sur-Orge*
for their cooperation and assistance.

Collège Eugène Delacroix

Contents

UNITÉ 1

Salut Nathalie! Ça va?

Ça va bien! Et toi?

Moi aussi!

 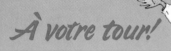

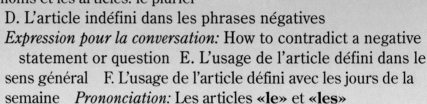

La France de l'an 2000°

France is a country of Western Europe with a population of close to 60 million people. On the map of the world, France may look tiny when compared to such giant countries as the United States, Canada, China, India, Russia or Australia. Yet, in spite of its relatively small size and population, France plays a major role in world affairs. It is a founding member of the United Nations and one of the five permanent members of the Security Council, along with the United States, Great Britain, Russia and China. As such, it must approve and can veto any decision taken by this world organization.

Economically, France is a highly developed nation, and its citizens enjoy one of the highest standards of living in the world. It is a pioneer and leader in many advanced technological and scientific fields, such as pharmaceutical and medical research, aeronautics and space exploration, rapid urban transportation, electronics, software engineering, and telecommunications.

The France of 2000 draws much of its prosperity and vitality from its integration into an economically unified Europe. **The European Union** (or **Union européenne**, as it is called in French), has taken nearly fifty years to build, but now has become a reality for nearly 400 million people. The first steps occurred in the 1950s when the leaders of France and Germany, two countries which had historically been very bitter enemies, decided to form a zone of free exchange between themselves and their immediate neighbors. At first the European Union had only six members, but now it includes fifteen countries of western, northern and southern Europe.

In addition to forming a powerful economic bloc, the creation of the European Union has provided many benefits for the citizens of its member countries and especially for its young people who can study, work and travel in any country of their choice within the Union without needing a passport, visa or permit of any kind. When shopping, they use the euro, the common European currency which has replaced the local currencies since 2002 and has the same value no matter in which country it is earned or spent. The creation of the euro is useful not only for Europeans, but also for the millions of American tourists who visit Europe every year and who no longer have to convert dollars into French francs, francs into German marks, marks into Italian liras, and liras into Spanish pesetas as they travel from country to country.

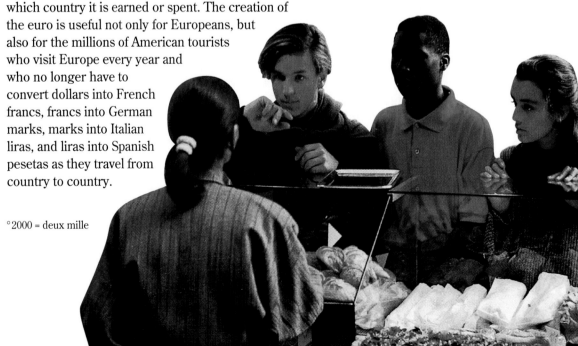

°2000 = deux mille

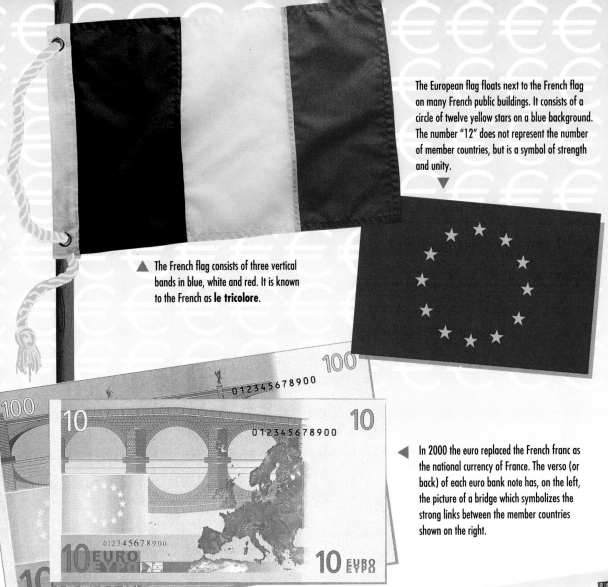

The European flag floats next to the French flag on many French public buildings. It consists of a circle of twelve yellow stars on a blue background. The number "12" does not represent the number of member countries, but is a symbol of strength and unity.

▲ The French flag consists of three vertical bands in blue, white and red. It is known to the French as **le tricolore**.

◀ In 2000 the euro replaced the French franc as the national currency of France. The verso (or back) of each euro bank note has, on the left, the picture of a bridge which symbolizes the strong links between the member countries shown on the right.

 ◀ The euro is divided into 100 **cents** or **centimes**. Its symbol is the capital letter "E" (for **Europa**) formed by a partial circle crossed with two horizontal bars.

THE COUNTRIES OF THE EUROPEAN UNION

ORIGINAL MEMBERS	NEW MEMBERS	
Belgium	Austria	Ireland
France	Denmark*	Portugal
Germany	Finland	Spain
Italy	Great Britain*	Sweden*
Luxembourg	Greece*	
Netherlands		

In 1999, all of the above countries voted to use the euro as their national currency, except for the four marked with an asterisk (*).

▲ The first French stamp celebrating the euro and denominated in both the new currency (0,46 euro) and the old currency (3,00 francs).

Parlons français!

The people portrayed on these pages represent many different backgrounds. Some live in France, some in the United States. They are from Europe, Africa, Asia, and North America. They do, however, have one thing in common. They all speak French. Let's meet them.

1
Sophie Lafont, 14, is from Toulouse, a city in southern France. She is a student at the Lycée Saint-Exupéry. (A **lycée** is the equivalent of an American high school.)

2
Philippe Martin, 15, lives in Paris and goes to the Collège Eugène Delacroix.

3
Stéphanie Malle, 14, also lives in Paris and attends the Collège Eugène Delacroix. Her family is from Martinique, a French island in the Caribbean.

4
Ahmed Belkacem, 14, lives in Lyon, France, and goes to the Lycée Jean Moulin. His parents are from Algeria and speak French and Arabic. Ahmed, who was born in France, speaks only French.

5
Fredy Vansattel, 20, lives near Lausanne, a city in French-speaking Switzerland. He is a student at the well-known École Hôtelière. In addition to French, Fredy also speaks English and German.

6
Prak Maph, 15, left Cambodia with his family when he was four. He lives in Paris and goes to the Lycée Claude Monet. Maph speaks French as well as Khmer, the national language of Cambodia.

7

Amélan Konan, 13, lives in Abidjan, a large city in Ivory Coast, a country of West Africa. Amélan goes to the Collège Moderne Voltaire, where many of the teachers are from France. Amélan is fluent in both French and Baoulé, the tribal language that she speaks with her relatives.

8

Pauline Lévêque, 14, is from Quebec City in the province of Quebec, in Canada. Pauline goes to the École Louis-Jolliet. She speaks both French and English, but she prefers to speak French with her friends and family.

9

Moustapha Badid is a French athlete of North African origin who lives in Paris. At age 23, he won the wheelchair title at the Boston Marathon and established a world record in the event. In that same year, he also won an Olympic gold medal. He speaks French, Arabic, and some English.

10

Dr. Michèle Klopner, a clinical psychologist, grew up in Haiti, where her family resides. She came to the United States to study at the University of Michigan and Rutgers University. Dr. Klopner speaks French, Haitian Creole, and English. She uses all these languages in her work at the Cambridge Hospital in Cambridge, Massachusetts.

11

Marie-Christine Mouis was born in Canada of a French father and a Canadian mother. At the age of 16, Marie-Christine joined the Paris Opera Ballet, becoming the youngest dancer in the world's oldest ballet company. She was the principal ballerina of the Boston Ballet for ten years.

12

Dr. Larry Phan was born in Vietnam. At the age of ten, he went to France, where he received his high school education. In 1976, he came to the United States to pursue a medical career. He attended the University of California and Tufts School of Dental Medicine. Dr. Phan is on the staff of the Children's Hospital in Boston.

ACTIVITÉS CULTURELLES

1. On a world map or globe, locate the cities and countries of origin for each of the people pictured.
2. Do you know any people in your community who have French names or people who speak French? Where are their families originally from?

Bonjour, le monde français!

*I*n today's world, French is an international language spoken daily by more than 100 million people. French is understood by another 100 million in many countries and regions of the globe.

IN NORTH AMERICA

■ In Canada, about one third of the population speaks French. These French speakers live mainly in the province of Quebec **(le Québec)**. They are descendants of French settlers who came to Canada in the 17th and 18th centuries.

■ In the United States, French is understood and spoken in many families whose French and French-Canadian ancestors came to Louisiana **(la Louisiane)** and New England **(la Nouvelle-Angleterre)** at various times in our history.

■ In the Caribbean, French and Creole are spoken in the Republic of Haiti **(Haïti)**. French is also spoken on the islands of Martinique **(la Martinique)** and Guadeloupe **(la Guadeloupe)**; the inhabitants of these two islands are French citizens.

IN OTHER PARTS OF THE WORLD

■ French is spoken as far away as Tahiti **(Tahiti)** and New Caledonia **(la Nouvelle-Calédonie)**, two French territories in the South Pacific.

■ In the Middle East, French is still taught and spoken in Lebanon **(le Liban)**.

■ French is also used and understood by many Vietnamese and Cambodian families who have left their countries **(le Viêt-nam, le Cambodge)** to settle in other parts of the world.

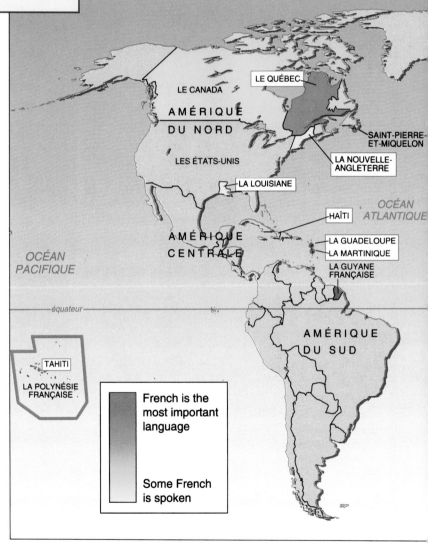

LE QUÉBEC

LE CANADA

AMÉRIQUE DU NORD

LES ÉTATS-UNIS

SAINT-PIERRE-ET-MIQUELON

LA NOUVELLE-ANGLETERRE

LA LOUISIANE

HAÏTI

OCÉAN ATLANTIQUE

AMÉRIQUE CENTRALE

LA GUADELOUPE
LA MARTINIQUE
LA GUYANE FRANÇAISE

OCÉAN PACIFIQUE

équateur

AMÉRIQUE DU SUD

TAHITI

LA POLYNÉSIE FRANÇAISE

French is the most important language

Some French is spoken

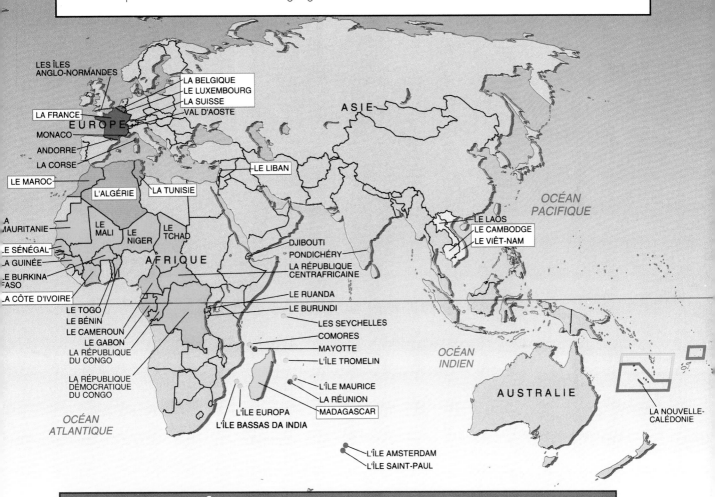

IN EUROPE

French is not only spoken in France **(la France)** but also in parts of Belgium **(la Belgique)**, Switzerland **(la Suisse)**, and Luxembourg **(le Luxembourg)**.

IN AFRICA

French is an important language in countries which have strong commercial and cultural ties to France.

■ In Western and Central Africa, about 20 countries have adapted French as their official language.

These countries include Senegal **(le Sénégal)**, the Ivory Coast **(la Côte d'Ivoire)**, and the Democratic Republic of Congo **(la République démocratique du Congo)**. French is also spoken on the large island of Madagascar **(Madagascar)**.

■ In North Africa, French is understood and spoken by many people of Algeria **(l'Algérie)**, Morocco **(le Maroc)**, and Tunisia **(la Tunisie)**. More than two million people from these countries have emigrated to France and have become French citizens.

ACTIVITÉS CULTURELLES

1. Name at least six African countries where French is spoken. Find out the capital of each country. (Source: atlas, encyclopedia)
2. Collect clippings from newspapers and magazines in which a French-speaking country is mentioned. Try to find one clipping for each of the areas on the map.

NOTE: You may also wish to refer to the reference map of the French-speaking world on pages R2–R3.

Bonjour, la France!

L'ANGLETERRE

LA BELGIQUE

la Manche

Lille

LE LUXEMBOURG

L'ALLEMAGNE

Rouen

LA NORMANDIE

Paris

Strasbourg

la Seine

L'ALSACE

LA BRETAGNE

l'océan Atlantique

Nantes

Tours

LA TOURAINE

la Loire

LA SUISSE

LA FRANCE

Lyon

Château d'Azay-le-Rideau, Touraine

Grenoble

le Rhône

L'ITALIE

Bordeaux

les Alpes

la Garonne

aerospatiale

LA PROVENCE

Nice

MONACO

Toulouse

Marseille

Toulon

les Pyrénées

la Méditerranée

LA CORSE

L'ESPAGNE

Les Pyrénées

Eguisheim, Alsace

Les Alpes, Chamonix

Menton, Côte d'Azur

*B*efore starting your study of French, you may be interested in learning a few facts about France.

■ In area, France is the second-largest country in Western Europe.

■ Economically, France is one of the most developed countries of the world with a sophisticated high-tech industry.

■ France is the only European country with a space exploration program. French communication satellites provide 400 million Europeans with direct TV transmission.

■ France is a country with a strong cultural tradition. French philosophers, writers, and artists have influenced our ways of thinking and looking at the world.

■ France has a long history reaching back through Roman times into distant prehistory.

■ Geographically, France is a very diversified country with the highest mountains in Europe **(les Alpes et les Pyrénées)** and an extensive coastline along the Atlantic **(l'océan Atlantique)** and the Mediterranean **(la Méditerranée)**.

■ France consists of many different regions which have maintained their traditions, their culture, and—in some cases—their own language. Some of the traditional provinces are Normandy and Brittany **(la Normandie et la Bretagne)** in the west, Alsace **(l'Alsace)** in the east, Touraine **(la Touraine)** in the center, and Provence **(la Provence)** in the south.

ACTIVITÉS CULTURELLES

1. Find the countries which have a common border with France. What are their capitals? (Source: atlas, encyclopedia)
2. Imagine that you are spending a year in France. Where would you go if you wanted to ski in the winter? Which provinces would you want to visit in the summer if you wanted to swim in the Atlantic? in the Mediterranean? Are there any particular parts of France you would like to explore?

NOTE: You may also wish to refer to the reference map of France on page R4.

Bonjour! Je m'appelle ...

Here is a list of some traditional French names. As you begin your study of the French language, you may want to "adopt" a French name from the list.

Alain	Geoffroy	Mathieu
Albert	Georges	Michel
André	Grégoire	Nicolas
Antoine	Guillaume	Olivier
Bernard	Henri	Patrick
Bertrand	Jacques	Paul
Charles	Jean	Philippe
Christophe	Jean-Claude	Pierre
Daniel	Jean-François	Raoul
David	Jean-Louis	Raymond
Denis	Jean-Paul	Richard
Dominique	Jérôme	Robert
Édouard	Joseph	Roger
Éric	Julien	Samuel
Étienne	Laurent	Simon
François	Marc	Thomas
Frédéric		

Sylvie

Alice

Alain

Jean-Paul

Éric

Laure

Olivier

Alice
Andrée
Anne
Anne-Marie
Barbara
Béatrice
Brigitte
Caroline
Catherine
Cécile
Charlotte
Christine
Claire
Corinne
Delphine
Denise
Diane
Dominique

Éléonore
Élisabeth
Émilie
Florence
Françoise
Hélène
Isabelle
Jeanne
Judith
Juliette
Karine
Laure
Lise
Louise
Lucie
Marguerite
Marie
Marie-Christine

Marthe
Michèle
Monique
Nathalie
Nicole
Patricia
Pauline
Rachel
Renée
Rose
Sophie
Stéphanie
Suzanne
Sylvie
Thérèse
Véronique
Virginie

Jean?   *Guillaume?*   *Georges?*
Henri?   *Philippe?*   *François?*
Jacques?   *Charles?*   *Michel?*
Sébastien?   *Gérard?*   *Paul?*
Jean-Paul?   *Pierre?*   *Marc?*
Lucien?   *Jean-Pierre?*   *Luc?*
    André?

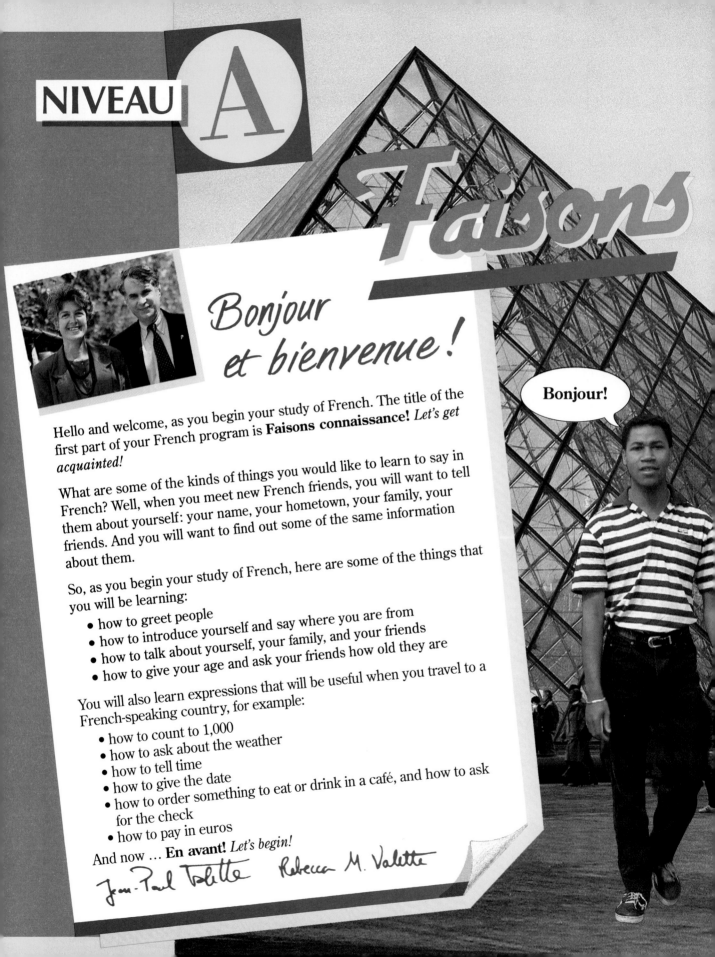

NIVEAU A

Faisons

Bonjour et bienvenue!

Bonjour!

Hello and welcome, as you begin your study of French. The title of the first part of your French program is **Faisons connaissance!** *Let's get acquainted!*

What are some of the kinds of things you would like to learn to say in French? Well, when you meet new French friends, you will want to tell them about yourself: your name, your hometown, your family, your friends. And you will want to find out some of the same information about them.

So, as you begin your study of French, here are some of the things that you will be learning:

- how to greet people
- how to introduce yourself and say where you are from
- how to talk about yourself, your family, and your friends
- how to give your age and ask your friends how old they are

You will also learn expressions that will be useful when you travel to a French-speaking country, for example:

- how to count to 1,000
- how to ask about the weather
- how to tell time
- how to give the date
- how to order something to eat or drink in a café, and how to ask for the check
- how to pay in euros

And now … **En avant!** *Let's begin!*

Jean-Paul Valette   Rebecca M. Valette

INTRODUCTION
culturelle

Salutations *(Greetings)*

How do you greet people in the United States? You may nod or smile. With adults, you may shake hands when you are introduced for the first time.

In France, people shake hands with friends and acquaintances each time they see one another, and not only to say hello but also when they say good-bye. Among teenagers, boys shake hands with boys. Girls kiss each other on the cheeks two or three times. (This is called **une bise**). Boys and girls who are close friends also greet each other with **une bise.**

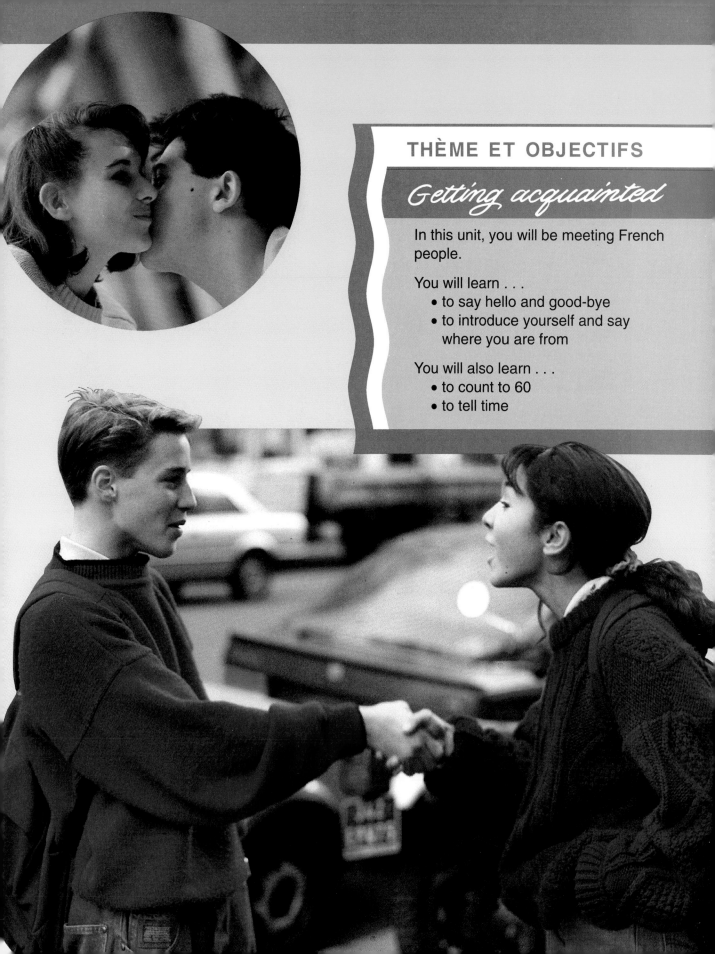

THÈME ET OBJECTIFS

Getting acquainted

In this unit, you will be meeting French people.

You will learn . . .
- to say hello and good-bye
- to introduce yourself and say where you are from

You will also learn . . .
- to count to 60
- to tell time

La rentrée

This is the first day of school. Students are greeting their friends and meeting new classmates.

Bonjour! Je m'appelle Philippe.

Et moi, je m'appelle Stéphanie.

«
—Bonjour! Je m'appelle Philippe.
—Et moi, je m'appelle Stéphanie. »

Je m'appelle Marc. Et toi?

Moi, je m'appelle Isabelle.

Comment t'appelles-tu?

Je m'appelle Nathalie.

«
—Je m'appelle Marc. Et toi?
—Moi, je m'appelle Isabelle. »

«
—Comment t'appelles-tu?
—Je m'appelle Nathalie.
—Bonjour.
—Bonjour. »

POUR COMMUNIQUER

Bonjour!

How to say hello:

Bonjour!   *Hello!*   —**Bonjour,** Nathalie!
      —**Bonjour,** Jean-Paul!

How to ask a classmate's name:

Comment t'appelles-tu?   *What's your name?*   —**Comment t'appelles-tu?**
Je m'appelle . . .   *My name is . . .*   —**Je m'appelle** Stéphanie.

OTHER EXPRESSIONS

moi   *me*   **Moi,** je m'appelle Marc.
et toi?   *and you?*   **Et toi,** comment t'appelles-tu?

■ NOTES ■ CULTURELLES

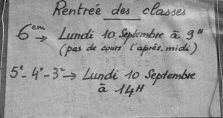

Rentrée des classes
6ᵉᵐ → Lundi 10 Septembre à 9ᴴ
(pas de cours l'après-midi)
5ᵉ-4ᵉ-3ᵉ → Lundi 10 Septembre à 14ᴴ

1 La rentrée *(Back to school)*

French and American students have about the same number of days of summer vacation. In France, summer vacation usually begins at the end of June and classes resume in early September. The first day back to school in fall is called **la rentrée.**

2 Les prénoms français
(French first names)

Many traditional French names have corresponding equivalents in English.

For boys:
Jean *(John)*
Pierre *(Peter)*
Marc *(Mark)*
Philippe *(Philip)*
Nicolas *(Nicholas)*

For girls:
Marie *(Mary)*
Monique *(Monica)*
Cécile *(Cecilia)*
Alice
Caroline

Often the names **Jean** and **Marie** are combined in double names such as **Jean-Paul** and **Marie-Christine.** In recent years, names of foreign origin, like **Dimitri** and **Karine,** have become quite popular.

Bonjour!
Je m'appelle Astérix.

1 **Bonjour!**

Say hello to the student nearest to you.

▶

Bonjour!

Bonjour!

Bonjour!

2 **Je m'appelle . . .**

Introduce yourself to your classmates.

▶ Je m'appelle (Paul).
▶ Je m'appelle (Denise).

3 **Et toi?**

Ask a classmate his or her name.

▶ —Comment t'appelles-tu?
—Je m'appelle (Christine).

4 **Bonjour, les amis!** *(Hello everyone!)*

Say hello to the following students.

▶ Bonjour, Marc!

Juliette

Jean-Paul

Isabelle

Marc

Stéphanie

Nathalie

Philippe

François

L'alphabet

A B C D E F G H I J K L
a bé cé dé e effe gé hache i ji ka elle

Les signes orthographiques *(Spelling marks)*

French uses accents and spelling marks that do not exist in English. These marks are part of the spelling and cannot be left out.

In French, there are four accents that may appear on vowels.

´	**l'accent aigu** *(acute accent)*	C**é**cile, St**é**phanie
`	**l'accent grave** *(grave accent)*	Mich**è**le, Hél**è**ne
^	**l'accent circonflexe** *(circumflex)*	Jér**ô**me
¨	**le tréma** *(diaeresis)*	No**ë**l, Jo**ë**lle

There is only one spelling mark used with a consonant. It occurs under the letter "**c**."

¸	**la cédille** *(cedilla)*	Fran**ç**ois

5 La rentrée

It is the first day of class. The following students are introducing themselves. Act out the dialogues with your classmates.

▶ Hélène et Philippe

Moi, je m'appelle Philippe.

Je m'appelle Hélène. Et toi?

1. Stéphanie et Marc
2. Cécile et Frédéric
3. Michèle et François
4. Béatrice et Joël
5. Céline et Jérôme

Les nombres de 0 à 10

0 zéro	**1** un	**2** deux	**3** trois
4 quatre	**5** cinq	**6** six	**7** sept
8 huit	**9** neuf	**10** dix	

6 Numéros de téléphone

Imagine you are visiting a family in Quebec. Give them your American phone number in French.

▶ 617-963-4028   six, un, sept — neuf, six, trois — quatre, zéro, deux, huit

M	**N**	**O**	**P**	**Q**	**R**	**S**	**T**	**U**	**V**	**W**	**X**	**Y**	**Z**
emme	enne	o	pé	ku	erre	esse	té	u	vé	double vé	ixe	i grec	zède

2

Tu es français?

It is the opening day of school and several of the students meet in the cafeteria (**la cantine**) at lunchtime. Marc discovers that not everyone is French.

Tu es français?

Oui, je suis français.

MARC: Tu es français?
JEAN-PAUL: Oui, je suis français.

MARC: Et toi, Patrick, tu es français aussi?
PATRICK: Non! Je suis américain. Je suis de Boston.

Non! Je suis américain.

MARC: Et toi, Stéphanie, tu es française ou américaine?
STÉPHANIE: Je suis française.
MARC: Tu es de Paris?
STÉPHANIE: Non, je suis de Fort-de-France.
MARC: Tu as de la chance!

Je suis française.

MARC: Are you French?
JEAN-PAUL: Yes, I'm French.

MARC: And you, Patrick, are you French too?
PATRICK: No! I'm American. I'm from Boston.

MARC: And you, Stéphanie, are you French or American?
STÉPHANIE: I'm French.
MARC: Are you from Paris?
STÉPHANIE: No, I'm from Fort-de-France.
MARC: You're lucky!

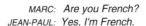

POUR
COMMUNIQUER

Tu es de Denver?

How to talk about where people are from:

Tu es de ...?	*Are you from . . . ?*	—**Tu es de** Denver?
Je suis de ...	*I'm from . . .*	—Non, **je suis de** Dallas.

How to talk about one's nationality:

Tu es ...?	*Are you . . . ?*	—Pierre, **tu es** français?
Je suis ...	*I am . . .*	—Oui, **je suis** français.

Les nationalités		
français	**française**
anglais	**anglaise**
américain	**américaine**
canadien	**canadienne**

OTHER EXPRESSIONS

oui	*yes*	Tu es français? **Oui,** je suis français.
non	*no*	Tu es canadien? **Non,** je suis américain.
et	*and*	Je suis de Paris. **Et** toi?
ou	*or*	Tu es français **ou** canadien?
aussi	*also, too*	Moi **aussi,** je suis française.

■ **NOTE** ■
CULTURELLE

LA MARTINIQUE

Fort-de-France et la Martinique

Fort-de-France is the capital of Martinique, a small French island in the Caribbean. Because Martinique is part of the French national territory, its inhabitants are French citizens. Most of them are of African origin. They speak French as well as a dialect called **créole.**

Martinique is also known as the Island of the Flowers (**l'Île aux Fleurs**) because of its warm tropical climate and magnificent vegetation. In the winter months, it attracts thousands of European and American tourists.

B A L A T A
jardin botanique

Petit commentaire

*The Statue of Liberty (**la statue de la Liberté**) was a gift to the United States from the French people on the occasion of the 100th anniversary of American independence. The Eiffel Tower (**la tour Eiffel**) was built to celebrate the 100th anniversary of the French Revolution.*

français, française

Names of nationalities may have two different forms, depending on whom they refer to:

	MASCULINE	FEMININE
Je suis . . . **Tu es . . . ?**	 français américain	française américaine

➡ Note that in written French the feminine forms always end in **-e.**

---

1 Et toi?

Give your name, your nationality, and your city of origin.

Bonjour!
Je m'appelle Bob Jones.
Je suis américain.
Je suis de Providence.

Bonjour!
Je m'appelle Linda Carlson.
Je suis américaine.
Je suis de Boston.

2 Français ou française?

You meet the following young people. Ask them if they are French. A classmate will answer you, as in the model. (Be sure to use **français** with boys and **française** with girls.)

▶ — Sophie, tu es française?
— Oui, je suis française. Je suis de Strasbourg.

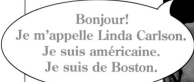

3 **Quelle nationalité?** *(Which nationality?)*

Greet the following young people and find out each one's nationality. A classmate will answer you, according to the model.

▶ —Bonjour, Marc. Tu es canadien?
—Oui, je suis canadien. Je suis de Montréal.

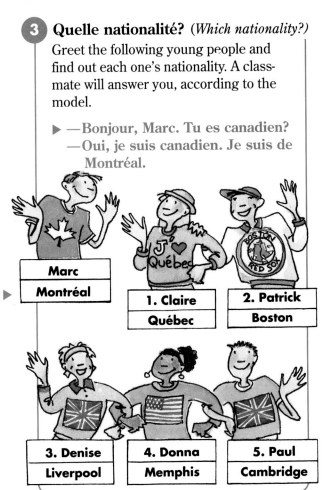

| Marc |
| Montréal |

| 1. Claire |
| Québec |

| 2. Patrick |
| Boston |

| 3. Denise |
| Liverpool |

| 4. Donna |
| Memphis |

| 5. Paul |
| Cambridge |

Les nombres de 10 à 20

10 dix	**11** onze	**12** douze
13 treize	**14** quatorze	**15** quinze
16 seize	**17** dix-sept	**18** dix-huit
19 dix-neuf	**20** vingt	

4 **La fusée Ariane**
(The Ariane rocket)

Give the countdown for the lift-off of the French rocket Ariane, from 20 to 0.

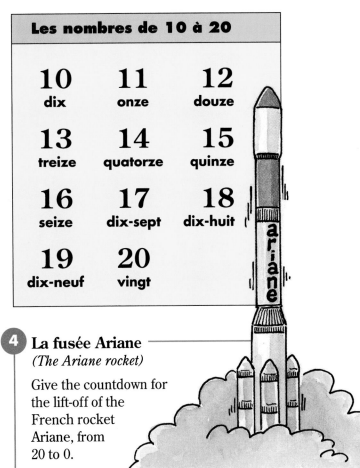

Prononciation

Les lettres muettes *(Silent letters)*

Paris

In French, the last letter of a word is often not pronounced.

- Final "**e**" is always silent.
  Répétez: **Sophie Philippe Stéphanie anglaise française onze douze treize quatorze quinze seize**

- Final "**s**" is almost always silent.
  Répétez: **Paris Nicolas Jacques anglais français trois**

- The letter "**h**" is always silent.
  Répétez: **Hélène Henri Thomas Nathalie Catherine**

LEÇON 3

Salut! Ça va?

On the way to school, François meets his friends.

Salut, Isabelle!

Salut! Ça va?

Ça va! Merci!

Salut, Nathalie! Ça va?

Ça va bien! Et toi?

Moi aussi!

Ça va, Philippe?

Ah non! Zut! Ça va mal.

François also meets his teachers.

Bonjour, monsieur.

Bonjour, François.

Bonjour, madame.

Bonjour, François.

Bonjour, mademoiselle.

Bonjour, François.

Monsieur Masson **Madame Chollet** **Mademoiselle Lacour**

After class, François says good-bye to his teacher and his friends.

Au revoir, mademoiselle.

Au revoir, François.

Au revoir, Nathalie.

Au revoir, François.

POUR COMMUNIQUER

How to greet a friend or classmate:

Salut!   *Hi!*

How to greet a teacher or another adult:

Bonjour!   *Hello!*   **Bonjour, monsieur.**
                              Bonjour, madame.
                              Bonjour, mademoiselle.

How to say good-bye:

Au revoir!   *Good-bye!*   **Au revoir, Philippe.**
                                  Au revoir, monsieur.

➡ In written French, the following abbreviations are commonly used:

M. Masson	Monsieur Masson
Mme Chollet	Madame Chollet
Mlle Lacour	Mademoiselle Lacour

➡ Young people often use **Salut!** to say good-bye to each other.

■ NOTE ■ CULTURELLE

Bonjour ou Salut?

French young people may greet one another with **Bonjour,** but they often prefer the less formal **Salut.** When they meet their teachers, however, they always use **Bonjour.** French young people are generally much more formal with adults than with their friends. This is especially true in their relationships with teachers, whom they treat with great respect.

Have you noticed that in France adults are addressed as **monsieur, madame,** or **mademoiselle?** The last name is almost never used in greeting people.

1 Bonjour ou salut?

You are enrolled in a French school.
Greet your friends and teachers.

▶ Salut, Sophie!

▶ Bonjour, mademoiselle!

Sophie

Mademoiselle Pinot

1. Anne

2. Monsieur Masson

3. Nathalie

4. Marc

5. Madame Albert

6. Mademoiselle Boucher

POUR *COMMUNIQUER*

How to ask people how they feel:

—**Ça va?** *How are you? How are things going? How's everything?*
—**Ça va!** *(I'm) fine. (I'm) okay. Everything's all right.*

Ça va . . . **très bien** **bien** **comme ci, comme ça** **mal** **très mal**

How to express one's feelings of frustration and appreciation:

Zut! *Darn!* **Zut!** Ça va mal! **Merci!** *Thanks!* Ça va, **merci.**

➡ **Ça va?** *(How are you?)* is an informal greeting that corresponds to the following expressions:

    Comment vas-tu? (when addressing a friend)
      Bonjour, Paul. Comment vas-tu?
    Comment allez-vous? (when addressing an adult)
      Bonjour, madame. Comment allez-vous?

2 Dialogue

Exchange greetings with your classmates and ask how they are doing.

▶ —Salut, (Thomas)! Ça va?
  —Ça va! Et toi?
  —Ça va bien. Merci.

3 Situations

Sometimes we feel good and sometimes we don't. How would you respond in the following situations?

▶ You have the flu.
—Ça va?
—Ça va mal!

1. You just received an "A" in French.
2. You lost your wallet.
3. Your uncle gave you five dollars.
4. Your grandparents sent you a check for 100 dollars.
5. You bent the front wheel of your bicycle.
6. Your parents bought you a new bicycle.
7. Your little brother broke your walkman.
8. It's your birthday.
9. You have a headache.
10. You just had an argument with your best friend.
11. Your favorite baseball team has just lost a game.
12. Your French teacher has just canceled a quiz.

Les nombres de 20 à 60

20 vingt	**30** trente	**40** quarante
vingt et un	trente et un	quarante et un
vingt-deux	trente-deux	quarante-deux
vingt-trois	trente-trois	quarante-trois
. . .	. . .	. . .
vingt-neuf	trente-neuf	quarante-neuf

50 cinquante	**60** soixante
cinquante et un	
cinquante-deux	
cinquante-trois	
. . .	
cinquante-neuf	

➡ Note the use of **et** in numbers with **un**:
vingt et un.

---

5 Loto

Read out loud the numbers on the French Loto tickets.

---

4 Ça va?

How would the following people answer the question **Ça va?**

Prononciation

Les consonnes finales
(Final consonants)

1 2 3
un deux trois

In French, the last consonant of a word is often not pronounced.

• Remember: Final "**s**" is usually silent.
  Répétez: **trois   français   anglais**

• Most other final consonants are usually silent.
  Répétez: **Richard   Albert   Robert   salut**
  américain   canadien   bien   deux

EXCEPTION: The following final consonants are usually pronounced: "**c**," "**f**," "**l**," and sometimes "**r**."

Répétez: **Éric   Daniel   Lebeuf   Pascal   Victor**

However, the ending **-er** is usually pronounced /e/.

Répétez: **Roger   Olivier**

▶▶▶▶▶▶▶▶▶▶▶▶▶▶▶▶▶▶▶▶▶▶▶

L'heure

A. Un rendez-vous

Jean-Paul and Stéphanie are sitting in a café.
Stéphanie seems to be in a hurry to leave.

STÉPHANIE: Quelle heure est-il?
JEAN-PAUL: Il est trois heures.
STÉPHANIE: Trois heures?
JEAN-PAUL: Oui, trois heures.
STÉPHANIE: Oh là là. J'ai un rendez-vous
avec David dans vingt minutes.
Au revoir, Jean-Paul.
JEAN-PAUL: Au revoir, Stéphanie. À bientôt!

STÉPHANIE: *What time is it?*
JEAN-PAUL: *It's three o'clock.*
STÉPHANIE: *Three o'clock?*
JEAN-PAUL: *Yes, three o'clock.*
STÉPHANIE: *Uh, oh! I have a date with David in
twenty minutes. Good-bye, Jean-Paul.*
JEAN-PAUL: *Good-bye, Stéphanie. See you soon!*

POUR
COMMUNIQUER

How to talk about the time:

Il est huit heures!

Quelle heure est-il?   *What time is it?*
Il est ...   *It's ...*

une heure	**deux heures**	**trois heures**	**quatre heures**	**cinq heures**	**six heures**

sept heures	**huit heures**	**neuf heures**	**dix heures**	**onze heures**	**midi**	**minuit**

1 Quelle heure est-il?

Ask your classmates what time it is.

▶

2 L'heure d'été *(Daylight savings time)*

Philippe forgot to set his watch ahead for daylight savings time, so he is an hour off. Isabelle gives him the correct time.

▶ PHILIPPE: **Il est sept heures.**
　ISABELLE: **Mais non, il est huit heures!**

▶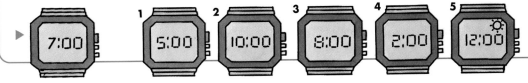

➡ Although *o'clock* may be left out in English, the expression **heure(s)** must be used in French when giving the time.

　　It's ten. (It's ten o'clock.)　**Il est dix heures.**

➡ To distinguish between A.M. and P.M., the French use the following expressions:

du matin	*in the morning*	Il est dix heures **du matin.**
de l'après-midi	*in the afternoon*	Il est deux heures **de l'après-midi.**
du soir	*in the evening*	Il est huit heures **du soir.**

NOTE DE PRONONCIATION: In telling time, the NUMBER and the word **heure(s)** are linked together. Remember, in French the letter "**h**" is always silent.

une heure　　deux heures　　trois heures　　quatre heures　　cinq heures　　six heures

sept heures　huit heures　　neuf heures　　dix heures　　　onze heures

B. À quelle heure est le film?

Stéphanie and David have decided to go to a movie.

STÉPHANIE: Quelle heure est-il?
DAVID: Il est trois heures et demie.
STÉPHANIE: Et à quelle heure est le film?
DAVID: À quatre heures et quart.
STÉPHANIE: Ça va. Nous avons le temps.

STÉPHANIE: *What time is it?*
DAVID: *It's three-thirty (half past three).*
STÉPHANIE: *And at what time is the movie?*
DAVID: *At four-fifteen (quarter past four).*
STÉPHANIE: *That's okay. We have time.*

POUR COMMUNIQUER

À quelle heure est le dîner?

How to ask at what time something is scheduled:

À quelle heure est ...?   *At what time is ... ?*
—**À quelle heure est le concert?**   *At what time is the concert?*
—**Le concert est à huit heures.**   *The concert is at eight.*

How to say that you have an appointment or a date:

J'ai un rendez-vous à ...   *I have an appointment*   **J'ai un rendez-vous à**
                              (a date) at . . .   deux heures.

How to indicate the minutes:

Il est ...   dix heures   six heures   sept heures   deux heures
                   dix   vingt-cinq   trente-cinq   cinquante-deux

How to indicate the half hour and the quarter hours:

 **et quart**    **et demie**   moins le quart

 Il est une heure **et quart.**   Il est deux heures **et demie.**   Il est trois heures **moins le quart.**

3 L'heure

Give the times according to the clocks.

▶ **Il est une heure et quart.**

4 À quelle heure?

Ask your classmates at what time certain activities are scheduled. They will answer according to the information below.

▶ 8 h 50   le film

—À quelle heure est le film?
—Le film est à huit heures cinquante.

1. 7 h 15 le concert
2. 2 h 30 le match de football *(soccer)*
3. 3 h 45 le match de tennis
4. 5 h 10 le récital
5. 7 h 45 le dîner

M'O Musée d'Orsay
Festival de cinéma
12h15

5 Rendez-vous

Isabelle has appointments with various classmates and teachers. Look at her notebook and act out her dialogues with Philippe.

▶ ISABELLE: **J'ai un rendez-vous avec Marc.**
PHILIPPE: **À quelle heure?**
ISABELLE: **À onze heures et demie.**

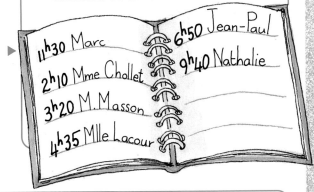

11h30 Marc
2h10 Mme Chollet
3h20 M. Masson
4h35 Mlle Lacour
6h50 Jean-Paul
9h40 Nathalie

6 À la gare *(At the train station)*

You are at the information desk of a French train station. Travelers ask you the departure times for the following trains. Answer them according to the posted schedule.

▶ le train de Nice

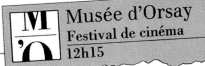

À quelle heure est le train de Nice?

Le train de Nice est à six heures dix.

DÉPARTS			
NICE	◆ 6 h 10	TOULON	◆ 9 h 35
LYON	◆ 7 h 15	COLMAR	◆ 10 h 40
CANNES	◆ 7 h 30	TOULOUSE	◆ 10 h 45
TOURS	◆ 8 h 12	MARSEILLE	◆ 10 h 50
DIJON	◆ 8 h 25	BORDEAUX	◆ 10 h 55

À votre tour!

1 Nathalie et Marc

It is the first day of school. Nathalie is talking to Marc and you hear parts of their conversation. For each of Nathalie's greetings or questions, select Marc's reply from the suggested responses on the right.

1. Salut!
2. Ça va?
3. Comment t'appelles-tu?
4. Tu es français?
5. Quelle heure est-il?
6. Au revoir!

a. Bonjour!
b. Au revoir!
c. Non, je suis canadien.
d. Il est deux heures moins le quart.
e. Marc Boutin.
f. Oui, ça va bien! Merci!

2 Et toi?

You and Nathalie meet at a sidewalk café. Respond to her greetings and questions.

1. Salut! Ça va?
2. Comment t'appelles-tu?
3. Tu es canadien (canadienne)?
4. Quelle heure est-il?
5. Oh là là. J'ai un rendez-vous dans (in) dix minutes. Au revoir.

3 Conversation dirigée

Two students, Jean-Pierre and Janet, meet on the Paris-Lyon train. With a partner, compose and act out their dialogue according to the suggested script.

Jean-Pierre				Janet
	says hello	→ ↙	responds and asks how things are	
	says things are fine	⇗	asks him what his name is	
	says his name is Jean-Pierre . . . asks her name	→ ↙	says her name is Janet	
	asks her if she is English	→ ↙	says no and responds that she is American	
	asks her if she is from New York	→	replies that she is from San Francisco	

4 Minidialogues

Create original dialogues on the basis of the pictures below.

1. David et Nicole

2. Monsieur Bertin et Mademoiselle Laval

3. Florence et Alain

4. Jean-Pierre et Sylvie

5. Thomas et Nicole

5 En scène

With a classmate, act out the following scene.

CHARACTERS:

You and a French exchange student

SITUATION:

You are at a party and meet a French exchange student who is happy to respond to your greetings and questions.

- Greet the student.
- Ask how things are going.
- Introduce yourself and ask his/her name.
- Ask if he/she is French.
- Ask if he/she is from Paris.
- Say good-bye.

6 Les nombres

1. Select any number between 0 and 15 and give the next five numbers in sequence.

2. Select a number between 1 and 9. Use that number as a starting point and count by tens to 60.

▶ deux

   douze, vingt-deux, trente-deux, etc.

Oui, vous parlez français!

Yes, you speak French! If you were visiting a French city, you would be able to understand many of the signs around you.

Look at the words on the following signs and compare them to their English equivalents. Which ones are spelled exactly the same? Which ones are spelled a little differently? What are the differences?

Office de Tourisme

AVENUE DE L'OPÉRA

Hôpital ·SILENCE·

AÉROPORT ORLY

DÉPARTS

ARRIVÉES

TAXI

AUTOBUS

musée

cathédrale

THÉÂTRE

station-service

DIRECTION BORDEAUX

AVENUE FRANKLIN ROOSEVELT

Parking Municipal

GARAGE

HÔTEL

HOTEL

téléphone

restaurant

TOILETTES

ATTENTION! DANGER!

La présence FRANÇAISE en Amérique

Between 1600 and 1750, the French explored large parts of Canada and the United States, which they called **La Nouvelle France** *(New France).* Today many American towns have French names, as you will see on the map below.

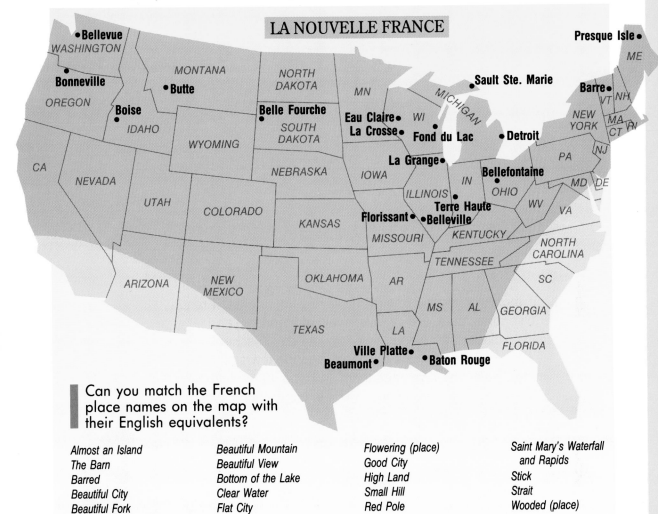

LA NOUVELLE FRANCE

| Can you match the French place names on the map with their English equivalents? |

Almost an Island
The Barn
Barred
Beautiful City
Beautiful Fork
Beautiful Fountain

Beautiful Mountain
Beautiful View
Bottom of the Lake
Clear Water
Flat City

Flowering (place)
Good City
High Land
Small Hill
Red Pole

Saint Mary's Waterfall
  and Rapids
Stick
Strait
Wooded (place)

Un jeu (game)

Many American cities were also named after:

- French people (such as King Louis XIV and his patron Saint Louis, General La Fayette, Napoleon, and of course, explorers like Champlain, Jolliet, Marquette, La Salle, Duluth, Dubuque)
- French cities (such as Paris, Montpellier, La Rochelle, Orléans)

In teams of three or four, see how many cities with French names you can locate on a map of the United States.

Les copains et la famille

INTRODUCTION

culturelle

L'amitié *(Friendship)*

Is friendship important to you? Friendship is very important to French teenagers. Of course, there are various levels of friendship and different types of friends: classmates whom we see every day in school, friends with whom we spend time outside of school, and the few special friends who are always there when we need them and who will remain our friends for the rest of our lives. As you will see, the French have different words to describe these various relationships.

THÈME ET OBJECTIFS

Talking about people

In this unit, you will be talking about people you know. You will learn . . .
- to identify friends, family, and relatives
- to say how old you are and find out someone's age
- to talk about birthdays and holidays

You will also learn . . .
- to count from 60 to 1,000
- to give the date and the day of the week

Copain ou copine?

In French, there are certain girls' and boys' names that sound the same. Occasionally this can be confusing.

> Dominique? Qui est-ce? Un copain ou une copine?

Scène 1. Philippe et Jean-Paul

Philippe is at home with his friend Jean-Paul. He seems to be expecting someone. Who could it be . . . ? The doorbell rings.

PHILIPPE: Tiens! Voilà Dominique!
JEAN-PAUL: Dominique? Qui est-ce?
Un copain ou une copine?
PHILIPPE: C'est une copine.

Scène 2. Philippe, Jean-Paul, Dominique

PHILIPPE: Salut, Dominique! Ça va?
DOMINIQUE: Oui, ça va! Et toi?
JEAN-PAUL: *(thinking)* C'est vrai! C'est une copine!

> Salut, Dominique! Ça va?

Scene 1. Philippe and Jean-Paul

PHILIPPE: *Hey! There's Dominique!*
JEAN-PAUL: *Dominique? Who's that?*
A boy(friend) or a girl(friend)?
PHILIPPE: *A girl(friend).*

Scene 2. Philippe, Jean-Paul, Dominique

PHILIPPE: *Hi, Dominique! How's everything?*
DOMINIQUE: *Fine! And you?*
JEAN-PAUL: *(thinking) It's true! She is a girlfriend!*

POUR *COMMUNIQUER*

> Tiens! Voilà Caroline! C'est une copine!

How to introduce or point out someone:

Voici . . .   *This is . . . , Here come(s) . . .*

Voici Jean-Paul.
Voici Nathalie et François.
Voilà Isabelle.
Voilà Philippe et Dominique.

Voilà . . .   *This (That) is . . . , There's . . .*

How to find out who someone is:

Qui est-ce?   *Who's that? Who is it?*
C'est . . .   *It's . . . , That's . . . , He's . . . , She's . . .*

—**Qui est-ce?**
—**C'est** Patrick. **C'est** un copain.

How to get someone's attention or to express surprise:

Tiens!   *Look! Hey!*

Tiens, voilà Dominique!

Les personnes

un garçon	*boy*
un ami	*friend (male)*
un copain	*friend (male)*

une fille	*girl*
une amie	*friend (female)*
une copine	*friend (female)*

un monsieur	*gentleman*
un prof	*teacher*

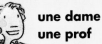

une dame	*lady*
une prof	*teacher*

■ NOTE ■ CULTURELLE

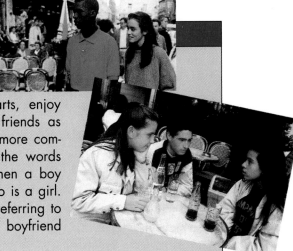

Amis et copains

French young people, like their American counterparts, enjoy spending time with their friends. They refer to their friends as **un ami** (for a boy) and **une amie** (for a girl) or — more commonly — as **un copain** or **une copine.** Note that the words **copain, copine** can also have special meanings. When a boy talks about **une copine,** he is referring to a friend who is a girl. However, when he says **ma** *(my)* **copine,** he may be referring to his girlfriend. Similarly, a girl would call her boyfriend **mon copain.**

C'EST UN CHAMPION!

MAIS NON! C'EST UNE CHAMPIONNE.

Petit commentaire

Cycling is a popular competitive sport throughout France. The most popular races are the **Tour de France** *and the* **Tour de France féminin,** *which take place every year in July. French women cyclists have won many world titles.*

---

un garçon, une fille

In French, all NOUNS are either MASCULINE or FEMININE.
Nouns referring to boys or men are almost always MASCULINE.
   They are introduced by **un** *(a, an).*
Nouns referring to girls or women are almost always FEMININE.
   They are introduced by **une** *(a, an).*

MASCULINE		FEMININE	
un garçon	*a boy*	**une** fille	*a girl*
un ami	*a friend (male)*	**une** amie	*a friend (female)*

---

1 Copain ou copine?

Say that the following people are your friends. Use **un copain** or **une copine,** as appropriate.

▶ **Christine est une copine.**

Christine

1. Alice

2. Marie-Jeanne

3. Éric

4. David

5. Sylvie

2 Les amis

The same young people are visiting your school. Point them out to your classmates, using **un ami** or **une amie,** as appropriate.

▶ —**Tiens, voilà Christine!**
   —**Qui est-ce?**
   —**C'est une amie.**

3 Un ou une?

Identify the people below by completing the sentences with **un** or **une.**

1. Voici . . . fille.
2. Voilà . . . garçon.
3. Voici . . . dame.
4. C'est . . . amie.
5. Olivier est . . . ami.
6. Jean-Paul est . . . copain.
7. Cécile est . . . copine.
8. Voici Mlle Lacour. C'est . . . prof.
9. Voici M. Masson. C'est . . . prof.
10. Voici Mme Chollet. C'est . . . prof.

4 **À la fenêtre** *(At the window)*

You and a friend are walking down the street and you see the following people at their windows. Identify them in short dialogues.

▶ —Tiens, voilà un monsieur!
—Qui est-ce?
—C'est Monsieur Mercier. ▶

Monsieur Mercier

1. Nicole

2. Mademoiselle Lasalle

3. Éric

4. Madame Albert

5. Monsieur Lavie

6. Alain

Les nombres de 60 à 79

60 soixante

61 soixante et un	66 soixante-six
62 soixante-deux	67 soixante-sept
63 soixante-trois	68 soixante-huit
64 soixante-quatre	69 soixante-neuf
65 soixante-cinq	

70 soixante-dix

71 soixante et onze	76 soixante-seize
72 soixante-douze	77 soixante-dix-sept
73 soixante-treize	78 soixante-dix-huit
74 soixante-quatorze	79 soixante-dix-neuf
75 soixante-quinze	

➡ Note that in counting from 70 to 79, the French continue adding numbers to 60:
70 = 60 + 10   71 = 60 + 11   72 = 60 + 12, etc.

---

5 **Numéros de téléphone**

Read aloud the phone numbers of Jean-Paul's friends in Paris.

▶ Philippe   zéro un,
quarante-deux,
soixante et un,
dix-neuf,
soixante-quinze

Philippe   01.42.61.19.75
Martine   01.41.33.64.79
Michèle   01.42.56.76.62
Stéphanie   01.45.68.77.55
François   01.49.78.13.62

Prononciation

La liaison

Pronounce the following words:

un ami   un Américain   un Anglais   un artiste

un ami

In general, the "**n**" of **un** is silent. However, in the above words, the "**n**" of **un** is pronounced as if it were the *first* letter of the next word. The two words are *linked* together in LIAISON.

Liaison occurs between two words when the second one begins with a VOWEL SOUND, that is, with "**a**", "**e**", "**i**", "**o**", "**u**", and sometimes "**h**" and "**y**".

➡ Although liaison is not marked in written French, it will be indicated in your book by the symbol ‿ where appropriate.

Contrastez et répétez:

LIAISON: **un ami   un Américain   un Italien   un artiste**

NO LIAISON: **un copain   un Français   un Canadien   un prof**

6

Une coïncidence

Isabelle is at a party with her new Canadian friend Marc.
She wants him to meet some of the other guests.

ISABELLE: *Do you know the girl over there?*
MARC: *No. Who is she?*
ISABELLE: *She's a friend. Her name is Juliette Savard.*

MARC: *Is she French?*
ISABELLE: *No, she's Canadian. She is from Montreal.*
MARC: *Me too!*
ISABELLE: *What a coincidence!*

POUR *COMMUNIQUER*

Tu connais la dame?

Oui, elle s'appelle Madame Leblanc.

How to inquire about people:

Tu connais . . . ?	*Do you know . . . ?*	**Tu connais** Jean-Paul?

How to describe people and give their nationalities:

Il est . . .	*He is . . .*	**Il est** canadien.
Elle est . . .	*She is . . .*	**Elle est** canadienne.

How to find out another person's name:

Comment s'appelle . . . ?	*What's the name of . . . ?*	**Comment s'appelle** le garçon?
		Comment s'appelle la fille?
Il s'appelle . . .	*His name is . . .*	**Il s'appelle** Marc.
Elle s'appelle . . .	*Her name is . . .*	**Elle s'appelle** Juliette.

■ NOTE ■ CULTURELLE

Montréal et la province de Québec

In population, metropolitan Montreal is the second-largest city in Canada. After Paris, it is also the second-largest French-speaking city in the world.

Montreal is located in the province of Quebec, where French is the official language. In fact, French speakers represent over 90% of the population. These people are the descendants of French settlers who came to Canada in the 17th and 18th centuries. If you visit Montreal, you will discover that the people of Quebec **(les Québécois)** are very proud of their heritage and dedicated to maintaining French as their language.

Petit commentaire

French teenagers are very much interested in the United States. They love American music and American movies. Every year, more and more French high school students come to visit our country either through exchange programs or summer homestays.

> BONJOUR!
>
> TU CONNAIS LE MONSIEUR?
>
> OUI, IL S'APPELLE ONCLE SAM. IL EST AMÉRICAIN.

le garçon, la fille

The French equivalent of *the* has two basic forms: **le** and **la.**

 MASCULINE
le garçon — *the boy*
le copain — *the friend*

 FEMININE
la fille — *the girl*
la copine — *the friend*

NOTE: Both **le** and **la** become **l'** before a vowel sound.

un copain	→	le copain	une copine	→ la copine
un ami	→	**l'**ami	une amie	→ **l'**amie

1 Qui est-ce?

Ask who the following people are, using **le, la,** or **l'.**

▶ une prof
   Qui est la prof?

1. un monsieur
2. une dame
3. une fille
4. un garçon
5. un prof
6. un ami
7. une amie

2 Tu connais . . . ?

Ask your classmates if they know the following people. They will answer that they do.

▶ une dame / Madame Vallée

> Oui, c'est Madame Vallée.
>
> Tu connais la dame?

1. un prof / Monsieur Simon
2. un garçon / Christophe
3. une fille / Sophie
4. une dame / Mademoiselle Lenoir
5. une prof / Madame Boucher
6. un monsieur / Monsieur Duval

3 Comment s'appelle . . . ?

Ask the names of the following people, using the words **le garçon, la fille.** A classmate will respond.

▶ —Comment s'appelle la fille?
  —Elle s'appelle Stéphanie.

Stéphanie	1. Marc	2. Juliette	3. François

4. Jean-Paul	5. Nathalie	6. Philippe	7. Isabelle

4 Français, anglais, canadien ou américain?

Give the nationalities of the following people.

▶ Jewel?
Elle est américaine.

1. le prince Charles?
2. Céline Dion?
3. Juliette Binoche?
4. Gwyneth Paltrow?
5. Pierre Cardin?
6. Matt Damon?
7. Oprah Winfrey?
8. Tom Cruise?
9. Hugh Grant?

Les nombres de 80 à 1000

80 quatre-vingts

81 quatre-vingt-un	86 quatre-vingt-six
82 quatre-vingt-deux	87 quatre-vingt-sept
83 quatre-vingt-trois	88 quatre-vingt-huit
84 quatre-vingt-quatre	89 quatre-vingt-neuf
85 quatre-vingt-cinq	

90 quatre-vingt-dix

91 quatre-vingt-onze	96 quatre-vingt-seize
92 quatre-vingt-douze	97 quatre-vingt-dix-sept
93 quatre-vingt-treize	98 quatre-vingt-dix-huit
94 quatre-vingt-quatorze	99 quatre-vingt-dix-neuf
95 quatre-vingt-quinze	

100 cent   **1000 mille**

➡ Note that in counting from 80 to 99, the French add numbers to the base of **quatre-vingts** (fourscore):

$$80 = 4 \times 20 \qquad 90 = 4 \times 20 + 10$$
$$85 = 4 \times 20 + 5 \qquad 99 = 4 \times 20 + 19$$

5 Au téléphone

In France, the telephone area code (**l'indicatif**) is always a four-digit number. Your teacher will name a city (**une ville**) from the chart. Give the corresponding area code.

▶ Nice?   **C'est le zéro quatre quatre-vingt-treize.**

VILLE	INDICATIF
Albi	0563
Avignon	0490
Cannes	0493
Dijon	0380
Marseille	0491
Montpellier	0467
Nancy	0383
Nice	0493
Nîmes	0466
Rennes	0299
Saint-Tropez	0494
Strasbourg	0388
Vichy	0470

Prononciation   /ɛ̃/

La voyelle nasale /ɛ̃/

In French, there are three nasal vowel sounds:

/ɛ̃/ **cinq** (5)   /ɔ̃/ **onze** (11)   /ɑ̃/ **trente** (30)

Practice the sound /ɛ̃/ in the following words. Note that this vowel sound can have several different spellings.

➡ Be sure not to pronounce an "**n**" or "**m**" after the nasal vowel.

Répétez: "**in**"   ci**n**q qui**n**ze vi**ngt** vi**ngt**-ci**n**q quatre-vi**ngt**-qui**n**ze
"**ain**"   américai**n** Alai**n** copai**n**
"**(i)en**" bie**n** canadie**n** tie**ns**!
"**un**"   u**n**

Tiens**! Voilà Alai**n**. Il est américai**n**.   E**t** Julie**n**? Il est canadie**n**.**

5
cinq

7 Les photos d'Isabelle

Isabelle is showing her family photo album to her friend Jean-Paul.

ISABELLE:	Voici ma mère.
JEAN-PAUL:	Et le monsieur, c'est ton père?
ISABELLE:	Non, c'est mon oncle Thomas.
JEAN-PAUL:	Et la fille, c'est ta cousine?
ISABELLE:	Oui, c'est ma cousine Béatrice. Elle a seize ans.
JEAN-PAUL:	Et le garçon, c'est ton cousin?
ISABELLE:	Non, c'est un copain.
JEAN-PAUL:	Un copain ou ton copain?
ISABELLE:	Dis donc, Jean-Paul, tu es vraiment trop curieux!

ma mère

mon oncle Thomas

ma cousine Béatrice

??

ISABELLE:	*This is my mother.*
JEAN-PAUL:	*And the man, is he your father?*
ISABELLE:	*No, that's my uncle Thomas.*
JEAN-PAUL:	*And the girl, is she your cousin?*
ISABELLE:	*Yes, that's my cousin Béatrice. She's sixteen.*

JEAN-PAUL:	*And the boy, is he your cousin?*
ISABELLE:	*No, that's a friend.*
JEAN-PAUL:	*A friend or a boyfriend?*
ISABELLE:	*Hey there, Jean-Paul, you are really too curious!*

POUR
COMMUNIQUER

Voici mon chien Malice.

How to introduce your family:

Voici mon père.   *This is my father.*
Et voici ma mère.   *And this is my mother.*

La famille *(Family)*

un frère	*brother*	**une soeur**	*sister*
un cousin	*cousin*	**une cousine**	*cousin*
un père	*father*	**une mère**	*mother*
un oncle	*uncle*	**une tante**	*aunt*
un grand-père	*grandfather*	**une grand-mère**	*grandmother*

Les animaux domestiques *(Pets)*

un chat   **un chien**

■ NOTE ■
CULTURELLE

La famille française

When you and your friends talk about your families, you usually are referring to your brothers, sisters, and parents. In French, however, **la famille** refers not only to parents and children but also to grandparents, aunts, uncles, cousins, as well as a whole array of more distant relatives related by blood and marriage.

Since the various members of a family often live in the same region, French teenagers see their grandparents and cousins fairly frequently. Even when relatives do not live close by, the family finds many occasions to get together: for weekend visits, during school and summer vacations, on holidays, as well as on special occasions such as weddings and anniversaries.

---

mon cousin, ma cousine

The French equivalents of *my* and *your* have the following forms:

MASCULINE		FEMININE	
mon cousin	*my cousin (male)*	**ma** cousine	*my cousin (female)*
mon frère	*my brother*	**ma** soeur	*my sister*
ton cousin	*your cousin (male)*	**ta** cousine	*your cousin (female)*
ton frère	*your brother*	**ta** soeur	*your sister*

➡ Note that the feminine **ma** becomes **mon** and the feminine **ta** becomes **ton** before a vowel sound. Liaison is required.

   une amie   →   **mon** amie   **ton** amie

---

1 L'album de photos

You are showing a friend your photo album. Identify the following people, using **mon** and **ma,** as appropriate.

▶ cousine Jacqueline   **Voici ma cousine Jacqueline.**

1. frère	5. père	9. copine Pauline	13. chien Toto
2. soeur	6. mère	10. amie Florence	14. chat Minou
3. tante Monique	7. copain Nicolas	11. grand-mère Michèle	15. cousine Sophie
4. oncle Pierre	8. ami Jérôme	12. grand-père Robert	

2 Comment s'appelle . . . ?

Ask your classmates to name some of their friends, relatives, and pets. They can invent names if they wish.

Comment s'appelle ton copain?

Mon copain s'appelle Bob.

▶ le copain

1. l'oncle	4. la cousine	7. la grand-mère
2. la tante	5. la copine	8. le chien
3. le cousin	6. le grand-père	9. le chat

POUR
COMMUNIQUER

How to find out how old a friend is:

Quel âge as-tu?	*How old are you?*
J'ai . . . ans.	*I'm . . . (years old).*

—**Quel âge as-tu?**
—**J'ai treize ans.**

Quel âge as-tu?

J'ai treize ans.

How to ask about how old others are:

—**Quel âge a ton père?**	*How old is your father?*
—**Il a quarante-deux ans.**	*He is 42 (years old).*
—**Quel âge a ta mère?**	*How old is your mother?*
—**Elle a trente-neuf ans.**	*She is 39 (years old).*

➡ Although *years old* may be left out in English, the word **ans** must be used in French when talking about someone's age.

Il a vingt ans.   *He's twenty. (He's twenty years old.)*

---

3 **Quel âge as-tu?**

Ask your classmates how old they are.

▶ —**Quel âge as-tu?**
  —**J'ai (treize) ans.**

4 **Joyeux anniversaire!**
(Happy birthday!)
Ask your classmates how old the following people are.

▶ —**Quel âge a Stéphanie?**
  —**Elle a quatorze ans.**

Stéphanie

1. Éric   **2. Mademoiselle Doucette**   **3. Monsieur Boucher**

4. Madame Dupont   **5. Monsieur Camus**   **6. Madame Simon**

5 **Curiosité**

Find out the ages of your classmates' friends and relatives. If they are not sure, they can guess or invent an answer.

▶ la copine   —**Quel âge a ta copine?**
            —**Ma copine a (treize) ans.**

1. le père	4. la tante	7. le grand-père
2. la mère	5. le cousin	8. la grand-mère
3. l'oncle	6. la cousine	

Prononciation   /ã/   /ɔ̃/

Les voyelles nasales /ã/ et /ɔ̃/

tante   oncle

The letters "**an**" and "**en**" usually represent the nasal vowel /ã/. Be sure not to pronounce an "**n**" after the nasal vowel.

Répétez: **ans   tante   grand-père   français
anglais   quarante   cinquante
trente   comment   Henri   Laurent**

The letters "**on**" represent the nasal vowel /ɔ̃/. Be sure not to pronounce an "**n**" after the nasal vowel.

Répétez: **non   mon   ton   bonjour   oncle
garçon   onze**

Contrastez: **an—on   tante—ton   onze—ans
Mon oncle François a trente ans.**

LEÇON 8

Le jour et la date

A. Quel jour est-ce?

For many people, the days of the week are not all alike.

Dialogue 1. Vendredi

PHILIPPE: Quel jour est-ce?
STÉPHANIE: C'est vendredi.
PHILIPPE: Super! Demain, c'est samedi!

Super! Demain, c'est samedi!

Dialogue 2. Mercredi

NATHALIE: Ça va?
MARC: Pas très bien.
NATHALIE: Pourquoi?
MARC: Aujourd'hui, c'est mercredi.
NATHALIE: Et alors?
MARC: Demain, c'est jeudi! Le jour de l'examen.
NATHALIE: Zut! C'est vrai! Au revoir, Marc.
MARC: Au revoir, Nathalie. À demain!

Demain, c'est jeudi! Le jour de l'examen.

Dialogue 1. Friday

PHILIPPE: *What day is it?*
STÉPHANIE: *It's Friday.*
PHILIPPE: *Great! Tomorrow is Saturday!*

Dialogue 2. Wednesday

NATHALIE: *How are things?*
MARC: *Not very good.*
NATHALIE: *Why?*
MARC: *Today is Wednesday.*

NATHALIE: *So?*
MARC: *Tomorrow is Thursday! The day of the exam.*
NATHALIE: *Darn! That's right! Good-bye, Marc.*
MARC: *Good-bye, Nathalie. See you tomorrow!*

POUR COMMUNIQUER

À samedi!

How to talk about days of the week:

Quel jour est-ce?   *What day is it?*
  Aujourd'hui, c'est mercredi.   *Today is Wednesday.*
  Demain, c'est jeudi.   *Tomorrow is Thursday.*

How to tell people when you will see them again:

À samedi!   *See you Saturday!*
À demain!   *See you tomorrow!*

Les jours de la semaine *(Days of the week)*

lundi	*Monday*	**vendredi**	*Friday*	**aujourd'hui**	*today*
mardi	*Tuesday*	**samedi**	*Saturday*	**demain**	*tomorrow*
mercredi	*Wednesday*	**dimanche**	*Sunday*		
jeudi	*Thursday*				

---

1 Questions

1. Quel jour est-ce aujourd'hui?
2. Et demain, quel jour est-ce?

2 Un jour de retard *(One day behind)*

Georges has trouble keeping track of the date. He is always one day behind. Monique corrects him.

▶ samedi

Aujourd'hui, c'est samedi?

Non, aujourd'hui, c'est dimanche!

1. lundi   3. jeudi   5. dimanche
2. mardi   4. vendredi   6. mercredi

3 Au revoir!

You are on the phone with the following friends. Say good-bye and tell them when you will see them.

▶ Christine / lundi
   Au revoir, Christine. À lundi.

1. David / dimanche
2. Roger / samedi
3. Delphine / mercredi
4. Sophie / vendredi
5. Alain / mardi
6. Éric / jeudi

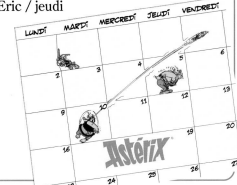

B. Anniversaire

François and Isabelle are on their way
to Nathalie's birthday party. As they are
talking, François wants to know when
Isabelle's birthday is.

FRANÇOIS:	C'est quand, ton anniversaire?
ISABELLE:	C'est le 18 mars!
FRANÇOIS:	Le 18 mars? Pas possible!
ISABELLE:	Si! Pourquoi?
FRANÇOIS:	C'est aussi mon anniversaire.
ISABELLE:	Quelle coïncidence!

FRANÇOIS:	*When is your birthday?*
ISABELLE:	*It's March 18!*
FRANÇOIS:	*March 18? That's not possible!*
ISABELLE:	*Yes, it is! Why?*
FRANÇOIS:	*It's my birthday too.*
ISABELLE:	*What a coincidence!*

POUR COMMUNIQUER

Quelle est la date?

How to talk about the date:

Quelle est la date?	*What's the date?*
C'est le 12 (douze) octobre.	*It's October 12.*
C'est le premier juin.	*It's June first.*

How to talk about birthdays:

—**C'est quand, ton anniversaire?**	*When is your birthday?*
—**Mon anniversaire est le 2 (deux) mars.**	*My birthday is March 2.*

Les mois de l'année *(Months of the year)*

janvier	**avril**	**juillet**	**octobre**
février	**mai**	**août**	**novembre**
mars	**juin**	**septembre**	**décembre**

La date

To express a date in French, the pattern is:

le	+	NUMBER	+	MONTH
le		11 (onze)		novembre
le		20 (vingt)		mai

EXCEPTION: The first of the month is **le premier.**

➡ In front of numbers, the French use **le** (and never **l'**): **le onze, le huit.**

➡ Note that when dates are abbreviated in French, the day always comes first.

2/8 **le deux** août **1/11** **le premier** novembre

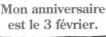

Les Backstreet Boys
à Paris
Au Parc des Princes
le 23 juin

---

4 **Anniversaires**

Ask your classmates when their birthdays are.

C'est quand, ton anniversaire?

Mon anniversaire est le 3 février.

---

5 **Quelle est la date?**

Ask what the date is.

▶ —Quelle est la date?
—C'est le douze septembre.

12 SEPTEMBRE

1 — **30** JUIN 2 — **8** MAI 3 — **4** MARS 4 — **21** NOVEMBRE 5 — **1** AVRIL 6 — **25** AOÛT

---

6 **Dates importantes**

Give the following dates in French.

▶ Noël *(Christmas):* 25/12 **C'est le vingt-cinq décembre.**

1. le jour de l'An *(New Year's Day):* 1/1
2. la fête *(holiday)* de Martin Luther King: 15/1
3. la Saint-Valentin: 14/2
4. la Saint-Patrick: 17/3
5. la fête nationale américaine: 4/7
6. la fête nationale française: 14/7
7. la fête de Christophe Colomb: 12/10

À votre tour!

1 Nathalie et Philippe

Nathalie is talking to Philippe and you hear parts of their conversation. For each of Nathalie's questions, select Philippe's response from the suggested answers.

1. Qui est-ce?
2. C'est ta soeur?
3. Quel âge as-tu?
4. C'est quand, ton anniversaire?
5. Quel âge a ton oncle?
6. Tu connais Stéphanie?
7. Comment s'appelle ta prof de français?
8. Quel jour est-ce aujourd'hui?

a. Vendredi.
b. Oui, c'est une copine.
c. Quinze ans.
d. Non, c'est ma cousine.
e. Quarante-cinq ans.
f. Elle s'appelle Madame Doucette.
g. Le dix-huit décembre.
h. C'est mon cousin Christophe.

2 Et toi?

You have just met Nathalie at a party. Answer her questions.

1. Quel âge as-tu?
2. Quel âge a ton copain (ta copine)?
3. C'est quand, ton anniversaire?
4. C'est quand, l'anniversaire de ton copain (ta copine)?
5. Comment s'appelle le (la) prof de français?

3 Conversation dirigée

Nathalie and Christophe are in a café. Christophe sees another girl that Nathalie seems to know. He wonders who she is.

Christophe			Nathalie
	asks Nathalie if she knows the girl	→ ↙	says she does and that she is a friend	
	asks Nathalie the name of her friend	→ ↙	says that her name is Michèle Lafontaine	
	asks if she is Canadian	→ ↙	says yes and adds that she is from Quebec City **(de Québec)**	
	says what a coincidence **(Quelle coïncidence!)** and adds that he is also from Quebec City			

4 Ma famille *(My family)*

You are showing your friends a picture of your family. Introduce everyone, giving their ages.

▶ **Voici ma soeur. Elle a douze ans.**

5 En scène

With a classmate, act out the following scene.

CHARACTERS:
You and a French guest

SITUATION:
You are in France. Your French friends have invited you to a picnic. You meet one of the guests and have a conversation.

- Greet the guest.
- Introduce yourself and ask the guest's name.
- Tell the guest how old you are and ask his/her age.
- Tell the guest the date of your birthday and ask the date of his/her birthday.
- *(The guest waves to a friend.)* Ask the guest the name of his/her friend.
- *(It is the end of the picnic.)* Say good-bye.

6 Le loto

Loto is a French version of Bingo. Read out loud the numbers on your board.

13	24		42			75	89
8		25	31		53	68	
	16		36		57		79	90

LES BRUITS FRANÇAIS *(French sounds)*

People in various countries can hear the same noises and interpret them differently. Notice how the French express certain common sounds.

TIC-TAC

TOC! TOC!

DRING DRING

PLOC... PLOC...

BOUM!

DING DONG

What sounds do animals make in France? They make French sounds, of course!

HI-HAN

MEUH

l'âne

COT... COT... CODÈT

la poule

OUAF OUAF

MIAOU

COIN COIN

la vache

le chien

le chat

le canard

ASTÉRIX
en action

Astérix and his friends lead an action-packed life. Can you match the sounds with the corresponding cartoon frames?

a ¡CRAAAC!

b POM POM! POM!

c RRROAÂOOO! GRRRAOOR!

d GLOU! GLOU! GLOU! GLOU! GLOU!

e TATARARA TATA!

f PAFFF!

1 From ASTÉRIX LE GAULOIS

2 From ASTÉRIX GLADIATEUR

AU NOM DE CÉSAR, OUVREZ!

3 From ASTÉRIX CHEZ LES BRETONS

4 From ASTÉRIX CHEZ LES BRETONS

5 From ASTÉRIX GLADIATEUR

6 From ASTÉRIX LE GAULOIS

3 Bon appétit!

INTRODUCTION

culturelle

Bon appétit!

Where do you go when you want something to eat or drink? Maybe to a fast-food restaurant or an ice cream place?

   French teenagers also have a large choice of places to go when they are hungry or thirsty. Some go to a bakery **(une boulangerie)** or a pastry shop **(une pâtisserie)** to buy croissants, éclairs, or other small pastries. Some may buy pizzas, crepes, hot dogs, or ice-cream cones from street vendors. Still others may go to a fast-food restaurant **(un fast-food).** But the favorite place to get something to eat or drink is the café. There are cafés practically everywhere in France. As you will see, the café plays an important role in the social life of all French people.

THÈME ET OBJECTIFS

Having a snack in France

When in France, you will often want to buy something to eat or drink. In this unit, you will learn . . .
- to order some common foods and beverages in a café
- to ask about prices and pay the check
- to ask friends to give or lend you something

You will also learn . . .
- to identify French money
- to talk about the weather
- to name the seasons

LEÇON 9

Tu as faim?

Pierre, Philippe, and Nathalie are on their way home from school. They stop by a street vendor who sells sandwiches and pizza. Today it is Pierre's turn to treat his friends.

Scène 1. Pierre et Nathalie

PIERRE: Tu as faim?

NATHALIE: Oui, j'ai faim.

PIERRE: Tu veux un sandwich ou une pizza?

NATHALIE: Donne-moi une pizza, s'il te plaît.

PIERRE: Voilà.

NATHALIE: Merci.

Scène 2. Pierre et Philippe

PIERRE: Et toi, Philippe, tu as faim?

PHILIPPE: Oh là là, oui, j'ai faim.

PIERRE: Qu'est-ce que tu veux? Un sandwich ou une pizza?

PHILIPPE: Je voudrais un sandwich . . . euh . . . et donne-moi aussi une pizza.

PIERRE: C'est vrai! Tu as vraiment faim!

Scene 1. *Pierre and Nathalie*

PIERRE: *Are you hungry?*

NATHALIE: *Yes, I'm hungry.*

PIERRE: *Do you want a sandwich or a pizza?*

NATHALIE: *Give me a pizza, please.*

PIERRE: *Here you are.*

NATHALIE: *Thanks.*

Scene 2. *Pierre and Philippe*

PIERRE: *And you, Philippe, are you hungry?*

PHILIPPE: *Oh yes, I'm hungry.*

PIERRE: *What do you want? A sandwich or a pizza?*

PHILIPPE: *I would like a sandwich . . . er . . . and give me a pizza too.*

PIERRE: *It's true! You are really hungry!*

POUR *COMMUNIQUER*

> J'ai faim!
> Tu as faim?

How to say that you are hungry:

J'ai faim.	*I'm hungry.*
Tu as faim?	*Are you hungry?*

How to offer a friend something:

Tu veux . . . ?	*Do you want . . . ?*	**Tu veux** un sandwich?
Qu'est-ce que tu veux?	*What do you want?*	**Qu'est-ce que tu veux?** Un sandwich ou une pizza?

How to ask a friend for something:

Je voudrais . . .	*I would like . . .*	**Je voudrais** un sandwich.
Donne-moi . . .	*Give me . . .*	**Donne-moi** une pizza.
S'il te plaît . . .	*Please . . .*	**S'il te plaît,** François, donne-moi une pizza.

Les nourritures *(Foods)*

un croissant   **un sandwich**    **un steak**    **un steak-frites**   **un hamburger**    **un hot dog**

 une salade    **une pizza**   **une omelette**    **une crêpe**   **une glace**

■ NOTE ■ CULTURELLE

Les jeunes et la nourriture

In general, French teenagers eat their main meals at home with their families. On weekends or after school, however, when they are with friends, they often stop at a fast-food restaurant or a café for something to eat.

At fast-food restaurants, French teenagers order pretty much the same types of foods as Americans: hamburgers, hot dogs, and pizza.

At a café, teenagers may order a croissant, a sandwich, or a dish of ice cream. Some favorite sandwiches are ham **(un sandwich au jambon),** Swiss cheese **(un sandwich au fromage),** or salami **(un sandwich au saucisson).** And, of course, they are made with French bread, which has a crunchy crust. Another traditional quick café meal is a small steak with French fries **(un steak-frites).**

J'AI FAIM! JE VOUDRAIS UN SANDWICH.

Petit commentaire

In France, sandwiches are traditionally very simple: a piece of French bread with a slice of ham or cheese. Usually sandwiches are not made with mayonnaise or lettuce.

un sandwich, une pizza

You may have noted that the names of some foods are masculine and others are feminine. In French, ALL NOUNS, whether they designate people or things, are either MASCULINE or FEMININE.

MASCULINE NOUNS	FEMININE NOUNS
un sandwich **le** sandwich **un** croissant **le** croissant	**une** pizza **la** pizza **une** salade **la** salade

1 Au choix *(Your choice)*

Offer your classmates a choice between the following items. They will decide which one they would like.

▶ une pizza ou un sandwich?

1. un hamburger ou un steak?
2. un hot dog ou un sandwich?
3. une salade ou une omelette?
4. un steak-frites ou une pizza?
5. une crêpe ou un croissant?
6. une glace à la vanille ou une glace au chocolat?

Qu'est-ce que tu veux? Une pizza ou un sandwich?

Donne-moi un sandwich s'il te plaît.

2 Au café

You are in a French café. Ask for the following dishes.

 1
 2
3

▶ Je voudrais un croissant.

 4
 5
 6

3 Tu as faim?

You have invited French friends to your home. Ask if they are hungry and offer them the following foods.

▶ —Tu as faim?
— Oui, j'ai faim.
— Tu veux un hamburger?
— Oui, merci.

1
2
3
4
5
6

4 Qu'est-ce que tu veux?

Say which foods you would like to have in the following circumstances.

▶ You are very hungry.

Je voudrais un steak-frites.

1. You are at an Italian restaurant.
2. You are on a diet.
3. You are a vegetarian.
4. You are having breakfast.
5. You would like a dessert.
6. You want to eat something light for supper.

Prononciation

L'intonation

When you speak, your voice rises and falls. This is called INTONATION. In French, as in English, your voice goes down at the end of a statement.

Voici un steak . . . et une salade.

However, in French, your voice rises after each group of words in the middle of a sentence. (This is the opposite of English, where your voice drops a little when you pause in the middle of a sentence.)

Répétez: **Je voudrais une pizza.**

Je voudrais une pizza et un sandwich.

Je voudrais une pizza, un sandwich et un hamburger.

Voici un steak.

Voici un steak et une salade.

Voici un steak, une salade et une glace.

10 Au café

This afternoon Jean-Paul and Isabelle went shopping. They are now tired and thirsty. Jean-Paul invites Isabelle to a café.

Tu as soif?

Vous désirez, mademoiselle?

Scène 1. Jean-Paul, Isabelle

JEAN-PAUL: Tu as soif?
ISABELLE: Oui, j'ai soif.
JEAN-PAUL: On va dans un café? Je t'invite.
ISABELLE: D'accord!

Scène 2. Le garçon, Isabelle, Jean-Paul

LE GARÇON: Vous désirez, mademoiselle?
ISABELLE: Un jus d'orange, s'il vous plaît.
LE GARÇON: Et pour vous, monsieur?
JEAN-PAUL: Donnez-moi une limonade,* s'il vous plaît.

C'est pour vous, mademoiselle?

Scène 3. Le garçon, Isabelle, Jean-Paul

LE GARÇON: *(à Isabelle)* La limonade, c'est pour vous, mademoiselle?
JEAN-PAUL: Non, c'est pour moi.
LE GARÇON: Ah, excusez-moi. Voici le jus d'orange, mademoiselle.
ISABELLE: Merci.

Scene 2. *The waiter, Isabelle, Jean-Paul*

WAITER: *May I help you, Miss?*
ISABELLE: *An orange juice, please.*
WAITER: *And for you, Sir?*
JEAN-PAUL: *Give me a "limonade," please.*

Scene 1. *Jean-Paul, Isabelle*

JEAN-PAUL: *Are you thirsty?*
ISABELLE: *Yes, I'm thirsty.*
JEAN-PAUL: *Shall we go to a café? I'm treating (inviting) you.*
ISABELLE: *Okay!*

Scene 3. *The waiter, Isabelle, Jean-Paul*

WAITER: *The "limonade" is for you, Miss?*
JEAN-PAUL: *No, it's for me.*
WAITER: *Oh, excuse me. Here is the orange juice, Miss.*
ISABELLE: *Thank you.*

*****Une limonade** is a popular inexpensive soft drink with a slight lemon flavor.

POUR
COMMUNIQUER

> Donnez-moi une limonade, s'il vous plaît!

How to say that you are thirsty:

J'ai soif.	*I'm thirsty.*
Tu as soif?	*Are you thirsty?*

How to order in a café:

Vous désirez?	*May I help you?*	**—Vous désirez?**
Je voudrais . . .	*I would like . . .*	**—Je voudrais** un Perrier.

How to request something . . .

from a friend:	*from an adult:*	
S'il te plaît, donne-moi . . .	**S'il vous plaît, donnez-moi . . .**	*Please, give me . . .*

➡ Note that French people have two ways of saying *please.* They use
s'il te plaît with friends, and
s'il vous plaît with adults.

As we will see later, young people address their friends as **tu** and adults that they do not know very well as **vous.**

Les boissons *(Beverages)*

un soda	un jus d'orange	un jus de pomme	un jus de tomate	un jus de raisin*	une limonade	un café	un thé	un chocolat

---

■ NOTE ■
CULTURELLE

Le café

The café is a favorite gathering place for French young people. They go there not only when they are hungry or thirsty but also to meet their friends. They can sit at a table and talk for hours over a cup of coffee or a glass of juice. French young people also enjoy mineral water and soft drinks, which they order by brand name (**un Coca, un Orangina, un Pepsi, un Schweppes, un Perrier**). In a French café, a 15% service charge is included in the check. However, most people also leave some small change as an added tip.

*****Jus de raisin** is a golden-colored juice made from grapes.

1 Tu as soif?

You have invited a French friend to your house. You offer a choice of beverages and your friend (played by a classmate) responds.

▶ un thé ou un chocolat?
—Tu veux un thé ou un chocolat?
—Donne-moi un chocolat, s'il te plaît.

1. un thé ou un café?
2. une limonade ou un soda?
3. un jus de pomme ou un jus d'orange?   4. un jus de raisin ou un jus de tomate?

2 Au café

You are in a French café. Get the attention of the waiter **(Monsieur)** or the waitress **(Mademoiselle)** and place your order. Act out the dialogue with a classmate.

3 **Que choisir?** *(What to choose?)*

You are in a French café. Decide what beverage you are going to order in each of the following circumstances.

▶ You are very thirsty.
  S'il vous plaît, une limonade (un jus de pomme) . . .

1. It is very cold outside.
2. You do not want to spend much money.
3. You like juice but are allergic to citrus fruits.
4. It is breakfast time.
5. You have a sore throat.

4 **La faim et la soif** *(Hungry and thirsty)*

You are having a meal in a French café. Order the food suggested in the picture. Then order something to drink with that dish. A classmate will play the part of the waiter.
Note: **Et avec ça?** means *And with that?*

1

2

3

4

Vous désirez?

Je voudrais un steak-frites.

Et avec ça?

Un Orangina, s'il vous plaît.

Prononciation

L'accent final

In French, the rhythm is very even and the accent always falls on the *last* syllable of a word or group of words.

Répétez: **Philippe   Thomas   Alice   Sophie   Dominique**

un café	Je voudrais un café.
une salade	Donnez-moi une salade.
un chocolat	Donne-moi un chocolat.

ŭn chŏcŏlāt

If you want French people to understand you, the most important thing is to speak with an even rhythm and to stress the last syllable in each group of words. (Try speaking English this way: people will think you have a French accent!)

Ça fait combien?

At the café, Jean-Paul and Isabelle have talked about many things. It is now time to go. Jean-Paul calls the waiter so he can pay the check.

JEAN-PAUL:	S'il vous plaît?
LE GARÇON:	Oui, monsieur.
JEAN-PAUL:	Ça fait combien?
LE GARÇON:	Voyons, un jus d'orange, 4 euros, et une limonade, 3 euros. Ça fait 7 euros.
JEAN-PAUL:	7 euros . . . Très bien . . . Mais, euh . . . Zut! Où est mon porte-monnaie . . . ? Dis, Isabelle, prête-moi 10 euros, s'il te plaît.

Dis, Isabelle, prête-moi 10 euros, s'il te plaît.

JEAN-PAUL:	*Excuse me? (Please?)*
WAITER:	*Yes, Sir.*
JEAN-PAUL:	*What do I owe you? (How much does that make?)*
WAITER:	*Let's see, one orange juice, 4 euros, and one "limonade" 3 euros. That comes to (makes) 7 euros.*
JEAN-PAUL:	*7 euros . . . Very well . . . But, uh . . . Darn! Where is my wallet . . . ? Hey, Isabelle, loan me 10 euros, please.*

■ NOTE ■
CULTURELLE

L'argent européen *(European money)*

France uses the euro **(l'euro)** as its monetary unit. The euro is the common currency of eleven European countries and has the same value in each country. It is divided into 100 **cents,** also called **centimes** or **eurocentimes** in France. The euro-currency consists of bills and coins. The 7 euro bills are of different colors and different sizes, the greater the value, the larger the bill: 5, 10, 20, 50, 100, 200, and 500 euros. The face of a euro bill shows an archway, door or window to symbolize opportunity and opening to new ideas. The bridge on the back of each bill emphasizes the strong links among the various European countries shown in the map underneath the bridge. The 8 euro coins are issued in the following values: 1, 2, 5, 10, 20, and 50 cents, and 1 and 2 euros.

Prior to 2002, the French used the **franc** as their national currency. Unlike the euro, the franc could be used only in France.

POUR
COMMUNIQUER

C'est combien?

How to ask how much something costs:

C'est combien?	*How much is it?*	—**C'est combien?**
Ça fait combien?	*How much does that come to (make)?*	—**Ça fait combien?**
Ça fait . . .	*That's . . . , That comes to . . .*	—**Ça fait** 10 euros.
Combien coûte . . . ?	*How much does . . . cost?*	—**Combien coûte** le sandwich?
Il/Elle coûte . . .	*It costs . . .*	—**Il coûte** 5 euros.

How to ask a friend to lend you something:

Prête-moi . . .	*Lend me . . . , Loan me . . .*	**Prête-moi** 30 euros, s'il te plaît.

➡ Note that masculine nouns can be replaced by **il** and feminine nouns can be replaced by **elle.**

| Voici **une glace.** | **Elle** coûte 2 euros. | ***It*** *costs 2 euros.* |
| Voici **un sandwich.** | **Il** coûte *5 euros.* | ***It*** *costs 5 euros.* |

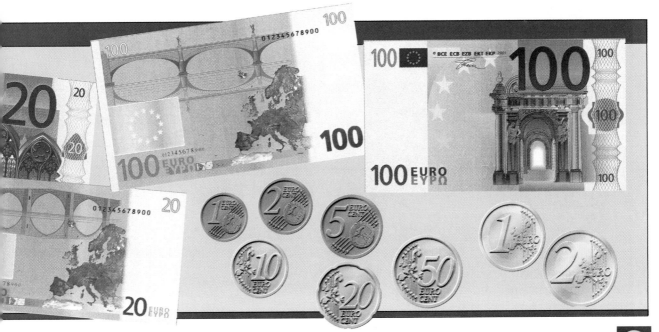

1 S'il te plaît . . .

You have been shopping in Paris and discover that you did not exchange enough money. Ask a friend to loan you the following sums.

▶ 10 euros
   S'il te plaît, prête-moi dix euros.

1. 20 euros	4. 60 euros	7. 85 euros
2. 30 euros	5. 75 euros	8. 90 euros
3. 45 euros	6. 80 euros	9. 95 euros

2 Décision

Before ordering at a café, Stéphanie and Émilie are checking the prices. Act out the dialogues.

▶ le chocolat

Combien coûte le chocolat?

Il coûte deux euros cinquante.

1. le thé
2. le jus d'orange
3. la salade de tomates
4. la glace à la vanille
5. le café
6. le steak-frites
7. le hot dog
8. l'omelette
9. la salade mixte
10. le jus de raisin

LE SELECT

— **BOISSONS** —

café	2€
chocolat	2€50
thé	2€80
limonade	3€
jus d'orange	3€50
jus de raisin	3€

— **GLACES** —

glace au chocolat	2€50
glace à la vanille	2€50

— **SANDWICHS** —

sandwich au jambon	4€
sandwich au fromage	4€

— **ET AUSSI . . .** —

steak-frites	5€25
salade mixte	3€50
salade de tomates	4€
omelette	5€25
hot dog	3€50
croissant	3€50
pizza	4€50

LE SELECT
P. SOULIE
CAFÉ RESTAURANT*
Tél. 01.45.22.46.29
30, boulevard des Batignolles 75017 Paris

3 Ça fait combien?

You have gone to Le Select with your friends and have ordered the following items. Now you are ready to leave the café, and each one wants to pay. Check the prices on the menu for Le Select, and act out the dialogue.

▶ —Ça fait combien, s'il vous plaît?
—Ça fait deux euros cinquante.
—Voici deux euros cinquante.
—Merci.

1   2

3

4   5

4 Au «Select»

You are at Le Select. Order something to eat and drink. Since you are in a hurry, ask for the check right away. Act out the dialogue with a classmate who will play the part of the waiter/waitress.

Monsieur, s'il vous plaît!

Vous désirez?

Je voudrais un sandwich au jambon et un café. Ça fait combien?

Ça fait 6 euros.

Prononciation

La consonne «r»   /r/

The French consonant "**r**" is not at all like the English "**r**." It is pronounced at the back of the throat. In fact, it is similar to the Spanish "jota" sound of José.

Répétez: **Marie Paris orange Henri
franc très croissant fromage
bonjour pour Pierre quart
Robert Richard Renée Raoul**

Marie, prête-moi trente euros.

Marie

LEÇON 12

Le temps

It is nine o'clock Sunday morning. Cécile and her brother Philippe have planned a picnic for the whole family. Cécile is asking about the weather.

CÉCILE: Quel temps fait-il?
PHILIPPE: Il fait mauvais!
CÉCILE: Il fait mauvais?
PHILIPPE: Oui, il fait mauvais! Regarde!
Il pleut!
CÉCILE: Zut, zut et zut!
PHILIPPE: !!!???
CÉCILE: Et le pique-nique?
PHILIPPE: Le pique-nique? Ah oui, le pique-nique! . . .
Écoute, ça n'a pas d'importance.
CÉCILE: Pourquoi?
PHILIPPE: Pourquoi? Parce que Papa va
nous inviter au restaurant.
CÉCILE: Super!

CÉCILE: How's the weather?
PHILIPPE: It's bad!
CÉCILE: It's bad?
PHILIPPE: Yes, it's bad! Look! It's raining!
CÉCILE: Darn, darn, darn!
PHILIPPE: !!!???
CÉCILE: And the picnic?
PHILIPPE: The picnic? Oh yes, the picnic! . . .
Listen, it's not important (that has no importance).
CÉCILE: Why?
PHILIPPE: Why? Because Dad is going to take us out (invite us) to a restaurant.
CÉCILE: Great!

POUR COMMUNIQUER

Quel temps fait-il?

How to talk about the weather:

Quel temps fait-il?   *How's the weather?*

Il fait beau.

Il fait bon.

Il fait chaud.

Il fait frais.

Il fait froid.

Il fait mauvais.

Il pleut.

Il neige.

Les saisons *(Seasons)*

le printemps	*spring*	**au printemps**	*in (the) spring*
l'été	*summer*	**en été**	*in (the) summer*
l'automne	*fall, autumn*	**en automne**	*in (the) fall*
l'hiver	*winter*	**en hiver**	*in (the) winter*

---

1 **Ta région**

Tell Cécile what the weather is like in your part of the country.

▶ en juillet

En juillet, il fait chaud.

1. en août
2. en septembre
3. en novembre
4. en janvier
5. en mars
6. en mai

2 **Les quatre saisons**

Describe what the weather is like in each of the four seasons in the following cities.

▶ à Miami

En été, il fait chaud. En automne, il fait chaud aussi. En hiver, il fait frais. Au printemps, il fait bon.

1. à Chicago
2. à San Francisco
3. à Denver
4. à Boston
5. à Seattle
6. à Dallas

À votre tour!

1 Isabelle et Jean-Paul

Isabelle is talking to Jean-Paul. You hear parts of their conversation. For each of Isabelle's questions, select Jean-Paul's response from the suggested answers.

1. Tu as faim?
2. Tu veux un jus de pomme?
3. Combien coûte le café au Café Français?
4. Quel temps fait-il?
5. Quelle est ta saison favorite?

a. Il fait chaud.
b. Trois euros.
c. Oui, merci, j'ai soif.
d. C'est le printemps.
e. Oui, je voudrais un sandwich.

2 Et toi?

Now Isabelle is phoning you. Answer her questions.

1. Quel temps fait-il aujourd'hui?
2. Quel temps fait-il en hiver?
3. Quelle est ta saison favorite?

3 Conversation dirigée

Stéphanie is in a café called Le Petit Bistrot. The waiter is taking her order. With a partner, compose and act out a dialogue according to the script suggested below.

le garçon			Stéphanie
greets client and asks if he may help her	→ ↙	says that she would like a croissant and asks how much an orange juice costs	
answers 3 euros	→ ↙	asks for an orange juice . . . calls the waiter and asks how much she owes	
says 8 euros cinquante	→ ↙	gives waiter 10 euros **(Voici . . .)**	
says thank you			

4 Au café

You are in a French café. Call the waiter/waitress and order the following items. A classmate will play the part of the waiter/waitress.

▶ —**Monsieur (Mademoiselle), s'il vous plaît!**
—**Vous désirez?**
—**Un croissant, s'il vous plaît!**
   (Donnez-moi un croissant, s'il vous plaît!)
   (Je voudrais un croissant, s'il vous plaît!).

5 En scène

With two classmates, act out the following scene.

CHARACTERS:

You, a French friend, and the waiter in the café

SITUATION:

A French friend has been showing you around Paris. You invite your friend to a café and discover too late that you have not changed enough money. Your friend will respond to your questions.

- Ask your friend if he/she is thirsty.
- Ask if he/she wants a soft drink.
- Ask if he/she is hungry.
- Ask if he/she wants a sandwich.
- When the waiter comes, your friend orders and you ask for a croissant and a cup of hot chocolate.
- Ask the waiter how much everything is.
- Ask your friend to please lend you 20 euros.

6 La date, la saison et le temps

Look at the calendar days. For each one, give the date, the season, and the weather.

▶ **C'est le dix avril.**
C'est le printemps.
Il pleut.

Une chanson: Alouette

Alouette *(The Lark)* is a popular folksong of French-Canadian origin. As the song leader names the various parts of the bird's anatomy, he points to his own body. The chorus repeats the refrain with enthusiasm.

Alouette

A - lou - et - te, gen - tille a - lou - et - te, a - lou - et - te, je te plu - me - rai. Je te plu - me - rai la tête, je te plu - me - rai la tête. Et la tête, et la tête, a - lou - ette, a - lou - ette, oh!

le bec
la tête
le cou
le dos
les ailes
la queue
les pattes

1. Alouette, gentille alouette,
   Alouette, je te plumerai.

   Je te plumerai la tête,
   Je te plumerai la tête.

   Et la tête—et la tête
   Alouette—Alouette
   Oh oh oh oh

2. Alouette, gentille alouette
   Alouette, je te plumerai.

   Je te plumerai le bec,
   Je te plumerai le bec.

   Et le bec—et le bec
   Et la tête—et la tête
   Alouette—Alouette
   Oh oh oh oh

3. Je te plumerai le cou . . .

4. Je te plumerai les ailes . . .

5. Je te plumerai le dos . . .

6. Je te plumerai les pattes . . .

7. Je te plumerai la queue . . .

Québec

Les parties du corps

(Parts of the body)

l'oeil (les yeux)
le nez
la bouche
le bras
le ventre
la jambe

les cheveux
la tête
l'oreille
le cou
le dos
la main
le pied

Un jeu **Jacques a dit**

The French sometimes play a game called **Jacques a dit** *(Jim said)*. The rules are the same as the English game of Simon Says. Everyone stands up to play.

The game leader says: **Jacques a dit: Les mains sur la tête!** placing her hands on her head. The other players also place their hands on their head.

Then the game leader may say: **Les mains sur le dos!** placing her hands on her back. This time, however, the other players should not move, because the game leader did not first say **Jacques a dit.** Any player that did move must sit down.

The game continues until only one player is left standing.

À l'école en France

BONJOUR, Nathalie!

Bonjour!

Je m'appelle Nathalie Aubin.

J'ai 15 ans et j'habite° à Savigny-sur-Orge avec ma famille. (Savigny est une petite° ville° à 20 kilomètres au sud° de Paris.)

J'ai un frère, Christophe, 17 ans, et deux sœurs, Céline, 13 ans, et Florence, 7 ans.

Mon père est programmeur. (Il travaille° à Paris.)

Ma mère est dentiste. (Elle travaille à Savigny.)

Je vais au lycée Jean-Baptiste Corot.

Je suis élève° de seconde°. Et vous?

Nathalie

j'habite *I live* **petite** *small* **ville** *city* **sud** *south*
travaille *works* **élève** *student* **seconde** *tenth grade*

mon père

moi

**ma soeur
Florence**

Voici ma famille.

ma mère   **ma soeur Céline**

**mon frère
Christophe**

Voici mon école.°
Le lycée Jean-Baptiste
Corot est dans°
un château!°

Voici ma maison.°
(C'est une maison confortable,
mais° ce n'est pas un château!)

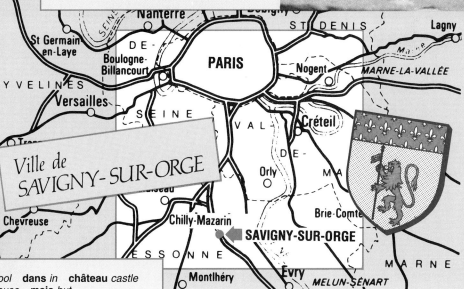

Ville de
SAVIGNY-SUR-ORGE

école *school* **dans** *in* **château** *castle*	
maison *house* **mais** *but*	

Un jour de classe

Le matin

À la maison

Nathalie gets up every morning at seven. After a light breakfast (toasted bread with butter and jam, hot chocolate), she leaves for school.

Nathalie sur sa mobylette

Since she does not live too far from her lycée, she goes there on her moped **(sa mobylette).** Students who live farther away take the school bus.

La classe de sciences-éco

Nathalie arrives at school at about 8:25, five minutes before her first class. Today, Thursday, her first class is economics **(les sciences économiques),** which is her favorite subject.

L'après-midi

À la cantine

At 12:30, Nathalie goes to the school cafeteria **(la cantine)** for lunch. As in American schools, the food is served cafeteria-style. During lunch break, Nathalie meets with her friends from other classes.

La classe d'anglais

Classes start again at two o'clock. Today they finish at four.

Après les classes

Depending on when her last class ends, Nathalie either goes home right after school or participates in one of the many school clubs.

Le soir

Dans la salle à manger

The Aubins have dinner around 7:30. Everyone helps with the kitchen chores. Today it is Christophe's turn.

Nathalie does her homework after dinner. She usually has about one or two hours of homework every night. When she is finished, she reads or listens to cassettes for a while, then goes to bed around 11 P.M.

Nathalie dans sa chambre

L'emploi du temps

	LUNDI	MARDI	MERCREDI	JEUDI	VENDREDI	SAMEDI
8h30 à 9h30	Histoire	Allemand				
9h30 à 10h30	Anglais	Français	Anglais	Sciences économiques		Français
10h30 à 11h30	Sport	Français	Sciences économiques	Sciences physiques (13h30)	Allemand	Français
11h30 à 12h30	Français	Latin	Maths	Maths (13h30)	Latin	Latin
13h00 à 14h00					Sciences physiques	Histoire ou Civilisation
14h00 à 15h00	Sciences physiques	Maths				
15h00 à 16h00	Géographie	Maths			Allemand	
16h00 à 17h00	Civilisation	Anglais		Histoire		

■ NOTE ■
CULTURELLE

Le programme scolaire

At the lycée, all students take a certain number of required subjects. These include French, math, one foreign language, history and geography, physical sciences, natural sciences, and physical education. Depending on their career plans, French students also have to choose among certain electives: a second foreign language, economics, computer science, biology, music.

Here are some of the subjects taught in French secondary schools. How many can you identify?

le français	**l'histoire**	**les maths**
l'anglais	**la géographie**	**la biologie**
l'espagnol	**les sciences**	**la physique**
l'allemand	** économiques**	**la chimie**
le latin	**l'éducation civique** *(civics)*	**l'informatique** *(computer science)*
	la musique	
	le dessin	**les sciences naturelles**
	l'éducation physique	**la philosophie**

ACTIVITÉS CULTURELLES

1. Look carefully at Nathalie's class schedule. You may have noted certain differences between the French and the American school systems.
   - French students have more class hours than American students. How many hours of classes does Nathalie have each week?
   - French students learn more foreign languages than American students. In France, the study of foreign languages is compulsory. What languages is Nathalie learning?
   - French students usually have Wednesday afternoon free. Does Nathalie have school on Saturday morning? on Saturday afternoon?
2. Write out your own class schedule in French.

Le lycée Jean-Baptiste Corot

un pastel de Corot

Jean-Baptiste Corot

Like many French schools, the lycée Jean-Baptiste Corot of Savigny-sur-Orge is named after a famous French person. Jean-Baptiste Corot is a 19th century painter, remembered especially for his landscapes.

The lycée Jean-Baptiste Corot is both very old and very modern. It was created in the 1950's on the grounds of a historical castle dating from the 12th century. The castle, which serves as the administrative center, is still surrounded by a moat. The lycée itself has many modern facilities which include:

- **les salles de classe** *(classrooms)*
- **la cantine** *(cafeteria)*
- **le stade** *(stadium)* **et le terrain de sport** *(playing field)*

Plan du lycée Jean-Baptiste Corot

une salle de classe

la cantine

le terrain de sport

NOTES CULTURELLES

1 L'école secondaire

There are two types of secondary schools in France:
- **le collège,** which corresponds to the U.S. middle school (grades 6 to 9)
- **le lycée,** which corresponds to the U.S. high school (grades 10 to 12)

On the following chart, you will notice that each grade **(une classe)** is designated by a number (as in the United States): **sixième (6e), cinquième (5e), quatrième (4e),** etc. However, the progression from grade to grade is the opposite in France. The secondary school begins in France with **sixième** and ends with **terminale.**

École	Classe	Âge des élèves	Équivalent américain
Le collège	sixième (6e)	11–12 ans	*sixth grade*
	cinquième (5e)	12–13 ans	*seventh grade*
	quatrième (4e)	13–14 ans	*eighth grade*
	troisième (3e)	14–15 ans	*ninth grade*
Le lycée	seconde (2e)	15–16 ans	*tenth grade*
	première (1re)	16–17 ans	*eleventh grade*
	terminale	17–18 ans	*twelfth grade*

2 Le bulletin de notes

At the end of each term, French students receive a report card **(le bulletin de notes),** which must be signed by their parents. Most schools assign grades on a scale of 0 (low) to 20 (high). Most teachers also write a brief evaluation of the student's progress in each subject.

Here is a report card for the first semester.

LYCÉE J.-B. COROT   91605 SAVIGNY - SUR - ORGE   CLASSE 2e

PICARD Laurent

PREMIER TRIMESTRE

	NIVEAU A B C D E	Appréciations des Professeurs
Math. M. Antoine	13,5	Élève sérieux.
Sc. Phys. Mme Durin	+ 11,2	Un premier devoir médiocre. Depuis, c'est mieux. Il faut continuer.
Sc. Nat. M. Lemaire	+ 12,5	ASSEZ BON ENSEMBLE.
Hist. et Géogr. M. Brunier	- 13	Bien.
Français M. Rivaud	11	Bon travail.
Anglais I M. Narre	16	Très bien.
Allemand II Mme Dumet	15,2	Excellent élève.

ENSEMBLE DES RÉSULTATS : A Très satisfaisant **(B)** Satisfaisant
C Tout juste suffisant   **D** Insuffisant   **E** Très insuffisant
Appréciations du Proviseur - du Proviseur Adjoint
du Conseiller Principal d'Éducation - du Professeur Principal
Bon trimestre

ACTIVITÉ CULTURELLE

1. What is the name of the student?
2. What is the name of his school?
3. What grade is he in?
4. What is his best subject? What grade did he get?
5. What is his weakest subject? What grade did he get?
6. How many foreign languages is he studying? Which ones?

Expressions pour la classe

Le professeur dit . . .

Écoutez!

à une élève   à un élève   à la classe

Regarde! *(Look!)*	**Regardez!**
Regarde la vidéo.	Regardez la vidéo.
Écoute! *(Listen!)*	**Écoutez!**
Écoute la cassette *(tape).*	Écoutez la cassette.
Parle! *(Speak!)*	**Parlez!**
Parle plus fort *(louder).*	Parlez plus fort.
Réponds! *(Answer!)*	**Répondez!**
Réponds à la question.	Répondez à la question.
Répète! *(Repeat!)*	**Répétez!**
Répète la phrase *(sentence).*	Répétez la phrase.
Lis! *(Read!)*	**Lisez!**
Lis l'exercice.	Lisez l'exercice.
Écris! *(Write!)*	**Écrivez!**
Écris dans ton cahier.	Écrivez dans vos cahiers.

Prends *(Take)*	une feuille de papier.	**Prenez**	une feuille de papier.
	un crayon		un crayon
Ouvre *(Open)*	ton livre.	**Ouvrez**	vos livres.
	la porte		la porte
Ferme *(Close)*	ton cahier.	**Fermez**	vos cahiers.
	la fenêtre		la fenêtre

Viens! *(Come!)*	**Venez!**
Viens ici.	Venez ici.
Va! *(Go!)*	**Allez!**
Va au tableau.	Allez au tableau.
Lève-toi! *(Stand up!)*	**Levez-vous!**
Assieds-toi! *(Sit down!)*	**Asseyez-vous!**

Apporte-moi *(Bring me)*		**Apportez-moi**	
Donne-moi *(Give me)*	ton devoir.	**Donnez-moi**	vos devoirs.
Montre-moi *(Show me)*		**Montrez-moi**	

Quelques objets

un crayon

un livre

un vidéodisque, un CD vidéo

un disque optique (le CD-ROM)

une feuille de papier

une cassette

un stylo

un cahier

un lecteur de CD vidéo

une vidéocassette

un devoir

un morceau de craie

un (disque) compact, un CD

un ordinateur

un lecteur optique externe/de CD-ROM

un disque optique (le CD-ROM)

une télé

une carte

une porte

un bureau

un tableau

un magnétoscope

une table

une chaise

une fenêtre

Tu dis ...

Je sais.	*I know.*
Je ne sais pas.	*I don't know.*
Je ne comprends pas.	*I don't understand.*
Que veut dire . . . ?	*What does . . . mean?*
Comment dit-on . . . en français?	*How does one say . . . in French?*

83

La vie de

Félicitations!

Congratulations! Now that you have learned how to meet and greet people in French, you are going to discover more about everyday life in France: **La vie de tous les jours.**

What are some of the aspects of daily life that you and your friends often talk about? You probably discuss home and family, things you own, and people you know. You talk about what you like to do, where you like to go, and what your weekend plans are. If you were going to France, you would discover that French young people are interested in the same topics.

In this second part of your book, you will learn . . .
- how to talk about your daily activities (both in school and out of school)
- how to make future plans: what you are going to do
- how to describe people you know
- how to describe objects you own
- how to talk about your home and your family
- how to express your opinions

You will also learn . . .
- how to ask your way around in a French city
- how to extend and accept invitations

In order to express yourself accurately, you will also begin to learn how the French language works: how to ask and answer questions, how to describe people, places, and things.

En avant et bon courage!

Jean-Paul Valette　　*Rebecca M. Valette*

tous les jours

THÈME ET OBJECTIFS

Daily activities

In this unit, you will be talking about the things you do every day, such as working and studying, as well as watching TV and listening to the radio.

You will learn . . .
- to describe some of your daily activities
- to say what you like and do not like to do
- to ask and answer questions about where others are and what they are doing

You will also learn . . .
- to invite friends to do things with you
- to politely accept or turn down an invitation

13 Mes activités

Accent sur ... Les activités de la semaine

French teenagers, as well as their parents, put a lot of emphasis on doing well in school. On the whole, French students spend a great deal of time on their studies. French schools have a longer class day than American schools, and teachers tend to assign quite a lot of homework.

However, French teenagers do not study all the time. They also watch TV and listen to music. Many participate in various sports activities, but to a lesser extent than young Americans. On weekends, French teenagers like to go out with their friends. Some go shopping. Others go to the movies. Many enjoy dancing and going to parties. Sunday is usually a family day for visiting relatives or going for a drive in the country.

Au cinéma
Des copains sont au cinéma.

Au café
Stéphanie est au café.

Une boum
Dominique et Stéphanie
sont à une boum.

**Le terrain de foot
au lycée Corot**
Des jeunes jouent au foot.

En classe
Marc et Patrick sont en classe.

A. Préférences

Est-ce que tu aimes parler français?

How to talk about what you like and don't like to do:

Est-ce que tu aimes . . .?	*Do you like . . .?*	**Est-ce que tu aimes** parler *(to speak)* français?
J'aime . . .	*I like . . .*	Oui, **j'aime** parler français.
Je n'aime pas . . .	*I don't like . . .*	Non, **je n'aime pas** parler français.
Je préfère . . .	*I prefer . . .*	**Je préfère** parler anglais.

J'aime . . .

| **téléphoner** | **parler français** | **parler anglais** | **parler espagnol** |
| *to phone* | *to talk, speak French* | *to speak English* | *to speak Spanish* |

| **manger** | **chanter** | **danser** | **nager** |
| *to eat* | *to sing* | *to dance* | *to swim* |

1 Et toi?

Indicate what you like to do in the following situations by completing the sentences.

1. En classe,
   j'aime . . .
   mais je préfère . . .
   - étudier
   - écouter le professeur
   - parler avec *(with)* un copain
   - parler avec une copine

2. En été,
   j'aime . . .
   mais je préfère . . .
   - travailler
   - nager
   - voyager
   - jouer au volley

J'aime aussi *(also)* . . .

jouer au tennis
to play tennis

jouer au volley
to play volleyball

jouer au basket
to play basketball

jouer au foot
to play soccer

Mais *(but)* **je préfère** . . .

regarder la télé
to watch TV

écouter la radio
to listen to the radio

dîner au restaurant
to have dinner at the restaurant; to eat out

voyager
to travel

Je n'aime pas toujours *(always)* . . .

étudier
to study

travailler
to work

HAVE YOU NOTED?

1. French people like to shorten words. For example, the words **volleyball, basketball, football,** and **télévision** are often shortened to **volley, basket, foot,** and **télé.**
2. In French, **foot** (or **football**) refers to *soccer.*

---

3. Avec mes *(my)* copains,
   j'aime . . .
   mais je préfère . . .

   - chanter
   - manger
   - écouter la radio
   - jouer au basket

4. Avec ma famille,
   j'aime . . .
   mais je préfère . . .

   - voyager
   - regarder la télé
   - jouer à «Nintendo»
   - dîner au restaurant

5. À la maison *(At home)*,
   j'aime . . .
   mais je préfère . . .

   - étudier
   - téléphoner
   - manger
   - écouter mon walkman

2 Tu aimes ou tu n'aimes pas?

Say whether or not you like to do the following things.

▶ parler français?

J'aime parler français.

Je n'aime pas parler français.

1. parler anglais?
2. étudier?
3. danser?
4. chanter?
5. jouer au basket?
6. jouer au tennis?

7. regarder la télé?
8. dîner au restaurant?
9. manger?
10. travailler?
11. écouter la radio?
12. téléphoner?

3 Préférences

Ask your classmates if they like to do the following things.

▶ —Est-ce que tu aimes téléphoner?
—Oui, j'aime téléphoner. (Non, je n'aime pas téléphoner.)

4 Dialogue

Philippe is asking Hélène if she likes to do certain things. She replies that she prefers to do other things. Play both roles. Note: "??" means you can invent an answer.

▶ PHILIPPE: Est-ce que tu aimes nager?
HÉLÈNE: Oui, mais je préfère jouer au tennis.

B. Souhaits *(Wishes)*

Je voudrais voyager en France.

How to talk about what you want, would like, and do not want to do:

Je veux . . .	*I want . . .*	**Je veux** parler français.
Je voudrais . . .	*I would like . . .*	**Je voudrais** voyager en France.
Je ne veux pas . . .	*I don't want . . .*	**Je ne veux pas** étudier aujourd'hui.

5 **Ce soir** *(Tonight)*

Say whether or not you want to do the following things tonight.

▶ étudier?
Oui, je veux étudier.
(Non, je ne veux pas étudier.)

1. parler français?
2. travailler?
3. jouer au ping-pong?
4. chanter?
5. danser?
6. regarder la télé?
7. écouter la radio?
8. dîner avec une copine?
9. parler à *(to)* mon frère?
10. téléphoner à mon cousin?

6 **Weekend**

Caroline and her friends are discussing their weekend plans. What do they say they would like to do?

▶ CAROLINE: **Je voudrais jouer au tennis.**

▶ **Caroline**
1. Jérôme
2. Monique
3. Jean-Louis
4. Céline
5. Patrick

7 **Trois souhaits** *(Three wishes)*

Read the list of suggested activities and select the three that you would like to do most.

parler français	voyager avec ma cousine
parler espagnol	voyager en France
parler avec *(with)* Oprah Winfrey	chanter comme *(like)* Will Smith
dîner avec le Président	jouer au tennis avec Venus Williams
dîner avec Tom Cruise	jouer au basket comme Michael Jordan

▶ Je voudrais parler espagnol.
Je voudrais chanter comme Will Smith.
Je voudrais voyager en France.

C. Invitations

Est-ce que tu veux jouer au tennis?

▶ *How to invite a friend:*

Est-ce que tu veux ...?	*Do you want to . . . ?*	**Est-ce que tu veux** jouer au tennis?
Est-ce que tu peux ...?	*Can you . . . ?*	**Est-ce que tu peux** parler à mon copain?
avec moi/toi	*with me/you*	Est-ce que tu veux dîner **avec moi?**

▶ *How to accept an invitation:*

Oui, bien sûr ...	*Yes, of course . . .*	
Oui, merci ...	*Yes, thanks . . .*	
Oui, d'accord ...	*Yes, all right, okay . . .*	
je veux bien.	*I'd love to.*	**Oui, bien sûr, je veux bien.**
je veux bien ...	*I'd love to . . .*	**Oui, merci, je veux bien** dîner avec toi.

▶ *How to turn down an invitation:*

Je regrette, mais	*I'm sorry, but*	**Je regrette, mais je ne peux pas**
je ne peux pas ...	*I can't . . .*	dîner avec toi.
Je dois ...	*I have to, I must . . .*	**Je dois** étudier.

---

8 Invitations

Imagine a French exchange group is visiting your school. Invite the following French students to do things with you. They will accept. (Your classmates will play the parts of the students.)

▶ Monique / dîner

Monique, est-ce que tu veux dîner avec moi?

Oui, d'accord, je veux bien dîner avec toi.

1. Éric / parler français
2. Philippe / étudier
3. Céline / jouer au tennis
4. Anne / manger une pizza
5. Jean-Claude / chanter
6. Caroline / danser

9 Conversation

Ask your classmates if they want to do the following things. They will answer that they cannot and explain what they have to do.

▶ jouer au basket? (étudier)
  —**Est-ce que tu veux jouer au basket?**
  —**Non, je ne peux pas. Je dois étudier.**

1. jouer au volley? (travailler)
2. jouer au ping-pong? (téléphoner à ma cousine)
3. étudier avec moi? (étudier avec ma copine)
4. dîner avec moi? (dîner avec ma famille)
5. nager? (jouer au foot à deux heures)

À votre tour!

Est-ce que tu veux **jouer au tennis** avec moi?

Non, je ne peux pas. Je dois travailler.

1 Créa-dialogue

Ask your classmates if they want to do the following things with you. They will answer that they cannot and will give one of the excuses in the box.

▶ jouer au tennis

1. jouer au basket
2. manger une pizza
3. regarder la télé
4. jouer au ping-pong
5. dîner au restaurant

Excuses:
étudier
travailler
téléphoner à une copine

dîner avec ma cousine
parler avec ma mère
chanter avec la chorale *(choir)*

2 Conversation dirigée

Philippe is phoning Stéphanie. Write out their conversation according to the directions. You may want to act out the dialogue with a classmate.

Philippe				**Stéphanie**
	asks Stéphanie how she is	⤢	answers that she is fine	
	asks her if she wants to eat out	⤢	asks at what time	
	says at 8 o'clock	⤡	says that she is sorry but that she has to study	
	says it is too bad (**Dommage!**)			

3 Expression personnelle

What we like to do often depends on the circumstances. Complete the sentences below saying what you like and don't like to do in the following situations.

▶ En hiver . . .
En hiver, j'aime regarder la télé. J'aime aussi jouer au basket. Je n'aime pas nager.

1. En été . . .
2. En automne . . .
3. Le samedi *(On Saturdays)* . . .
4. Le dimanche . . .
5. Le soir *(In the evening)* . . .
6. En classe . . .
7. Avec mes *(my)* amis . . .
8. Avec ma famille . . .

4 Composition

Write three things that you like to do and three things that you do not like to do.

▶

J'aime jouer au volley. Je n'aime pas jouer au foot.

5 Correspondance

This summer, you are going to spend two weeks in France. Your pen pal Philippe has written, asking what you like and don't like to do on vacation (**en vacances**). Write a postcard answering his questions.

▶

Cher Philippe,
En vacances, j'aime . . .

PHILIPPE RAYMOND
12 AV. VICTOR HUGO
PARIS 75116
FRANCE

Qui est là?

It is Wednesday afternoon. Pierre is looking for his friends but cannot find anyone. Finally he sees Hélène at the Café Bellevue and asks her where everyone is.

PIERRE: <u>Où</u> est Jacqueline?	*Where*
HÉLÈNE: Elle est <u>à la maison</u>.	*at home*
PIERRE: Et Jean-Claude? Il est <u>là</u>?	*here*
HÉLÈNE: Non, il n'est pas là.	
PIERRE: Où est-il?	
HÉLÈNE: Il est <u>en ville</u> avec une copine.	*in town*
PIERRE: Et Nicole et Sandrine? Est-ce qu'elles sont <u>ici</u>?	*here*
HÉLÈNE: Non, elles sont au restaurant.	
PIERRE: <u>Alors</u>, qui est là?	*So*
HÉLÈNE: Moi, je suis ici.	
PIERRE: C'est <u>vrai</u>, tu es ici! Eh bien, <u>puisque</u> tu es là, <u>je t'invite au cinéma</u>. D'accord?	*true / since* *I'll invite you to the movies*
HÉLÈNE: Super! Pierre, tu es un <u>vrai</u> copain!	*real*

Compréhension

Indicate where the following people are by selecting the appropriate completions.

1. Jacqueline est . . .   a) au café
2. Jean-Claude est . . .   b) à la maison
3. Nicole et Sandrine sont . . .   c) en ville
4. Hélène et Pierre sont . . .   d) au restaurant

■ NOTE ■
CULTURELLE

Le mercredi après-midi

French high school students do not have classes on Wednesday afternoons. They use this free time to go out with their friends or to catch up on their homework. For some students, Wednesday afternoon is also the time for music and dance lessons as well as sports club activities. However, in contrast to the United States, many French schools have classes on Saturday mornings.

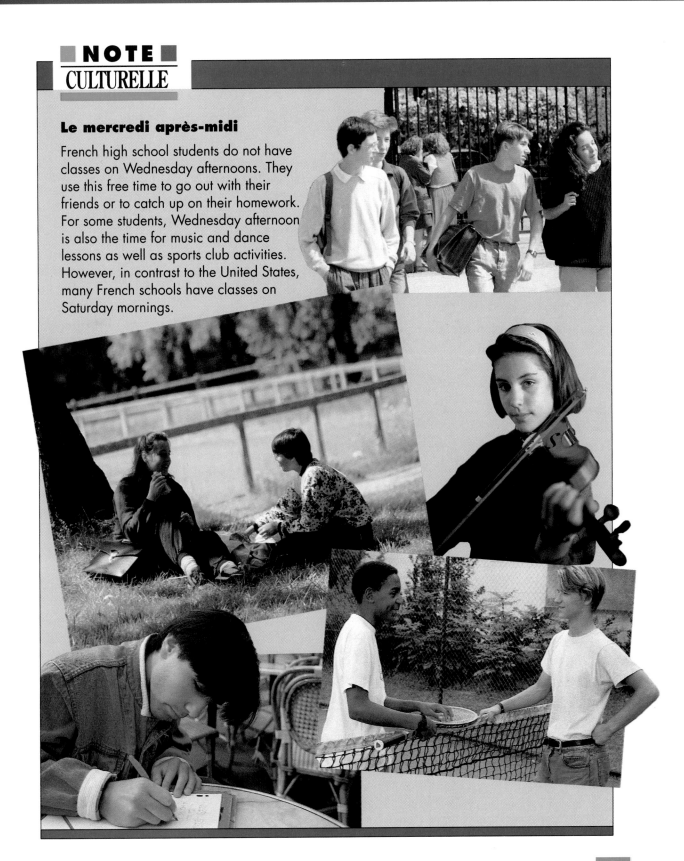

A. Le verbe *être* et les pronoms sujets

Être *(to be)* is the most frequently used verb in French. Note the forms of **être** in the chart below.

	être	*to be*	
SINGULAR	je **suis**	*I am*	Je **suis** américain.
	tu **es**	*you are*	Tu **es** canadienne.
	il/elle **est**	*he/she is*	Il **est** anglais.
PLURAL	nous **sommes**	*we are*	Nous **sommes** à Paris.
	vous **êtes**	*you are*	Vous **êtes** à San Francisco.
	ils/elles **sont**	*they are*	Ils **sont** à Genève.

➡ Note the liaison in the **vous** form:

    Vous êtes français?

➡ Note the expression **être d'accord** *(to agree):*

    —Tu **es** d'accord   *Do you agree*
        avec moi?   *with me?*

    — Oui, je **suis** d'accord!   *Yes, I agree.*

TU or *VOUS?*

When talking to ONE person, the French have two ways of saying *you:*

- **tu** ("familiar *you*") is used to talk to someone your own age (or younger) or to a member of your family
- **vous** ("formal *you*") is used when talking to anyone else

When talking to TWO or more people, the French use **vous.**

REMINDER: You should use . . .
- **vous** to address your teacher
- **tu** to address a classmate

Tu es français?

Vous êtes français?

Vous êtes français?

ILS or ELLES?

The French have two ways of saying *they:*

- **ils** refers to two or more males or to a mixed group of males and females
- **elles** refers to two or more females

Ils sont à Paris.   *Ils sont à Bordeaux.*
Ils sont à Lyon.   *Elles sont à Nice.*

1 En France

The following students are on vacation in France.
Which cities are they in?

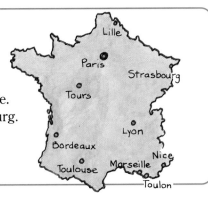

▶ Alice . . . à Nice.   **Alice est à Nice.**

1. Philippe . . . à Toulon.
2. Nous . . . à Paris.
3. Vous . . . à Marseille.
4. Je . . . à Lyon.
5. Tu . . . à Tours.
6. Michèle et Francine . . . à Lille.
7. Éric et Vincent . . . à Strasbourg.
8. Ma cousine . . . à Toulouse.
9. Mon copain . . . à Bordeaux.

Vocabulaire: *Où?*

Où est Cécile?   *Where is Cécile?*

Elle est . . .

ici *(here)*	**là** *(here, there)*	**là-bas** *(over there)*
à Paris *(in Paris)*	**à** Boston	**à** Québec
en classe *(in class)*	**en ville** *(downtown, in town, in the city)*	
en vacances *(on vacation)*	**en** France *(in France)*	
au café *(at the café)*	**au restaurant**	**au cinéma** *(at the movies)*
à la maison *(at home)*		

---

2 À Nice

Catherine is spending her summer vacation in Nice at the home of her pen pal Stéphanie Lambert. Catherine has met many different people and is asking them various questions. Complete her questions with **Tu es** or **Vous êtes,** as appropriate.

▶ *(Stéphanie's brother)* . . . en vacances?
  Tu es en vacances?

▶ *(Monsieur Lambert)* . . . de *(from)* Tours?
  Vous êtes de Tours?

1. *(Mélanie, a friend of Stéphanie's)* . . . canadienne?
2. *(Olivier, Stéphanie's boyfriend)* . . . souvent *(often)* avec Stéphanie?
3. *(Monsieur Tardif, the neighbor)* . . . en vacances?
4. *(the mailman)* . . . de Nice?
5. *(Frédéric, Stéphanie's young cousin)* . . . souvent à Nice?
6. *(a woman in the park)* . . . française?
7. *(a little girl at the beach)* . . . en vacances?
8. *(a man reading Time magazine)* . . . américain?

Où sont-ils?

Corinne is wondering if some of the people she knows are in certain places. Tell her she is right, using **il, elle, ils,** or **elles** in your answers.

▶ —Ta cousine est à Chicago?
—Oui, elle est à Chicago.

▶ —Pierre et Vincent sont au café?
—Oui, ils sont au café.

1. Stéphanie est à Lyon?
2. Monsieur Thomas est à San Francisco?
3. Suzanne et Monique sont à Genève?
4. Cécile et Charlotte sont au café?

5. Ta soeur est en ville?
6. Ton cousin est en vacances?
7. Claire, Alice et Éric sont au cinéma?
8. Monsieur et Madame Joli sont à Montréal?

Où?

You want to know where certain people are. A classmate will answer you on the basis of the illustrations.

▶ —Où est Céline?
—Elle est à New York.

Céline

1. Daniel

2. Caroline

3. Jean-Louis

4. Robert

5. Florence

6. Hélène

7. Julien

B. Les questions à réponse affirmative ou négative

The sentences on the left are statements. The sentences on the right are questions. These questions are called YES/NO QUESTIONS because they can be answered by *yes* or *no.* Note how the French questions begin with **est-ce que.**

STATEMENTS	YES/NO QUESTIONS	
Stéphanie est ici.	**Est-ce que** Stéphanie est ici?	*Is Stéphanie here?*
Tu es français.	**Est-ce que** tu es français?	*Are you French?*
Paul et Marc sont au café.	**Est-ce que** Paul et Marc sont au café?	*Are Paul and Marc at the café?*
Tu veux dîner avec moi.	**Est-ce que** tu veux dîner avec moi?	*Do you want to have dinner with me?*

Yes/no questions can be formed according to the pattern:

est-ce que + STATEMENT?	**Est-ce que** Pierre est ici?
↓	
est-ce qu' (+ VOWEL SOUND)	**Est-ce qu'**il est en ville?

➡ In yes/no questions, the voice goes up at the end of the sentence.

Est-ce que Paul et Florence sont au café?

➡ In casual conversation, yes/no questions can be formed without **est-ce que** simply by letting your voice rise at the end of the sentence.

Tu es français?   Cécile est en ville?

OBSERVATION: When you expect someone to agree with you, another way to form a yes/no question is to add the tag **n'est-ce pas** at the end of the sentence.

Tu es américain, **n'est-ce pas?**   *You are American, **aren't you?***
Tu aimes parler français, **n'est-ce pas?**   *You like to speak French, **don't you?***
Vous êtes d'accord, **n'est-ce pas?**   *You agree, **don't you?***

5 **Nationalités** ─────────────

You are attending an international music camp. Ask about the nationalities of the other participants.

▶ Marc/canadien?   **Est-ce que Marc est canadien?**

1. Jim/américain?   3. Paul et Philippe/français?   5. vous/anglais?   7. Ellen et Carol/
2. Luisa/mexicaine?   4. tu/canadien?   6. Anne/française?   américaines?

Expressions pour la conversation

How to answer a yes/no question:

Oui!	*Yes!*	**Non!**	*No!*
Mais oui!	*Sure!*	**Mais non!**	*Of course not!*
Bien sûr!	*Of course!*		
Peut-être . . .	*Maybe . . .*		

---

6 **Conversation** ──────────────

Ask your classmates the following questions. They will answer, using an expression from **Expressions pour la conversation.**

▶ Ton cousin est français?

1. Ta mère est à la maison?
2. Ta cousine est en France?
3. Ton copain est en classe?
4. Tu veux dîner avec moi?
5. Tu veux jouer au tennis avec moi?

Mais oui!   (Mais non!)

Alice, est-ce que ton cousin est français?

C. La négation

Compare the affirmative and negative sentences below:

AFFIRMATIVE	NEGATIVE	
Je **suis** américain.	Je **ne suis pas** français.	*I'm not French.*
Nous **sommes** en classe.	Nous **ne sommes pas** en vacances.	*We are not on vacation.*
Claire **est** là-bas.	Elle **n'est pas** ici.	*She is not here.*
Vous **êtes** à Paris.	Vous **n'êtes pas** à Lyon.	*You are not in Lyon.*
Tu **es** d'accord avec moi.	Tu **n'es pas** d'accord avec Marc.	*You do not agree with Marc.*

Negative sentences are formed as follows:

SUBJECT + **ne** + VERB + **pas** . . . ↓ **n'** (+ VOWEL SOUND)	Éric et Anne **ne** sont **pas** là. Michèle **n'**est **pas** avec moi.

Je suis en classe.

Je **ne** suis **pas** à la maison.

7 Non!

Answer the following questions negatively.

▶ —Est-ce que tu es français (française)?
—**Non, je ne suis pas français (française).**

1. Est-ce que tu es canadien (canadienne)?
2. Est-ce que tu es à Québec?
3. Est-ce que tu es à la maison?
4. Est-ce que tu es au café?
5. Est-ce que tu es en vacances?
6. Est-ce que tu es au cinéma?

8 D'accord

It is raining. François suggests to his friends that they go to the movies. Say who agrees and who does not, using the expression **être d'accord.**

▶ ☹ Philippe  Philippe n'est pas d'accord.

▶ ☺ Hélène Hélène est d'accord.

1. ☺ nous
2. ☺ je
3. ☹ tu
4. ☺ Patrick et Marc
5. ☹ Claire et Stéphanie
6. ☹ vous
7. ☺ ma copine
8. ☹ mon frère

Vocabulaire: Mots utiles *(Useful words)*

à	at	Je suis **à** la maison **à** dix heures.
	in	Nous sommes **à** Paris.
de	from	Vous êtes **de** San Francisco.
	of	Voici une photo **de** Paris.
et	and	Anne **et** Sophie sont en vacances.
ou	or	Qui est-ce? Juliette **ou** Sophie?
avec	with	Philippe est **avec** Pauline.
pour	for	Je veux travailler **pour** Monsieur Martin.
mais	but	Je ne suis pas français, **mais** j'aime parler français.

➡ **De** becomes **d'** before a vowel sound:
   Patrick est **de** Lyon.   François est **d'**Annecy.

Fête Nationale
mardi 14 juillet
à 22h

P A R I S

9 **Le mot juste** *(The right word)*

Complete the sentences below with the word in parentheses that fits logically.

1. Monsieur Moreau est en France. Aujourd'hui, il est . . . Lyon. (à/de)
2. Martine est canadienne. Elle est . . . Montréal. (de/et)
3. Florence n'est pas ici. Elle est . . . Jean-Claude. (et/avec)
4. Alice . . . Paul sont au restaurant. (avec/et)
5. Jean-Pierre n'est pas à la maison. Il est au café . . . au cinéma. (ou/et)
6. J'aime jouer au tennis . . . je ne veux pas jouer avec toi. (ou/mais)
7. Je dois travailler . . . mon père. (pour/à)

10 **Être ou ne pas être** *(To be or not to be)*

We cannot be in different places at the same time. Express this according to the model.

▶ Aline est en ville. (ici)
   Aline n'est pas ici.

1. Frédéric est là-bas. (à la maison)
2. Nous sommes en classe. (au restaurant)
3. Tu es à Nice. (à Toulon)
4. Vous êtes au café. (au cinéma)
5. Jérôme est avec Sylvie. (avec Catherine)
6. Juliette et Sophie sont avec Éric. (avec Marc)

Prononciation

/a/

La voyelle /a/

The letter "**a**" alone always represents the sound /a/ as in the English word *ah*. It never has the sound of "*a*" as in English words like *class*, *date*, or *cinema*.

chat

Répétez: **ch**a**t ç**a **v**a **à l**a l**à**-b**a**s **a**vec **a**mi voil**à**
cla**sse c**a**fé s**a**l**a**de d**a**me d**a**te M**a**d**a**me C**a**n**a**d**a**

Anne est **a**u C**a**n**a**d**a** **a**vec M**a**d**a**me L**a**v**a**l.

À votre tour!

1 Allô!

Jacques is phoning some friends. Match his questions on the left with his friends' answers on the right.

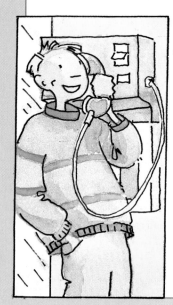

1. Où es-tu?

2. Où est ta soeur?

3. Est-ce que ton frère est à la maison?

4. Tes parents sont en vacances, n'est-ce pas?

5. Ta soeur est avec une copine?

a. Non, il est au cinéma.

b. Oui, elles sont au restaurant.

c. Je suis à la maison.

d. Elle est en classe.

e. Oui! Ils sont à Paris.

2 Où sont-ils?

Read what the following people are saying and decide where they are.

▶ Anne et Éric sont au café.

Une limonade, s'il vous plaît.

▶ **Anne et Éric**

Le film est excellent.

1. nous

Où est le musée *(museum)*?

2. les touristes

Une pizza, s'il vous plaît.

3. vous

Bonjour, Maman.

4. tu

Stéphanie, est-ce que tu veux nager?

5. Paul

3 Créa-dialogue

You are working for a student magazine in France. Your assignment is to interview tourists who are visiting Paris. Ask them where they are from. (Make sure to address the people appropriately as **tu** or **vous**.) Remember: The symbol "??" means you may invent your own responses.

Nationalité	**Villes** *(Cities)*	
▶ anglaise	Londres? *(London)* Liverpool	

▶ — Bonjour. <u>Vous êtes anglaise?</u>
— Oui, je suis <u>anglaise</u>.
— Est-ce que <u>vous êtes</u> de <u>Londres</u>?
— Mais non, je ne suis pas de <u>Londres</u>. Je suis de <u>Liverpool</u>.

Nationalité	**Villes**	
1 américaine	New York? Washington	
2 canadien	Québec? Montréal	
3 française	Paris? Nice	
4 mexicain	Mexico? Puebla	
5 ??	?? ??	
6 ??	?? ??	

4 Composition: Et toi?

Write a short paragraph about yourself and your friends.

1. Say what city you are from. **(Je suis de …)**
2. Say what city your father or your mother is from. **(Mon père / ma mère est de …)**
3. Say where one of your friends is from. **(Mon copain / ma copine …)**
4. Name an activity you like to do with a friend. **(J'aime … avec …)**
5. Name an activity you want to do with two friends. **(Je veux …)**
6. Name an activity you would like to do with one of your relatives. **(Je voudrais …)**

5 Composition: Personnellement

On a separate piece of paper, or on a computer, write where you are and where you are not at each of the following times.

▶ à 9 heures du matin
- à 4 heures
- à 7 heures du soir
- samedi
- dimanche
- en juillet

À neuf heures du matin, je suis en classe. Je ne suis pas à la maison.

Une boum

Jean-Marc has been invited to a party. He is trying to decide whether to bring Béatrice or Valérie. First he talks to Béatrice.

JEAN-MARC:	<u>Dis</u>, Béatrice, tu aimes danser?	*Hey*
BÉATRICE:	Bien sûr, j'aime danser!	
JEAN-MARC:	Est-ce que tu danses bien?	
BÉATRICE:	Oui, je danse très, <u>très bien</u>.	*very well*
JEAN-MARC:	Et ta cousine Valérie? Est-ce qu'elle danse bien?	
BÉATRICE:	Non, elle ne danse pas très bien.	
JEAN-MARC:	<u>Alors</u>, c'est Valérie <u>que</u> j'invite à la <u>boum</u>.	*So / that / party*
BÉATRICE:	Mais <u>pourquoi</u> elle? Pourquoi pas moi?	*why*
JEAN-MARC:	Écoute, Béatrice, <u>je ne sais pas</u> danser! <u>Alors</u>, je préfère inviter une fille qui ne danse pas très bien. C'est normal, non?	*don't know how / So*

● Compréhension: Vrai ou faux?

Read the following statements and say whether they are true (**C'est vrai!**) or false (**C'est faux!**).

1. Béatrice aime danser.
2. Elle danse bien.
3. Valérie danse très bien.
4. Jean-Marc invite Béatrice.
5. Il invite Valérie.

■ NOTE ■
CULTURELLE

Une boum

On weekends, French teenagers like to go to parties that are organized at a friend's home. Often the guests contribute something to the buffet: sandwiches or soft drinks. There is also a lot of music and dancing. (French teenagers love to dance!)

These informal parties have different names according to the age group of the participants. For students at a **collège** (or junior high), a party is sometimes known as **une boum** or **une fête.** For older students at a **lycée** (or high school), it is called **une soirée** or **une fête.**

A. Les verbes en -er: le singulier

Many French verbs end in **-er** in the infinitive.
Most of these verbs are conjugated like
parler *(to speak)* and **habiter** *(to live)*.
Note the forms of the present tense of these
verbs in the singular. Pay attention to their
endings.

> **Learning about language**
> The basic form of the VERB is the INFINITIVE:
> **jouer** *(to play)*   **travailler** *(to work)*
> In French dictionaries, verbs are listed by
> their infinitives.

INFINITIVE	parler	habiter	ENDINGS
STEM	parl-	habit-	
PRESENT TENSE (SINGULAR)	Je **parle** français. Tu **parles** anglais. Il / Elle **parle** espagnol.	J' **habite** à Paris. Tu **habites** à Boston. Il / Elle **habite** à Madrid.	-e -es -e

The present tense forms of -er verbs consist of two parts:

> STEM + ENDING

- The STEM does not change. It is the infinitive minus **-er:**
   parler   parl-   **habiter**   habit-
- The ENDINGS change with the subject:
   je → -e   tu → -es   il / elle → -e

➡ The above endings are silent.

➡ **Je** becomes **j'** before a vowel sound.
   je parle   **j'**habite

> **Learning about language**
> Verbs conjugated like **parler** and **habiter**
> follow a *predictable pattern.*
> They are called REGULAR VERBS.

---

1 **Curiosité**

At the party, Olivier wants to learn more about Isabelle.
She answers his questions affirmatively. Play both roles.

Tu parles anglais?   *Oui, je parle anglais.*

▶ parler anglais?

1. parler espagnol?
2. habiter à Paris?
3. étudier ici?
4. jouer au volley?
5. jouer au basket?
6. chanter?

Vocabulaire: Les verbes en -er

Verbs you already know:

chanter	*to sing*	**nager**	*to swim*
danser	*to dance*	**parler**	*to speak, talk*
dîner	*to have dinner*	**regarder**	*to watch, look at*
écouter	*to listen (to)*	**téléphoner**	*to phone, call*
étudier	*to study*	**travailler**	*to work*
jouer	*to play*	**voyager**	*to travel*
manger	*to eat*		

New verbs:

aimer	*to like*	Tu **aimes** Paris?
habiter	*to live*	Philippe **habite** à Toulouse?
inviter	*to invite*	J'**invite** un copain.
organiser	*to organize*	Sophie **organise** une **boum**/une **soirée**/une **fête** (party).
visiter	*to visit (places)*	Hélène **visite** Québec.

➡ **Regarder** has two meanings:

   to look (at)   Paul **regarde** Cécile.
   to watch   Cécile **regarde** la télé.

➡ Note the construction **téléphoner à**:

Hélène **téléphone**	**à**	Marc.
Hélène calls	. . .	*Marc.*

➡ Note the constructions with **regarder** and **écouter**:

Philippe **regarde**	. . .	Alice.
Philippe looks	*at*	*Alice.*

Alice **écoute**	. . .	le professeur.
Alice listens	*to*	*the teacher.*

---

2   **Quelle activité?**

Describe what the following people are doing by completing the sentences with one of the verbs below. Be logical in your choice of activity.

chanter   écouter   parler   travailler   manger   voyager   regarder   inviter

1. Je . . . un sandwich. Tu . . . une pizza.
2. Tu . . . anglais. Je . . . français.
3. Éric . . . la radio. Claire . . . un compact (un CD).
4. Jean-Paul . . . la télé. Tu . . . un match de tennis.
5. M. Simon . . . en (by) bus. Mme Dupont . . . en train.
6. Nicolas . . . Marie à la boum. Tu . . . Alain.
7. Mlle Thomas . . . dans (in) un hôpital. Je . . . dans un supermarché (supermarket).
8. Mick Jagger . . . bien. Est-ce que tu . . . bien?

3 Le télescope

Curious Georges has set up a telescope to observe what his neighbors are doing. Describe each person's activity.

▶ Monsieur Thomas dîne.

4 Où sont-ils?

You want to know where the following people are. A classmate will answer, telling you where the people are and what they are doing.

▶ Jacques? (en classe / étudier)

Où est Jacques?

Il est en classe.
Il étudie.

1. Pauline? (au restaurant / dîner)
2. Véronique? (à la maison / téléphoner)
3. Mme Dupont? (en ville / travailler)
4. M. Lemaire? (en France / voyager)
5. Jean-Claude? (à Paris / visiter la tour Eiffel)
6. André? (au Tennis Club / jouer au tennis)
7. Alice? (à l'Olympic Club / nager)

B. Les verbes en -er: le pluriel

Note the plural forms of **parler** and **habiter,** paying attention to the endings.

INFINITIVE	parler	habiter	ENDINGS
STEM	parl-	habit-	
PRESENT TENSE (PLURAL)	Nous **parlons** français. Vous **parlez** anglais. Ils / Elles **parlent** espagnol.	Nous **habitons** à Québec. Vous **habitez** à Chicago. Ils / Elles **habitent** à Caracas.	-ons -ez -ent

➡ In the present tense, the plural endings of -er verbs are:

nous → -ons   vous → -ez   ils / elles → -ent

➡ The -ent ending is silent.

➡ Note the liaison when the verb begins with a vowel sound:

Nous étudions.   Vous invitez Thomas.   Ils habitent en France.   Elles aiment Paris.

OBSERVATION: When the infinitive of the verb ends in -ger, the **nous**-form ends in -geons.

nager: nous na**geons**   manger: nous man**geons**   voyager: nous voya**geons**

5 Qui?

Stéphanie is speaking to or about her friends. Complete her sentences with **tu, elle, vous,** or **ils.**

▶ . . . étudient à Toulouse.
   Ils étudient à Toulouse.

1. . . . habitez à Tours.
2. . . . aime Paris.
3. . . . étudiez à Tours.
4. . . . aiment danser.
5. . . . organisent une boum.
6. . . . parlez espagnol.
7. . . . téléphone à Jean-Pierre.
8. . . . invites un copain.
9. . . . dîne avec Cécile.
10. . . . invitent Monique.

6 À la boum

At a party, Olivier is talking to two Canadian students, Monique and her friend. Monique answers yes to his questions.

▶ parler français?

> Oui, nous parlons français.

> Vous parlez français, n'est-ce pas?

1. parler anglais?
2. habiter à Québec?
3. étudier à Montréal?
4. voyager en France?
5. voyager en train?
6. visiter Paris?
7. aimer Paris?
8. aimer la France?

7 Le camp français

At summer camp, everything is organized according to a schedule. Describe the activities of the following campers by completing the sentences according to the illustrations.

▶ À cinq heures, Alice et Marc . . .   **À cinq heures, Alice et Marc jouent au volley.**

▶

1. À neuf heures, nous . . .
2. À quatre heures, vous . . .
3. À huit heures, Véronique et Pierre . . .
4. À sept heures, nous . . .
5. À trois heures, Thomas et François . . .
6. À six heures, vous . . .

8 Un voyage à Paris

A group of American students are visiting Paris. During their stay, they do all of the following things:

voyager en bus

téléphoner à un copain

visiter la tour Eiffel

dîner au restaurant

inviter une copine

écouter un opéra

Describe the trips of the following people.

▶ Jim   **Il voyage en bus, il visite la tour Eiffel . . .**

1. Linda   2. Paul et Louise   3. nous   4. vous

C. Le présent des verbes en *-er:* forme affirmative et forme négative

FORMS

Compare the affirmative and negative forms of **parler.**

AFFIRMATIVE	NEGATIVE
je **parle** tu **parles** il/elle **parle**	je **ne parle pas** tu **ne parles pas** il/elle **ne parle pas**
nous **parlons** vous **parlez** ils/elles **parlent**	nous **ne parlons pas** vous **ne parlez pas** ils/elles **ne parlent pas**

REMEMBER: The negative form of the verb follows the pattern:

SUBJECT + |ne| + VERB + |pas| ↓ |n'| (+ VOWEL SOUND)	Il **ne** travaille **pas** ici. Je **n'**invite **pas** Pierre.

Il <u>ne</u> travaille <u>pas</u>.

Ils <u>n'</u>écoutent <u>pas</u>.

Elle <u>ne</u> chante <u>pas</u> bien.

USES

In the present tense, French verbs have several English equivalents:

Je **joue** au tennis.
$\begin{cases} \text{I } \textbf{\textit{play}} \text{ tennis.} \\ \text{I } \textbf{\textit{do play}} \text{ tennis.} \\ \text{I } \textbf{\textit{am playing}} \text{ tennis.} \end{cases}$

Je **ne joue pas** au tennis.
$\begin{cases} \text{I } \textbf{\textit{do not play}} \text{ tennis. (I } \textbf{\textit{don't}} \text{ play tennis.)} \\ \text{I } \textbf{\textit{am not playing}} \text{ tennis. (I'm } \textbf{\textit{not playing}} \text{ tennis.)} \end{cases}$

Studying French helps you better appreciate how the English language works.

9 Non!

One cannot do everything. From the following list of activities, select at least three that you do *not* do.

▶ **Je ne joue pas au bridge.**

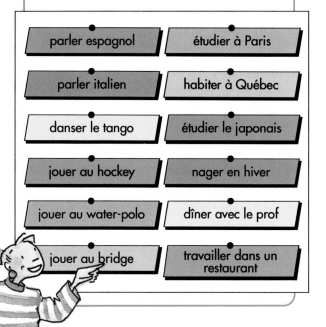

- parler espagnol
- étudier à Paris
- parler italien
- habiter à Québec
- danser le tango
- étudier le japonais
- jouer au hockey
- nager en hiver
- jouer au water-polo
- dîner avec le prof
- jouer au bridge
- travailler dans un restaurant

10 Pas aujourd'hui

Today the following people are tired and are not doing what they usually do. Express this according to the model.

▶ Pierre joue au tennis.
Aujourd'hui, il ne joue pas au tennis.

1. Je joue au foot.
2. Tu étudies.
3. Madame Simonet travaille.
4. Vous dînez à la maison.
5. Marc téléphone à Martine.
6. Nous nageons.
7. Jacques et Florence étudient.

11 Un jeu: Weekend!

On weekends, people like to do different things. For each person, pick an activity and say what that person does. Select another activity and say what that person does not do.

▶ **Antoine et Isabelle dansent.
Ils ne regardent pas la télé.**

je
tu
ma cousine
nous
Antoine et Isabelle
Monsieur Leblanc
Madame Jolivet
vous
le professeur

Vocabulaire: Mots utiles

bien	*well*	Je joue **bien** au tennis.
très bien	*very well*	Je ne chante pas **très bien**.
mal	*badly, poorly*	Tu joues **mal** au volley.
beaucoup	*a lot, much, very much*	Paul aime **beaucoup** voyager.
un peu	*a little, a little bit*	Nous parlons **un peu** français.
souvent	*often*	Charles invite **souvent** Nathalie.
toujours	*always*	Je travaille **toujours** en été.
aussi	*also, too*	Je téléphone à Marc. Je téléphone **aussi** à Véronique.
maintenant	*now*	J'étudie **maintenant**.
rarement	*rarely, seldom*	Vous voyagez **rarement**.

➡ In French, the above expressions *never* come *between* the subject and the verb. They usually come *after* the verb. Compare their positions in French and English.

Nous parlons **toujours** français.   *We **always** speak French.*
Tu joues **bien** au tennis.   *You play tennis **well**.*

12 Expression personnelle

Complete the following sentences with an expression from the list below.

bien	mal	très bien	toujours	souvent	rarement	un peu	beaucoup

1. Je chante . . .
2. Je nage . . .
3. Je regarde . . . la télé.
4. Je mange . . .
5. Je voyage . . . en bus.
6. Le prof parle . . . français.
7. Nous parlons . . . français en classe.
8. Les Rolling Stones chantent . . .
9. Michael Jordan joue . . . au basket.
10. Les Yankees jouent . . . au baseball.

Expressions pour la conversation

How to express approval or regret:

Super!   *Terrific!*   Tu parles français? **Super!**
Dommage!   *Too bad!*   Tu ne joues pas au tennis? **Dommage!**

> Tu parles français?
> Oui, je parle français.
> Super!

13 Conversation

Ask your classmates if they do the following things. Then express approval or regret, according to their answers.

▶ parler français?   —Est-ce que tu parles français?
    —Oui, je parle français. (Non, je ne parle pas français.)
    —Super! (Dommage!)

1. parler espagnol?
2. jouer au tennis?
3. danser bien?
4. voyager beaucoup?
5. dîner souvent au restaurant?
6. inviter souvent ton copain?

D. La construction: verbe + infinitif

Note the use of the infinitive in the following sentences.

J'aime **parler** français.   *I like **to speak** French. I like **speaking** French.*
Nous aimons **voyager**.   *We like **to travel**. We like **traveling**.*

Tu n'aimes pas **étudier**.   *You don't like **to study**. You don't like **studying**.*
Ils n'aiment pas **danser**.   *They don't like **to dance**. They don't like **dancing**.*

To express what they like and don't like to do, the French use these constructions:

SUBJECT + PRESENT TENSE + INFINITIVE . . . of **aimer**		SUBJECT + **n'** + PRESENT TENSE + **pas** + INFINITIVE . . . of **aimer**	
Nous	**aimons** **voyager**.	Nous	**n'aimons pas** **voyager**.

➡ Note that in this construction, the verb **aimer** may be affirmative or negative:
AFFIRMATIVE: Jacques **aime** voyager.   NEGATIVE: Philippe **n'aime pas** voyager.

➡ The above construction is used in questions: Est-ce que Paul **aime voyager?**

OBSERVATION: The infinitive is also used after the following expressions:

Je préfère . . .	*I prefer* . . .	**Je préfère travailler.**
Je voudrais . . .	*I would like* . . .	**Je voudrais voyager.**
Je (ne) veux (pas) . . .	*I (don't) want* . . .	**Je veux jouer** au foot.
Est-ce que tu veux . . .	*Do you want* . . .	**Est-ce que tu veux danser?**
Je (ne) peux (pas) . . .	*I can (I can't)* . . .	**Je ne peux pas dîner** avec toi.
Je dois . . .	*I have to* . . .	**Je dois étudier.**

14 Dialogue

Ask your classmates if they like to do the following things.

▶ chanter?
—**Est-ce que tu aimes chanter?**
—**Oui, j'aime chanter.**   (**Non, je n'aime pas chanter.**)

1. étudier?   4. danser?   7. nager en hiver?
2. voyager?   5. parler français en classe? 8. travailler le week-
3. téléphoner?   6. nager en été?   end *(on weekends)*?

15 Une excellente raison *(An excellent reason)*

The following people are doing certain things. Say that they like these activities.

▶ Thomas voyage.   **Il aime voyager.**

1. Monique chante.   7. Lise et Rose jouent au frisbee.
2. Charles étudie la musique. 8. Éric et Denis écoutent la radio.
3. Henri téléphone.   9. Nous travaillons.
4. Isabelle organise une boum. 10. Nous parlons espagnol.
5. Marc et Sophie nagent.   11. Vous regardez la télé.
6. Annie et Vincent dansent.   12. Vous mangez.

Prononciation

Les voyelles /i/ et /u/

/u/ **où?**   /i/ **ici!**

The vowel sounds /i/ and /u/ are easy to say. Remember to pronounce the French "**i**" as in **Mimi** and not as in the English *him*.

Répétez:
/i/   **ici   Philippe   il**
      Mimi   Sylvie   visite
Philippe visite Paris avec Sylvie.

/u/   **où   nous   vous**
      écoute   joue   toujours

Vous jouez au foot avec nous?

À votre tour!

1 Allô!

Sophie is phoning some friends. Match her questions on the left with her friends' answers on the right.

1 Est-ce que Marc est canadien?

2 Est-ce que tu joues au tennis?

3 Ton frère est à la maison?

4 Ta mère est en vacances?

5 Tu invites Christine et Juliette à la boum?

a Non, elle travaille.

b Oui, mais pas très bien.

c Bien sûr! Elles aiment beaucoup danser.

d Oui, il habite à Montréal.

e Non, il dîne au restaurant avec un copain.

2 Créa-dialogue

Find out how frequently your classmates do the following activities. They will respond using one of the expressions on the scale.

NON	OUI		
	un peu →	souvent →	beaucoup

▶ — **Robert**, est-ce que tu **joues au tennis?**
— Non, je **ne joue pas au tennis.**
— Est-ce que tu **écoutes la radio?**
— Oui, j'**écoute souvent la radio.**

3 Qu'est-ce qu'ils font?

(What do they do?)

Look at what the following students have put in their lockers and say what they like to do.

Éric aime jouer au tennis. Il aime aussi . . .

ÉRIC

HÉLÈNE & ANNE

LE FRANÇAIS PRATIQUE

NOUS

VOUS

¿QUÉ TAL?

4 Message illustré

Marc wrote about certain activities, using pictures. On a separate sheet, write out his description replacing these pictures with the missing words.

À la maison, ma soeur Catherine à une copine. Mon frère Éric . En général, nous à sept heures et demie. Après° le dîner, mes° parents . Moi, j' pour la classe de français. En vacances, nous . Je . Éric et Catherine . Parfois° mes parents au restaurant.

Après *After* **mes** *my* **Parfois** *Sometimes*

5 Point de vue personnel

Select one of the following situations. On a separate sheet of paper, or on a computer, write two things you do and one thing you do not do in that situation. Use complete sentences.

En classe, je...

À la maison,...

En vacances, . . .

Avec mes (my) copains,...

Avec mes Parents, . . .

Une interview

Nicolas is a reporter for *La Gazette des Étudiants,* the student newspaper. He has decided to write an article on the foreign students who attend his school. Today he is interviewing Fatou, a student from Senegal.

NICOLAS: Bonjour, Fatou. Est-ce que je peux <u>te poser</u>   *ask you some questions*
<u>quelques questions</u>?

FATOU: Oui, bien sûr.

NICOLAS: Tu es <u>sénégalaise</u>, n'est-ce pas?   *Senegalese*

FATOU: Oui, je suis sénégalaise.

NICOLAS: Où est-ce que tu habites?

FATOU: Je suis de Dakar, mais maintenant j'habite
à Paris avec ma famille.

NICOLAS: <u>Pourquoi</u> est-ce que vous habitez à Paris?   *Why*

FATOU: <u>Parce que</u> ma mère travaille pour l'Unesco.   *Because*

NICOLAS: Est-ce que tu aimes Paris?

FATOU: J'adore Paris.

NICOLAS: <u>Qu'est-ce que tu fais le weekend</u>?   *What do you do on weekends?*

FATOU: <u>Ça</u> dépend! Je regarde la télé ou je joue   *That*
au tennis avec <u>mes</u> copains.   *my*

NICOLAS: Merci beaucoup, Fatou.

FATOU: C'est <u>tout</u>?   *all*

NICOLAS: Oui, c'est tout!

■ NOTES ■
CULTURELLES

1 Le Sénégal

Senegal is a country in western Africa, whose capital is Dakar. Its population includes twelve different tribes, all speaking their own dialects. Because of the historical and cultural ties between Senegal and France, French has been adopted as the official language.

Most of the people of Senegal are Muslims. Some common names are **Awa** and **Fatou** (for girls), **Babacar** and **Mamadou** (for boys).

FATOU:	Bon. <u>Alors</u>, maintenant c'est mon <u>tour</u>!	*So / turn*
	Est-ce que je peux te poser une question?	
NICOLAS:	Bien sûr!	
FATOU:	Qu'est-ce que tu fais samedi?	
NICOLAS:	Euh . . . <u>je ne sais pas</u>.	*I don't know*
FATOU:	Alors, est-ce que tu veux <u>aller</u> à un concert	*to go*
	de musique africaine?	
NICOLAS:	Avec qui?	
FATOU:	Avec moi, bien sûr!	
NICOLAS:	D'accord! Où? <u>Quand</u>? Et à quelle heure?	*When*

2 L'Unesco

UNESCO (United Nations Educational Scientific and Cultural Organization) was founded in 1946 to promote international cooperation in education, science, and the arts. The organization has its headquarters in Paris and is staffed by people from all member countries.

Compréhension: Vrai ou faux?

Read the following statements and say whether they are true (**C'est vrai!**) or false (**C'est faux!**).

1. Fatou est française.
2. Elle habite à Paris.
3. Le père de Fatou travaille pour l'Unesco.
4. Le weekend, Fatou aime jouer au tennis.
5. Nicolas invite Fatou à un concert.
6. Fatou accepte l'invitation.

A. Les questions d'information

The questions below ask for specific information and are called INFORMATION QUESTIONS. The INTERROGATIVE EXPRESSIONS in heavy print indicate what kind of information is requested.

—**Où** est-ce que tu habites?   **Where** *do you live?*
—J'habite **à Nice.**   *I live **in Nice.***

—**À quelle heure** est-ce que vous dînez?   ***At what time** do you eat dinner?*
—Nous dînons **à sept heures.**   *We eat **at seven.***

In French, information questions may be formed according to the pattern:

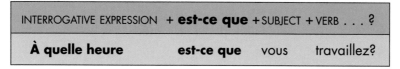

INTERROGATIVE EXPRESSION	+ **est-ce que**	+ SUBJECT	+ VERB . . . ?
À quelle heure	**est-ce que**	vous	travaillez?

➡ **Est-ce que** becomes **est-ce qu'** before a vowel sound.
    Quand **est-ce qu'**Alice et Roger dînent?

➡ In information questions, your voice rises on the interrogative expression and then falls until the last syllable.

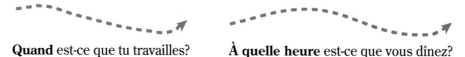

    Quand est-ce que tu travailles?   **À quelle heure** est-ce que vous dînez?

OBSERVATION: In casual conversation, French speakers frequently form information questions by placing the interrogative expression at the end of the sentence. The voice rises on the interrogative expression.

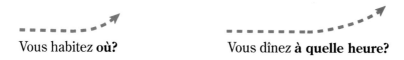

    Vous habitez **où?**   Vous dînez **à quelle heure?**

Vocabulaire: Expressions interrogatives

où	*where?*	**Où** est-ce que vous travaillez?
quand?	*when?*	**Quand** est-ce que ton copain organise une boum?
à quelle heure?	*at what time?*	**À quelle heure** est-ce que tu regardes la télé?
comment?	*how?*	**Comment** est-ce que tu chantes? Bien ou mal?
pourquoi?	*why?*	—**Pourquoi** est-ce que tu étudies le français?
parce que	*because*	—**Parce que** je veux voyager en France.

➡ **Parce que** becomes **parce qu'** before a vowel sound.
    Juliette invite Olivier **parce qu'**il danse bien.

1 Le Club International

The president of the International Club wants to know where some of the members are from. The secretary tells her where each one lives.

▶ Sylvie (à Québec)

LA PRÉSIDENTE: **Où est-ce que Sylvie habite?**

LE SECRÉTAIRE: **Elle habite à Québec.**

1. Jacques (à Montréal)
2. Awa (à Dakar)
3. Marc et Frédéric (à Toulouse)
4. Jean-Pierre (à Genève)
5. Sophie et Michèle (à Nice)
6. Isabelle (à Paris)

2 Curiosité

At a party in Paris, Nicolas meets Béatrice, a Canadian student. He wants to know more about her. Play both roles.

▶ où / habiter? (à Québec)

NICOLAS: **Où est-ce que tu habites?**

BÉATRICE: **J'habite à Québec.**

1. où/étudier? (à Montréal)
2. où/travailler? (dans [in] une pharmacie)
3. quand/parler français? (toujours)
4. quand/parler anglais? (souvent)
5. comment/jouer au tennis? (bien)
6. comment/danser? (très bien)
7. pourquoi/être en France? (parce que j'aime voyager)
8. pourquoi/être à Paris? (parce que j'ai [I have] un copain ici)

Expression pour la conversation

How to express surprise or mild doubt:

Ah bon?   *Oh? Really?*   —Stéphanie organise une soirée.
—**Ah bon?** Quand?

---

3 Au téléphone

When Philippe phones his cousin Michèle, he likes to tell her what his plans are. She asks him a few questions. Play both roles.

J'organise une soirée.

Samedi.

Ah bon? Quand est-ce que tu organises une soirée?

▶ organiser une soirée (quand? samedi)

1. organiser un pique-nique (quand? dimanche)
2. dîner avec Pauline (quand? lundi)
3. dîner avec Caroline (où? au restaurant Belcour)
4. regarder «Batman» (à quelle heure? à 9 heures)
5. jouer au tennis (quand ? demain)
6. inviter Brigitte (où? à un concert)
7. parler espagnol (comment? assez bien)
8. étudier l'italien (pourquoi? je veux voyager en Italie)

4 Questions personnelles

1. Où est-ce que tu habites? *(name of your city)*
2. Où est-ce que tu étudies? *(name of your school)*
3. À quelle heure est-ce que tu dînes?
4. À quelle heure est-ce que tu regardes la télé?
5. Quand est-ce que tu nages?
6. Quand est-ce que tu joues au tennis? (en mai? en juillet?)
7. Comment est-ce que tu chantes? (bien? très bien? mal?)
8. Comment est-ce que tu nages?

B. Les expressions interrogatives avec *qui*

To ask about PEOPLE, French speakers use the following interrogative expressions:

qui?	*who(m)?*	**Qui** est-ce que tu invites au concert?
à qui?	*to who(m)?*	**À qui** est-ce que tu téléphones?
de qui?	*about who(m)?*	**De qui** est-ce que vous parlez?
avec qui?	*with who(m)?*	**Avec qui** est-ce que Pierre étudie?
pour qui?	*for who(m)?*	**Pour qui** est-ce que Laure organise la boum?

To ask *who is doing something,* French speakers use the construction:

qui + VERB . . . ?	
Qui habite ici?	**Who** lives here?
Qui organise la boum?	**Who** is organizing the party?

---

5 **Précisions** *(Details)*

Anne is telling Hélène what certain people are doing. She asks for more details. Play both roles.

▶ Alice dîne. (avec qui? avec une copine)

1. Jean-Pierre téléphone. (à qui? à Sylvie)
2. Frédéric étudie. (avec qui? avec un copain)
3. Madame Masson parle. (à qui? à Madame Bonnot)
4. Monsieur Lambert travaille. (avec qui? avec Monsieur Dumont)
5. Juliette danse. (avec qui? avec Georges)
6. François parle à Michèle. (de qui? de toi)

Alice dîne.

Ah bon? Avec qui est-ce qu'elle dîne?

Elle dîne avec une copine.

---

6 **Un sondage** *(A poll)*

Take a survey to find out how your classmates spend their free time. Ask who does the following things.

▶ écouter la radio
   Qui écoute la radio?

1. voyager souvent	5. regarder la télé	9. regarder les clips *(music videos)*
2. aimer chanter	6. jouer au tennis	10. parler italien
3. nager	7. jouer au foot	11. étudier beaucoup
4. aimer danser	8. travailler	12. visiter souvent New York

7 Questions

Prepare short dialogues with your classmates, using the information in the illustrations.

où?

à la maison

▶ —Où est-ce que tu dînes?
—Je dîne à la maison.

1. à quelle heure?

à 8 heures

2. quand?

en septembre

3. comment?

BONJOUR!

très bien

4. avec qui?

avec Denise

5. à qui?

à mon cousin

6. de qui?

BLA BLA BLA...

de toi

7. pour qui?

pour M. Lambert

C. Qu'est-ce que?

Note the use of the interrogative expression **qu'est-ce que** *(what)* in the questions below.

Qu'est-ce que tu regardes?   Je regarde un match de tennis.
Qu'est-ce qu'Alice mange?   Elle mange une pizza.

To ask *what people are doing,* the French use the following construction:

qu'est-ce que + SUBJECT + VERB + . . . ?	**Qu'est-ce que** tu fais?
qu'est-ce qu' (+ VOWEL SOUND)	**Qu'est-ce qu'**elle fait?

8 La Boutique-Musique

People in Column A are at the Boutique-Musique, a local music shop. Use a verb from Column B to ask what they are listening to or looking at. A classmate will answer you, using an item from Column C.

A	B	C
tu	écouter?	une guitare
vous	regarder?	un poster
Alice		un compact (CD) de jazz
Éric		une cassette de rock
Antoine et Claire		un album de Paul Simon

Qu'est-ce qu'Éric écoute?

Il écoute un album de Paul Simon.

D. Le verbe *faire*

Faire *(to do, make)* is one of the most useful French verbs. It is an IRREGULAR verb since it does not follow a predictable pattern. Note the forms of **faire** in the present tense.

faire *(to do, make)*	
je **fais**	Je **fais** un sandwich.
tu **fais**	Qu'est-ce que tu **fais** maintenant?
il/elle **fait**	Qu'est-ce que ton copain **fait** samedi?
nous **faisons**	Nous **faisons** une pizza.
vous **faites**	Qu'est-ce que vous **faites** ici?
ils/elles **font**	Qu'est-ce qu'elles **font** pour la boum?

Vocabulaire: Expressions avec *faire*

faire un match	*to play a game (match)*	Mes cousins **font un match** de tennis.
faire une promenade	*to go for a walk*	Caroline **fait une promenade** avec Olivier.
faire un voyage	*to take a trip*	Ma copine **fait un voyage** en France.
faire attention	*to pay attention*	Est-ce que tu **fais attention** quand le professeur parle?

---

9 La boum de Juliette

Juliette's friends are helping her prepare food for a party. Use the verb **faire** to say what everyone is doing.

▶ Je . . . une crêpe.

Je fais une crêpe.

1. Nous . . . une salade.
2. Tu . . . une salade de fruits.
3. Vous . . . une tarte *(pie)*.
4. Cécile et Marina . . . un gâteau *(cake)*.
5. Christine . . . une pizza.
6. Marc . . . un sandwich.
7. Patrick et Thomas . . . une omelette.
8. Pierre et Karine . . . une quiche.

10 Qu'est-ce qu'ils font?

Read the descriptions below and say what the people are doing. Use the verb **faire** and an expression from the list below. Be logical.

un voyage   une promenade   une pizza   un match   attention

▶ Madame Dumont est en Chine.
Elle fait un voyage.

1. Nicolas travaille dans *(in)* un restaurant.
2. Nous sommes en ville.
3. Hélène et Jean-Paul jouent au tennis.
4. Je suis dans la cuisine *(kitchen)*.
5. Marc est dans le train Paris–Nice.
6. Vous jouez au volley.
7. Je suis dans le parc.
8. Monsieur Lambert visite Tokyo.
9. Nous écoutons le prof.

E. L'interrogation avec inversion

> ### Learning about language
>
> In conversational French, questions are usually formed with **est-ce que.** However, when the subject of the sentence is a pronoun, French speakers often use INVERSION, that is, they invert or reverse the order of the subject pronoun and the verb.
>
> REGULAR ORDER: **Vous parlez** français.   INVERSION: **Parlez-vous** anglais?
>   SUBJECT VERB   VERB   SUBJECT

Look at the two sets of questions below. They both ask the same thing. Compare the position of the subject pronouns in heavy print.

Est-ce que **tu** parles anglais?	Parles-**tu** anglais?	*Do you speak English?*
Est-ce que **vous** habitez ici?	Habitez-**vous** ici?	*Do you live here?*
Où est-ce que **nous** dînons?	Où dînons-**nous?**	*Where are we having dinner?*
Où est-ce qu'**il** est?	Où est-**il?**	*Where is he?*

Inverted questions are formed according to the patterns:

YES / NO	VERB / SUBJECT PRONOUN . . . ?	
QUESTION	**Voyagez-vous**	souvent?

INFORMATION	INTERROGATIVE EXPRESSION + VERB / SUBJECT PRONOUN . . . ?	
QUESTION	**Avec qui** **travaillez-vous**	demain?

➡ In inversion, the verb and the subject pronoun are connected by a hyphen.

OBSERVATION: In inversion, liaison is required before **il/elle** and **ils/elles.** If a verb in the singular ends on a vowel, the letter "**t**" is inserted between the verb and the subject pronoun so that liaison can occur:

Où travaille-**t**-il?	Où travaille-**t**-elle?
Avec qui dîne-**t**-il?	Avec qui dîne-**t**-elle?

11 Conversation

Get better acquainted with your classmates by asking them a few questions. Use inversion.

▶ où / habiter? —**Où habites-tu?**
　　　　　　　 —**J'habite à (Boston).**

1. à quelle heure / dîner?
2. à quelle heure / regarder la télé?
3. avec qui / parler français?
4. à qui / téléphoner souvent?
5. comment / nager?
6. avec qui / étudier?

Prononciation /y/

La voyelle /y/

S<u>u</u>per!

The vowel sound /y/ – represented by the letter "**u**" – does not exist in English. Here is a helpful trick for producing this new sound.

First say the French word **si**. Then round your lips as if to whistle and say **si** with rounded lips: /sy/. Now say **si-per.** Then round your lips as you say the first syllable: **super!**

Répétez:　/y/　**s<u>u</u>per　t<u>u</u>　ét<u>u</u>die　bien s<u>û</u>r**
　　　　　　　　L<u>u</u>cie L<u>u</u>c
　　　　　　　　T<u>u</u> ét<u>u</u>dies avec L<u>u</u>cie.

À votre tour!

1 Allô!

Awa is phoning some friends. Match her questions on the left with her friends' answers on the right.

1. Qu'est-ce que tu fais?

2. Qu'est-ce que vous faites samedi?

3. Où est ton père?

4. Quand est-ce que tu veux jouer au tennis avec moi?

5. Qui est-ce que tu invites au cinéma?

6. Pourquoi est-ce que tu étudies l'anglais?

a. Il fait une promenade.

b. Ma cousine Alice.

c. Dimanche. D'accord?

d. J'étudie.

e. Nous faisons un match de tennis.

f. Parce que je voudrais habiter à New York.

2 Les questions

The following people are answering questions. Read what they say and figure out what questions they were asked.

Je chante très mal.

▶ **Comment est-ce que tu chantes?**

J'habite à Québec.

1

Je dîne à sept heures.

2

Nous dînons à l'Hippopotame.

3

Je mange une pizza.

4

Je regarde un film.

5

J'invite Catherine.

6

3 Créa-dialogue

Ask your classmates what they do on different days of the week. Carry out conversations similar to the model. Note: "??" means you can invent your own answers.

▶ —Qu'est-ce que tu fais <u>lundi</u>?
—Je <u>joue au tennis</u>.
—Ah bon? À quelle heure est-ce que tu <u>joues</u>?
—<u>À deux heures</u>.
—Et avec qui?
—Avec <u>Anne-Marie</u>.

▶	lundi	mardi	mercredi	jeudi	vendredi	samedi	dimanche
ACTIVITÉ						??	??
À QUELLE HEURE?	2 heures	6 heures	??	??	??	??	??
AVEC QUI?	avec Anne-Marie	avec un copain	??	??	??	??	??

4 Faisons connaissance!
(Let's get acquainted!)

Get better acquainted with a classmate that you don't know very well. Ask questions in French. For instance:

- Where does he/she live?
- Does he/she study much at home?
- Does he/she speak French at home? (with whom?)
- Does he/she watch TV? (at what time?)
- Does he/she like to phone? (whom? [**à qui?**])

5 Interview

A famous rock star is visiting the United States. You are going to interview her for your school paper (perhaps even on the Internet!). Write out five questions you would want to ask the singer, addressing her as **vous.** For example, you may want to know . . .

- where she is singing
- why she is visiting your city
- how she is traveling
- how (well) she speaks English

6 Curiosité

Imagine that a French friend has just made the following statements. For each one, write down three or four related questions you could ask him or her.

Je joue au foot demain.

▶
- Avec qui est-ce que tu joues?
- Où est-ce que vous jouez?
- À quelle heure est-ce que vous jouez?
- Pourquoi est-ce que vous jouez au foot?

Je joue au tennis. **1**

2 Je dîne avec un copain.

3 Je fais une promenade.

4

J'organise une soirée.

Vive la différence!

Les activités quotidiennes

Nous sommes américains, français, anglais, canadiens . . . Nos° cultures ont° beaucoup de points communs, mais elles ne sont pas identiques.

Parlons° de la vie quotidienne.° Nous faisons les mêmes choses,° mais souvent nous faisons ces° choses un peu différemment.° Voici plusieurs° questions. Répondez° à ces questions. À votre avis,° quelles° sont les réponses des jeunes Français?°

1 **Quel jour de la semaine est-ce que vous préférez?**
- le lundi
- le vendredi
- le samedi
- le dimanche

Et les Français, quel jour est-ce qu'ils préfèrent?

3 **Voici quatre sports. Quel sport est-ce que vous pratiquez le plus?°**
- Je nage.
- Je joue au basket.
- Je fais du jogging.
- Je joue au football.

Et les jeunes Français, quel sport est-ce qu'ils pratiquent le plus?

5 **En moyenne,° combien d'heures° par jour° est-ce que vous regardez la télé?**
- une heure
- deux heures
- trois heures
- quatre heures ou plus°

Et les jeunes Français? Combien d'heures par jour est-ce qu'ils regardent la télé?

2 **Pendant° la semaine, qu'est-ce que vous préférez faire quand vous n'étudiez pas?**
- Je préfère regarder la télé.
- Je préfère lire.°
- Je préfère jouer au basket.
- Je préfère téléphoner à mes° copains.

Et les jeunes Français, qu'est-ce qu'ils préfèrent faire?

4 **À quelle heure est-ce que vous dînez en général?**
- entre° cinq heures et demie et six heures
- entre six heures et sept heures
- entre sept heures et huit heures
- après huit heures

Et les Français, à quelle heure est-ce qu'ils dînent?

6 **Qu'est-ce que vous préférez regarder à la télé?**
- les sports
- les films
- la publicité°
- les feuilletons°

Et les jeunes Français, qu'est-ce qu'ils préfèrent regarder?

Et les Français?
1. Ils préfèrent le samedi. 2. Ils préfèrent regarder la télé. 3. Ils jouent au football. 4. Ils dînent entre sept heures et huit heures. 5. Ils regardent la télé deux heures par jour. 6. Ils préfèrent regarder les films.

Nos *Our* **ont** *have* **Parlons** *Let's talk* **vie quotidienne** *daily life* **mêmes choses** *same things* **ces** *these* **différemment** *differently* **plusieurs** *several* **Répondez** *Answer* **À votre avis** *In your opinion* **quelles** *what* **jeunes Français** *young French people* **Pendant** *During* **lire** *to read* **mes** *my* **le plus** *the most* **entre** *between* **En moyenne** *On the average* **combien d'heures** *how many hours* **par jour** *per day* **plus** *more* **publicité** *commercials* **feuilletons** *series*

EN FRANCE

À la télé, ce weekend

In France, TV viewers have a choice of six main channels: **TF1**, **France 2**, **France 3**, **Arte**, **M6**, and **Canal Plus**. (People who want to watch **Canal Plus** need to have a special decoding machine for which they pay a monthly fee.)

Note that in TV listings, times are expressed using a 24-hour clock. In this system, 8 P.M. is **20.00 (vingt heures)**; 10 P.M. is **22.00 (vingt-deux heures)**.

Imagine that you are spending a month in Paris with a French family. This Friday and Saturday you have decided to stay home and watch TV. Look at the program listings at the right.

- 📺 Which programs would you like to watch on Friday? When do they start?

- 📺 Which programs would you choose on Saturday evening? When do they start?

- 📺 Your French hosts are soccer fans. What program would they want to watch and when? Which teams are playing? (Locate these cities on the map of France.)

- 📺 What program is featured on **France 2** on Saturday evening? Who are the guests on this program? Do you know any of them?

- 📺 How many different movies are being shown over the weekend? How many of these movies are American? Which movie would you choose to see? At what time and on which channel?

- 📺 You are interested in watching a French TV series. Which program would you select? On which channel? According to its title, what kind of a series do you think it is?

SÉLECTION DE LA SEMAINE

VEN | **SAM**

TF1

VEN	SAM
20.30 VARIÉTÉS **SALUT L'ARTISTE** Émission présentée par Yves Noël et Ophélie Winter	**20.35** SPECTACLE **HOLIDAY ON ICE** Mis en scène par Jérôme Savary
22.05 DOCUMENT **HISTOIRES NATURELLES**	**22.10** SÉRIE **DANS LA CHALEUR DE LA NUIT**

France 2

VEN	SAM
20.35 SÉRIE **HÔTEL DE POLICE** LE GENTIL MONSIEUR de Claude Barrois avec Cécile Magnet	**20.40** VARIÉTÉS **CHAMPS-ÉLYSÉES** Invités: Ricky Martin, Juliette Binoche, Ben Affleck
23.20 FILM **ALICE DANS LES VILLES** de Wim Wenders	**22.25** SÉRIE **MÉDECINS DE NUIT**

France 3

VEN	SAM
21.30 SÉRIE **LE MASQUE** MADEMOISELLE EVELYNE de Jean-Louis Fournier	**20.35** JEUNESSE **SAMDYNAMITE** DESSINS ANIMÉS Série : BATMAN
23.45 CONCERT **MUSIQUES, MUSIQUE**	**22.25** ENTRETIEN **LE DIVAN** Pierre Dumayet

arte

VEN	SAM
20.15 DOCUMENTAIRE **Cent ans de cinéma japonais**	**20.40** SÉRIE **Comédie visuelle**
23.20 MAGAZINE **Une vidéo inédite** de Lara Fabian	**21.45** DOCUMENTAIRE **Le monde des animaux**

M6

VEN	SAM
20.30 FILM TV **LE CINQUIÈME ÉLÉMENT** de Luc Besson avec Bruce Willis, Milla Jovovich	**20.35** FILM TV **L'ÉCLOSION DES MONSTRES** de J. Piquer Simon avec Yan Sera
22.05 THÉÂTRE **LE SEXE FAIBLE**	**22.20** SÉRIE **LE COMTE DE MONTE-CRISTO**

CANAL+

VEN	SAM
20.30 FOOTBALL **CAEN - TOULOUSE** Championnat de France 28e journée	**20.30** FILM **ALIENS, LE RETOUR** de James Cameron avec Sigourney Weaver
22.40 FILM **MALCOM X** de Spike Lee	**22.45** FILM **UNE NUIT À L'ASSEMBLÉE NATIONALE** de Jean-Pierre Mocky

Entre amis: Bonjour, Patrick!

Qu'est-ce que vous aimez faire? Dans° une lettre, Patrick répond° à cette question. Voici la lettre de Patrick.

Bonjour!

Je m'appelle Patrick Lacaze. J'ai 14 ans. J'habite à Tours avec ma famille. Je suis élève° de troisième.° J'étudie beaucoup, mais je n'étudie pas tout le temps.° Voici ce que° j'aime faire.

J'aime les boums parce que j'adore danser.

J'aime la musique. J'aime surtout° le rock. J'aimerais° jouer de la guitare, mais je ne sais pas.°

J'aime les sports. En hiver je skie et en été je nage et je joue au tennis. (Je ne suis pas un champion, mais je joue assez° bien.) J'aime jouer au basket, mais je préfère jouer au foot. (J'aime jouer au babyfoot, mais ce n'est pas un sport.) J'aime faire des promenades à vélo° le weekend avec mes copains.

J'aime mon école.° J'aime surtout l'anglais parce que le prof est sympa.° (Il s'appelle Mr. Ross, mais il est très gentil.°) Je n'aime pas trop° les maths.

À la maison, j'aime regarder la télé. J'adore les séries américaines! J'aime aussi écouter mes cassettes.

J'aime téléphoner à ma copine, mais je ne téléphone pas souvent. (Mon père n'aime pas ça.°)

J'aime jouer aux jeux° vidéo!

Et vous, qu'est-ce que vous aimez faire? Répondez-moi° vite.°

Amicalement,°

Patrick Lacaze

Dans *In* **répond** *answers* **élève** *student* **troisième** *ninth grade* **tout le temps** *all the time* **ce que** *what* **surtout** *especially* **aimerais** *would like* **je ne sais pas** *I don't know how* **assez** *rather* **promenades à vélo** *bike rides* **école** *school* **sympa** *nice* **gentil** *nice* **trop** *too much* **ça** *that* **jeux** *games* **Répondez-moi** *Answer me* **vite** *quickly* **Amicalement** *Cordially (In friendship)*

■ NOTES ■
CULTURELLES

1 Tours

Tours is an attractive city located about 150 miles southwest of Paris. It is the capital of Touraine, an area of France known for its beautiful castles.

Paris

Tours

2 Le babyfoot

Babyfoot is a tabletop soccer game in which two teams of two people each try to score goals by manipulating rows of toy players. **Babyfoot** is very popular among French teenagers, who play it in cafés or in youth clubs.

Comment lire *(Reading hints)*
GETTING THE MEANING

When you read French, try to understand the meaning. Don't look for a word-for-word English translation for each sentence.

- Sometimes the two languages use different constructions.

  Je m'appelle . . .   *(I call myself . . .)*   *My name is . . .*

- Sometimes French uses some words that English leaves out.

  J'aime le rock.   *I love rock.*
  J'aime jouer de la guitare.   *I like to play the guitar.*

- And sometimes French leaves out words that English uses.

  Je suis élève de troisième.   *I am a student in ninth grade.*

- Word order may also be different.

  des promenades à vélo   *bike rides*

Enrichissez votre vocabulaire
COGNATES

You have already discovered that there are many words in French that look like English words and have similar meanings. These are called COGNATES. Cognates let you increase your vocabulary effortlessly. But be sure to pronounce them the French way!

- Sometimes the spelling is the same, or almost the same.

  la radio   *radio*
  un champion   *champion*

- Sometimes the spelling is a little different.

  américain   *American*

Activité
Read the letter from Patrick again and find five more French-English cognates.

Activité: Une lettre à Patrick
You are writing a letter to Patrick in which you introduce yourself and explain what you like to do. You may tell him:

- if you like music (and what kind)
- what sports you like to do in fall or winter
- what sports you like to do in spring or summer
- what you like to do at home
- whether or not you like French and math
- what you like to do on weekends
- what programs you like to watch on TV

> You may start your letter with the words:
> **Mon cher Patrick,**
> *(My dear Patrick)*
> and end it with:
> **Amicalement,**

Mon cher Patrick,

Amicalement,

■NOTE■
CULTURELLE

Internet / CD-ROMs

Like young Americans, French teens are also interested in CD-ROMs and the internet. More and more teens are using **le Net** for all sorts of purposes: to look up phone numbers and addresses, to make ticket reservations (for concerts, movies, travel, etc.), and to meet and chat with international friends about school, sports, music, and just about everything else!

Le Net is becoming an exciting place for **les internautes:** there are cafés in Paris and many other cities and towns where you can **naviguer** or **netsurfer** while having lunch!

Le Minitel

Many teens still use France's popular online information service, **le Minitel.** The **Minitel** is a small computer terminal connected to the telephone. The most popular service is the **annuaire électronique** *(computerized phone directory).*

The **Minitel** has lots to offer. You can check plane and train schedules, reserve theater tickets, and send electronic messages. You can play all sorts of games. You can even win prizes like a pair of movie tickets or a trip abroad!

But there is a catch! Although the **Minitel** terminals are distributed free of charge, users are billed each month according to the services used and time spent online. Because **Minitel** use can be expensive, French parents insist on limiting its use.

Internet : bienvenue sur la planète virtuelle !

PASSEPORT TOURISME MINITEL

Le Louvre Fr CD #06831
50 euros
Découvrez avec ce CD interactif le plus grand musée du monde. Naviguez à travers le temps et les collections, attardez-vous sur les détails des œuvres grâce à la loupe, consultez les animations et commentaires.

Napoléon, l'Europe et l'Empire Fr CD
48 euros
Vous serez surpris par la qualité et la richesse historique et artistique de ce CD-Rom. Découvrez aux travers de liens hypertexte et du multimédia toute la vie de Napoléon; ses époque, ses rencontres marquantes de son des récits animés, ainsi que des anecdotes et citations. Infograme ..#07391

L'album des arts et métiers Fr CD #06829
44 euros
Plus de 1000 fiches décrivant les objets et la collection du Musée, 2000 photos ou gravures, 150 citations sonores et 150 animations font de ce CD un superbe album interactif.

Variétés

Cinq portraits

Cinq jeunes parlent de ce qu'ils font,° mais ils ne révèlent pas leur° identité. Est-ce que vous pouvez° identifier chacun?° Lisez° les paragraphes suivants° et faites correspondre° chaque° paragraphe à une photo.

Moussa Dembila
Abidjan, Côte d'Ivoire

1 Je ne suis pas français, mais je parle français. Je parle anglais aussi, mais je préfère parler français. J'aime les sports. Je joue au volley et au basket, mais mon sport préféré° est le hockey. Je m'appelle . . .

Catherine Miguel
Bordeaux, France

2 Je suis française, mais je n'habite pas à Paris. J'habite dans une île tropicale. Au lycée, j'étudie beaucoup. Mon sujet préféré est la biologie. (Je voudrais être médecin.°) J'aime la musique. J'aime beaucoup le reggae et j'adore chanter. J'aime les sports. Je nage souvent. Là où j'habite je peux nager en toute saison.° Je m'appelle . . .

3 Je n'habite pas à Paris. J'habite dans° une grande° ville° à 600 kilomètres de Paris. Je suis élève° dans un lycée. J'étudie beaucoup. Mes sujets préférés sont l'espagnol, la gymnastique, le français et la musique. J'aime beaucoup le jazz et le rock. J'adore danser. Je m'appelle . . .

Laurent Arnold
Genève, Suisse

4 Je n'habite pas en France, mais un jour je voudrais étudier à Paris. J'habite en Afrique. Je suis élève au Collège Moderne du Plateau. J'étudie l'anglais, les maths et la physique. Mon ambition est d'être architecte. Je m'appelle . . .

Isabelle Lamy
Trois Îlets, Martinique

5 J'habite dans un petit° pays° européen. Dans mon pays les gens° parlent des langues différentes. Moi, je parle français. En classe j'étudie l'anglais et l'allemand.° J'aime voyager. Je voudrais visiter le Canada. Ma cousine Christine habite là-bas. Je m'appelle . . .

Denis Lévêque
Montréal, Québec

ce qu'ils font *what they do*   **leur** *their*   **pouvez** *can*   **chacun** *each one*   **Lisez** *Read* **suivants** *following*   **faites correspondre** *match*   **chaque** *each*   **préféré** *favorite* **médecin** *doctor*   **en toute saison** *all year round (in any season)*   **dans** *in* **grande** *large*   **ville** *city*   **élève** *student*   **petit** *small*   **pays** *country*   **gens** *people* **allemand** *German*

Le monde personnel et familier

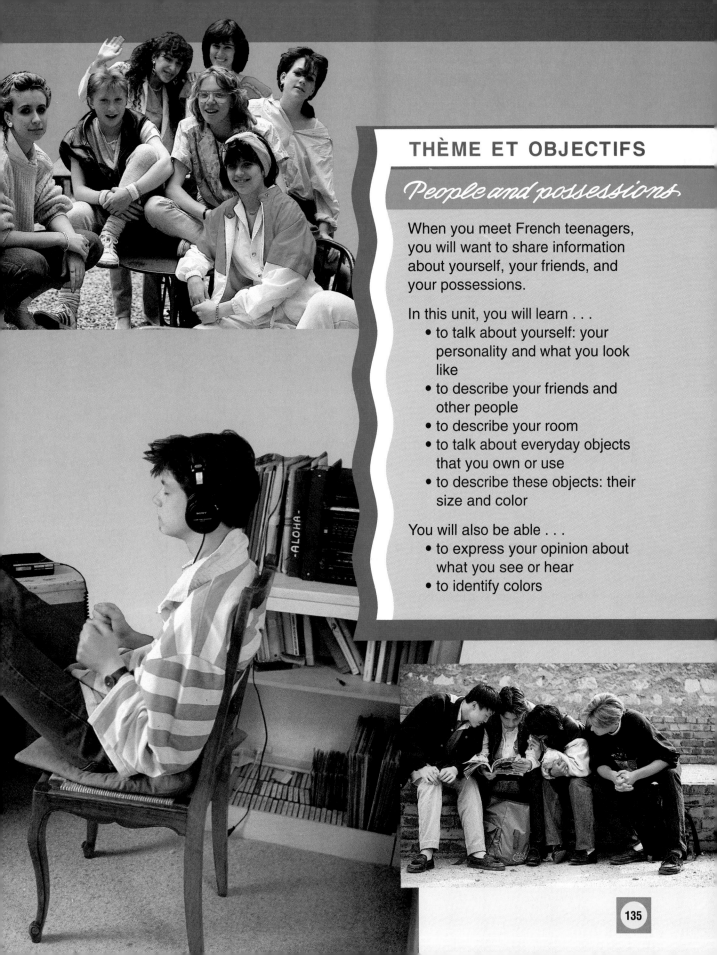

THÈME ET OBJECTIFS

People and possessions

When you meet French teenagers, you will want to share information about yourself, your friends, and your possessions.

In this unit, you will learn . . .
- to talk about yourself: your personality and what you look like
- to describe your friends and other people
- to describe your room
- to talk about everyday objects that you own or use
- to describe these objects: their size and color

You will also be able . . .
- to express your opinion about what you see or hear
- to identify colors

135

Les personnes et les objets

Accent sur . . . Les Français

France has a population of 60 million people. France is a European country, but its population includes people of many different ethnic backgrounds and cultural origins. There are many French citizens whose families have come from North Africa and French-speaking West Africa, as well as from Vietnam, Laos, and Cambodia.

- France is a country of Catholic tradition, but it also has:
  — the largest Jewish population of Western Europe (about 600,000 people).
  — the largest Muslim population of Western Europe (about five million people).

- France is a young country. Thirty percent of its population is under the age of 20.

- French young people tend to be idealists. They believe in freedom and democracy. They also believe in friendship and family. In fact, they rank these values far above money and material success.

- French young people in general have a positive attitude toward Americans. They like American music and would enjoy visiting the United States.

- Because language study is required in French secondary schools, many French teenagers can communicate in a second language, such as English or German.

Au Café Montparnasse
Stéphanie parle avec ses amis.

Chez le marchand de glaces
Philippe est chez le marchand
de glaces avec une copine.

À Paris
Des jeunes font une promenade
sur les Champs-Élysées.

Chez des amis
Stéphanie écoute des
disques avec un copain.

A. La description des personnes

> Qui est-ce?

> C'est un copain.

▶ *How to describe someone:*

Qui est-ce?
C'est un copain.

Comment s'appelle-t-il?
Il s'appelle Marc.

Quel âge a-t-il?
Il a seize ans.

Comment est-il?
Il est petit.
Il est blond.

Qui est-ce?
C'est une copine.

Comment s'appelle-t-elle?
Elle s'appelle Sophie.

Quel âge a-t-elle?
Elle a quinze ans.

Comment est-elle?
Elle est grande.
Elle est brune.

Les personnes

une **personne**

un **étudiant**	*(student)*
un **élève**	*(pupil)*
un **camarade**	*(classmate)*
un **homme**	*(man)*
un **professeur**, un **prof**	*(teacher)*
un **voisin**	*(neighbor)*

une **personne**

une **étudiante**	
une **élève**	
une **camarade**	
une **femme**	*(woman)*
un **professeur**, une **prof**	
une **voisine**	

➡ **Une personne** is always feminine whether it refers to a male or female person.

➡ **Un professeur** is always masculine whether it refers to a male or female teacher. However, in casual French, one distinguishes between **un prof** (male) and **une prof** (female).

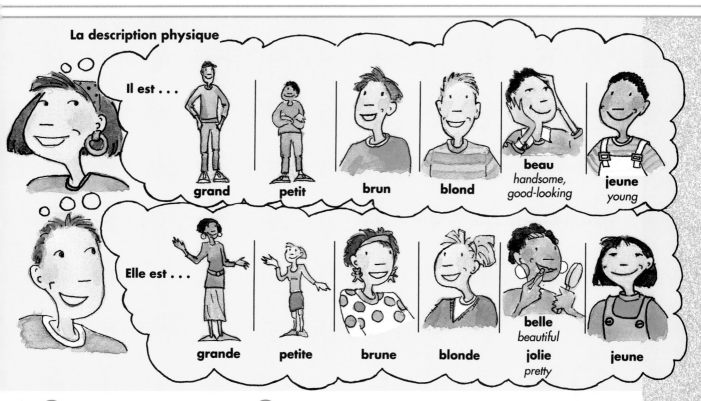

La description physique

Il est . . .

grand   **petit**   **brun**   **blond**   **beau** *handsome, good-looking*   **jeune** *young*

Elle est . . .

grande   **petite**   **brune**   **blonde**   **belle** *beautiful* **jolie** *pretty*   **jeune**

---

1 Oui ou non?

Describe the people below in affirmative or negative sentences.

▶ Michael Jordan / petit?
Michael Jordan n'est pas petit.

▶ Cameron Diaz / jolie?
Cameron Diaz est jolie.

1. Dennis Rodman / grand?
2. Leonardo DiCaprio / blond?
3. Dracula / beau?
4. mon copain / brun?
5. mon père / petit?
6. mon voisin / jeune?
7. Drew Barrymore / belle?
8. Meryl Streep / jeune?
9. Oprah Winfrey /grande?
10. ma copine / petite?
11. ma mère / brune?
12. ma voisine / jolie?

2 Vacances à Québec

You spent last summer in Quebec and have just had your photographs developed. Describe each of the people, giving name, approximate age, and two or three characteristics.

blond(e)   petit(e)
brun(e)   beau (belle)
grand(e)   jeune

▶ Il s'appelle Alain.
Il est brun.
Il a seize ans.
Il n'est pas grand.
Il est petit.

▶ **Alain**

1. Anne-Marie

2. Jean-Pierre

3. Claire

4. Mademoiselle Lévêque

5. Madame Paquette

6. Monsieur Beliveau

B. Les objets

Qu'est-ce que c'est?

▶ *How to identify something:*

| **Qu'est-ce que c'est?** | *What is it? What's that?* | —**Qu'est-ce que c'est?** |
| **C'est . . .** | *It's . . . , That's . . .* | —**C'est** une radio. |

▶ *How to say that you know or do not know:*

| **Je sais.** | *I know.* |
| **Je ne sais pas.** | *I don't know.* |

▶ *How to point out something:*

—**Regarde ça.**	*Look at that.*
—**Quoi?**	*What?*
—**Ça,** là-bas.	*That, over there.*

Quelques objets *(A few objects)*

un objet   un stylo   un crayon   un livre

un disque   un compact (un CD)   un sac

une chose *(thing)*   une raquette   une guitare

une affiche   une cassette

DO YOU REMEMBER?

In French, the names of objects are MASCULINE or FEMININE.

Masculine objects can be introduced by **un** or **le (l')**: **un disque, le disque, l'objet.**

Feminine objects can be introduced by **une** or **la (l')**: **une cassette, la cassette, l'affiche.**

3 Qu'est-ce que c'est?

Ask a classmate to identify the following objects.

4 S'il te plaît

Ask a classmate to give you the following objects.

▶ —S'il te plaît, donne-moi
la cassette.
—Voilà la cassette.
—Merci.

Est-ce que tu as une moto?

Oui, j'ai une moto.

C. Les possessions personnelles

How to talk about things you have:

| **Est-ce que tu as . . . ?** | Do you have . . . ? | —**Est-ce que tu as** un sac? |
| **Oui, j'ai . . .** | Yes, I have . . . | —**Oui, j'ai** un sac. |

Quelques objets

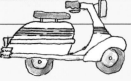

un répondeur

un téléphone

un vélo (une bicyclette)

un scooter

un magnétophone

un walkman

un appareil-photo

un ordinateur

un lecteur optique externe (un lecteur de CD-ROM)

un vidéodisque, un CD vidéo

un lecteur de CD vidéo

un (disque) compact, un CD

une souris

un disque optique (un CD-ROM)

une voiture (une auto)

une moto

une mobylette

une montre

une calculatrice

une radio

une radiocassette

une télé

une chaîne stéréo

How to ask if an object works:

| —Est-ce que la radio **marche?** | Does the radio **work?** |
| —Oui, elle **marche.** | Yes, it works. |

➡ The verb **marcher** has two meanings:

for people:
to walk — Nous **marchons.**

for things:
to work, to run — Le scooter ne **marche** pas bien.

5 Et toi?

1. J'ai . . .
   (Name 3 objects you own.)
2. Je voudrais . . .
   (Name 3 things you would like to have.)
3. Pour Noël / Hanoukka, je voudrais . . .
   (Name 2 gifts you would like to receive.)

6 Joyeux anniversaire
(Happy birthday)

For your birthday, a rich aunt is giving you the choice between different possible gifts. Indicate your preferences.

▶ vélo ou scooter?

1. mobylette ou moto?
2. montre ou radio?
3. appareil-photo ou walkman?
4. radiocassette ou chaîne stéréo?
5. télé ou ordinateur?
6. magnétophone ou calculatrice?

> Je préfère le vélo.

> Je préfère le scooter.

7 Qu'est-ce que tu as?

Philippe asks Christine if she has the following objects. She says that she does. Play both roles.

▶ PHILIPPE: **Est-ce que tu as une guitare?**
CHRISTINE: **Oui, j'ai une guitare.**

8 Est-ce qu'il marche bien?

Tell your classmates that you own the following objects. They will ask you if the objects are working. Answer according to the illustrations.

▶ —J'ai un vélo.
—Est-ce qu'il marche bien?
—Non, il ne marche pas bien.

▶ —J'ai une télé.
—Est-ce qu'elle marche bien?
—Oui, elle marche très bien.

D. Ma chambre *(My room)*

Dans ma chambre il y a une télé.

How to talk about what there is in a place:

il y a	there is	Dans *(In)* ma chambre, **il y a** une télé.
	there are	Dans le garage, **il y a** deux voitures.
est-ce qu'il y a . . . ?	is/are there . . . ?	**Est-ce qu'il y a** un ordinateur dans la classe?
qu'est-ce qu'il y a . . . ?	what is there . . . ?	**Qu'est-ce qu'il y a** dans le garage?

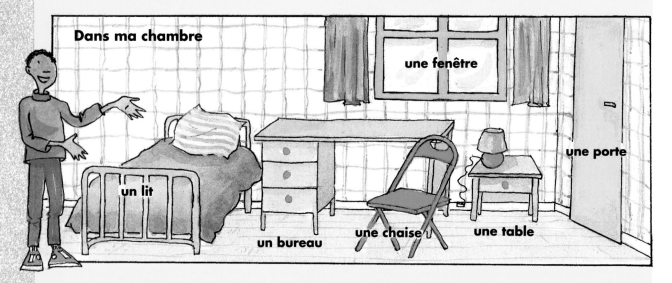

Dans ma chambre

une fenêtre

une porte

un lit

un bureau

une chaise

une table

How to say where something or someone is:

Où est Félix?
Félix est . . .

dans le lit

sur le lit

sous le lit

devant le lit

derrière le lit

9 Qu'est-ce qu'il y a?

Describe the various objects that are in the pictures.

1. Sur la table, il y a . . . 2. Sous le lit, il y a . . . 3. Dans le garage, il y a . . .

10 Ma chambre

Describe the various objects (pieces of furniture and personal belongings) that are in your room.

▶ **Il y a une radio, . . .**
Il y a aussi . . .

11 Où est le téléphone?

Michèle is looking for the telephone. Jean-Claude tells her where it is.

▶ MICHÈLE: **Où est le téléphone?**
JEAN-CLAUDE: **Il est sur la table.**

12 C'est étrange! *(It's strange!)*

Funny things sometimes happen. Describe these curious happenings by selecting an item from Column A and putting it in one of the places listed in Column B.

▶ Il y a un éléphant sous le lit!

▶ Il y a . . .

A	B
un rhinocéros	dans la classe
un éléphant	sur le bureau
une girafe	sous la table
un crabe	sous le lit
une souris *(mouse)*	derrière la porte
un ami de King Kong	sur la tour Eiffel
	dans le jardin *(garden)*
un extra-terrestre	devant le restaurant

13 La chambre de Nicole

Florence wants to borrow a few things from Nicole's room. Nicole tells her where each object is.

> Où est la raquette?
>
> Elle est sous le lit.

▶ la raquette

1. la télé
2. la guitare
3. le livre
4. le vélo
5. l'ordinateur

6. le sac
7. la radio
8. le compact
9. la cassette

14 Pauvre Monsieur Vénard *(Poor Mr. Vénard)*

Today Monsieur Vénard left on vacation, but he soon ran out of luck. Describe the four cartoons by completing the sentences below.

Le voyage de Monsieur Vénard

1. M. Vénard est ____ la voiture.
2. M. Vénard est ____ la voiture.
3. M. Vénard est ____ la voiture.
4. La contractuelle° est ____ la voiture.

la contractuelle *meter maid*

À votre tour!

1 Créa-dialogue

Daniel is showing Nathalie his recent photographs, and she is asking questions about the various people. Create similar dialogues and act them out in class.

▶
un copain
Éric/14

▶
—Qui est-ce?
—C'est <u>un copain</u>.
—Comment s'appelle-t-<u>il</u>?
—<u>Il</u> s'appelle <u>Éric</u>.
—Quel âge a-t-<u>il</u>?
—<u>Il</u> a <u>quatorze</u> ans.

1. une cousine	2. un camarade	3. une camarade	4. un voisin	5. une voisine	6. un professeur
Valérie/20	Philippe Boucher/13	Nathalie Masson/15	Monsieur Dumas/70	Madame Smith/51	Monsieur Laval/35

2 Conversation dirigée

Olivier is visiting his new friend Valérie. Act out the dialogue according to the instructions.

Olivier				Valérie
	asks Valérie if she has a boom box	⤢	answers affirmatively	
	asks her if it works well	⤢	says that it works very well and asks why	
	says he would like to listen to his new (**sa nouvelle**) cassette	→	says that the boom box is on the table in the living room (**le salon**)	

3 Mes possessions

Imagine that your family is going to move to another city. Prepare for the move by making a list of the objects you own. Use a separate sheet of paper.

4 Composition: Un objet

Write a short paragraph describing a real or an imaginary object. You may want to include a picture. (Use only vocabulary that you know.) You may begin your sentences with the following phrases:

▶
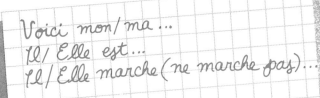
Voici mon/ma...
Il/Elle est...
Il/Elle marche (ne marche pas)...

18 Vive la différence!

We are not necessarily like our friends. Caroline, a French girl from Montpellier, describes herself. She also talks about her friend Jean-Pierre.

Caroline

Jean-Pierre

Je m'appelle Caroline.
J'habite à Montpellier.
J'ai des frères.

J'ai un chien.

J'ai un scooter.

J'aime le cinéma.
J'aime les films de science-fiction.
J'aime les sports.
J'étudie l'anglais.

Il s'appelle Jean-Pierre.
Il habite à Strasbourg.
Il n'a pas de frère,
    mais il a des soeurs.

Il n'a pas de chien,
    mais il a deux horribles chats.

Il a une moto.

Il préfère le théâtre.
Il préfère les westerns.
Il préfère la musique.
Il étudie l'espagnol.

Jean-Pierre et moi, nous sommes très différents . . . mais nous sommes copains.

C'est l'essentiel, non?

● Compréhension

Answer the questions below with the appropriate names: **Caroline, Jean-Pierre,** or **Caroline et Jean-Pierre.**

1. Qui habite en France?
2. Qui a des soeurs?
3. Qui n'a pas de frère?
4. Qui a un animal domestique?
5. Qui aime jouer au volley?
6. Qui préfère écouter un concert?
7. Qui étudie une langue *(language)*?

Et toi?

Describe yourself and your best friend by completing the sentences below with a phrase of your choice.

1. J'ai . . .
   Mon copain (ma copine) a . . .
   - un frère
   - une soeur
   - des frères
   - des soeurs

2. J'ai . . .
   Mon copain (ma copine) a . . .
   - un chien
   - un chat
   - un perroquet *(parrot)*
   - un poisson rouge *(goldfish)*

3. J'ai . . .
   Mon copain (ma copine) a . . .
   - un vélo
   - une moto
   - un scooter
   - une mobylette

4. J'aime . . .
   Mon copain (ma copine) aime . . .
   - le cinéma
   - le théâtre
   - la musique
   - les sports

5. Je préfère . . .
   Mon copain (ma copine) préfère . . .
   - les westerns
   - les comédies
   - les films d'aventures
   - les films de science-fiction

6. J'étudie . . .
   Mon copain (ma copine) étudie . . .
   - l'espagnol
   - le français
   - l'italien
   - l'allemand *(German)*

7. Mon ami(e) et moi,
   nous sommes . . .
   - assez *(rather)* différent(e)s
   - très différent(e)s
   - assez semblables *(similar)*
   - très semblables

■ NOTE ■ CULTURELLE

Montpellier et Strasbourg

Montpellier and Strasbourg are two very different cities.

- Montpellier is a city of more than 200,000 inhabitants located in southern France near the Mediterranean. It is an important university center with a School of Medicine founded in 1221.

- Strasbourg, a city of 255,000 inhabitants, is the capital of the French province of Alsace. Because of its location near Germany and Switzerland, it has always been an international city. Strasbourg is now the seat of important European institutions.

A. Le verbe *avoir*

The verb **avoir** *(to have, to own)* is irregular. Note the forms of this verb in the present tense.

avoir	to have	
j' **ai** tu **as** il/elle **a**	I have you have he/she has	J'**ai** une copine à Québec. Est-ce que tu **as** un frère? Philippe **a** une cousine à Paris.
nous **avons** vous **avez** ils/elles **ont**	we have you have they have	Nous **avons** un ordinateur. Est-ce que vous **avez** une moto? Ils n'**ont** pas ton appareil-photo.

➞ There is liaison in the forms: **nous avons, vous avez, ils ont, elles ont.**

Vocabulaire: Expressions avec *avoir*

avoir faim	to be hungry	J'**ai faim.** Et toi, est-ce que tu **as faim?**
avoir soif	to be thirsty	Paul **a soif.** Sylvie n'**a** pas **soif.**
avoir . . . ans	to be . . . (years old)	J'**ai** 14 **ans.** Le prof **a** 35 **ans.**

1 Les voitures

The people below own cars made in the countries where they live. Match each car with its owner.

> Monsieur Sato habite à Tokyo.

Il a une Toyota.

une Alfa Roméo
une Jaguar
une Renault
une Chevrolet
une Volvo
une Mercedes
une Toyota

1. Tu habites à Boston.
2. Vous habitez à Munich.
3. Madame Ericson habite à Stockholm.
4. J'habite à Paris.
5. Nous habitons à Oxford.
6. Mes cousines habitent à Rome.

2 Expression personnelle

How old are the following people? Complete the sentences below. If you don't know the exact age, make a guess.

1. J'ai . . .
2. *(The student on your right)* Tu as . . .
3. *(The teacher)* Vous . . .
4. Mon copain . . .
5. Ma copine . . .
6. La voisine . . .

3 Faim ou soif?

You are at a party with your classmates. Offer them the following foods and beverages. They will accept or refuse by saying whether they are hungry or thirsty.

1. une crêpe
2. un soda
3. un hamburger
4. un jus d'orange
5. un croissant
6. un jus de raisin
7. une pizza
8. un Perrier

> un sandwich
> une limonade

Tu veux un sandwich?

Oui, merci! J'ai faim.

(Non, merci! Je n'ai pas faim.)

Tu veux une limonade?

Oui, merci! J'ai soif.

(Non, merci! Je n'ai pas soif.)

B. Les noms et les articles: masculin et féminin

NOUNS

• Nouns designating PEOPLE
Nouns that designate male persons
are almost always *masculine:*
  un garçon   **un ami**
Nouns that designate female persons
are almost always *feminine:*
  une fille   **une amie**

> **Learning about language**
>
> NOUNS are words that designate people, animals, objects, and things.
>
> In French, all nouns have GENDER: they are either MASCULINE or FEMININE.

➡ EXCEPTIONS:
  une personne is always feminine (even when it refers to a male)
  un professeur is always masculine (even when it refers to a woman)

• Nouns designating ANIMALS, OBJECTS, and THINGS
There is no systematic way to determine whether these nouns are
masculine or feminine. Therefore, it is very important to learn these
nouns with their articles.

  MASCULINE: **un** disque   **un** vélo   **un** ordinateur
  FEMININE: **une** cassette **une** moto   **une** affiche

ARTICLES

Note the forms of the articles in the chart below.

> **Learning about language**
>
> Nouns are often introduced by ARTICLES. In French, ARTICLES have the *same* gender as the nouns they introduce.

	MASCULINE		FEMININE			
INDEFINITE ARTICLE	**un**	*a, an*	**une**	*a, an*	**un** garçon	**une** fille
DEFINITE ARTICLE	**le**	*the*	**la**	*the*	**le** garçon	**la** fille

➡ Both **le** and **la** become **l'** before a vowel sound:
  le garçon   **l'ami**
  la fille   **l'amie**

PRONOUNS

> **Learning about language**
>
> Nouns may be replaced by PRONOUNS. In French, PRONOUNS have the *same* gender as the nouns they replace.

Note the forms of the pronouns in the chart below.

MASCULINE	**il**	*he* / *it*	Où est **le** garçon? / Où est **le** disque?	**Il** est en classe. / **Il** est sur la table.
FEMININE	**elle**	*she* / *it*	Où est **la** fille? / Où est **la** voiture?	**Elle** est en ville. / **Elle** est là-bas.

4 Les célébrités

You and Jean-Pierre have been invited to a gala dinner attended by many American celebrities. Jean-Pierre asks you who each person is. Answer him using **un** or **une,** as appropriate.

Tiens, voilà Katie Couric!

Qui est-ce?

Une journaliste.

▶ Katie Couric / journaliste

1. Peter Jennings / journaliste
2. Cameron Diaz / actrice
3. Matt Damon / acteur
4. Whoopi Goldberg / comédienne
5. Lauryn Hill / chanteuse (singer)
6. Michael Jordan / athlète
7. Denzel Washington / acteur
8. Will Smith / chanteur

5 Sur la table ou sous la table?

Caroline is looking for the following objects. Cécile tells her where each one is: on or under the table.

▶ walkman
CAROLINE: **Où est le walkman?**
  CÉCILE: **Le walkman? Il est sur la table.**

1. ordinateur
2. sac
3. affiche
4. calculatrice
5. raquette
6. disque
7. radiocassette
8. télé

C. Les noms et les articles: le pluriel

Compare the singular and plural forms of the articles and nouns in the sentences below.

SINGULAR	PLURAL
Tu as **le disque?**	Tu as **les disques?**
Qui est **la fille** là-bas?	Qui sont **les filles** là-bas?
Voici **un livre.**	Voici **des livres.**
J'invite **une copine.**	J'invite **des copines.**

PLURAL NOUNS

In written French, the plural of most nouns is formed as follows:

> SINGULAR NOUN + **s** = PLURAL NOUN

Les sacs

⇒ If the noun ends in -**s** in the singular, the singular and plural forms are the same.
  Voici **un Français.**   Voici **des Français.**
⇒ In spoken French, the final -**s** of the plural is always silent.
⇒ NOTE: **des gens** *(people)* is always plural. Compare:

| **une personne** | *person* | Qui est **la personne** là-bas? |
| **des gens** | *people* | Qui sont **les gens** là-bas? |

SINGULAR AND PLURAL ARTICLES

The forms of the articles are summarized in the chart below.

	SINGULAR	PLURAL		
DEFINITE ARTICLE	**le (l')** *the* **la (l')**	**les** *the*	**les** garçons **les** filles	**les** ordinateurs **les** affiches
INDEFINITE ARTICLE	**un** *a, an* **une**	**des** *some*	**des** garçons **des** filles	**des** ordinateurs **des** affiches

➡ There is liaison after **les** and **des** when the next word begins with a vowel sound.

➡ **Des** corresponds to the English article *some.* While *some* is often omitted in English, **des** MUST be expressed in French. Contrast:

Il y a *There are*	des *some*	livres sur la table. *books on the table.*

Je dîne avec *I'm having dinner with*	des *. . .*	amis. *friends.*

6 Pluriel, s'il vous plaît

Give the plurals of the following nouns.

▶ une copine
  des copines

▶ l'ami
  les amis

1. un copain
2. une amie
3. un homme
4. une femme
5. un euro
6. une affiche
7. le voisin
8. l'élève
9. la cousine
10. le livre
11. l'ordinateur
12. la voiture

7 Shopping

You are in a department store in Montpellier looking for the following items. Ask the salesperson if he or she has these items. The salesperson will answer affirmatively.

▶ —Pardon, monsieur (madame). Est-ce que vous avez des sacs?
  —Bien sûr, nous avons des sacs.

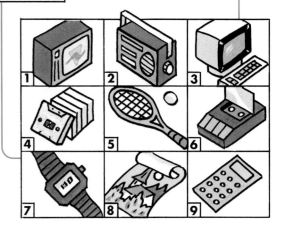

8 Qu'est-ce qu'il y a?

Explain what there is in the following places. Complete the sentences with **il y a** and a noun from the box. Be sure to use the appropriate articles: **un, une, des.** Be logical. Often several choices are possible.

▶ Dans le garage, . . .

Dans le garage, il y a une moto (des voitures . . .).

1. Sur le bureau, . . .
2. À la boum, . . .
3. Dans la classe, . . .
4. Au café, sur la table, . . .
5. Dans ma chambre, . . .
6. Dans la classe de maths, . . .

**limonade   stylo   livres   affiches   moto
professeur   lit   croissants   voitures   filles
ordinateur   garçons   élèves   table**

D. L'article indéfini dans les phrases négatives

Compare the forms of the indefinite article in affirmative and negative sentences.

AFFIRMATIVE	NEGATIVE	
Tu as **un** vélo?	Non, je n'ai **pas de** vélo.	*No, I don't have a bike.*
Est-ce que Paul a **une** radio?	Non, il n'a **pas de** radio.	*No, he doesn't have a radio.*
Vous invitez **des** copains demain?	Non, nous n'invitons **pas de** copains.	*No, we are not inviting any friends.*

After a NEGATIVE verb:

> **pas + un, une, des**   becomes   **pas de**

➡ Note that **pas de** becomes **pas d'** before a vowel sound.

    Alice a un ordinateur.   Paul n'a **pas d'**ordinateur.

    J'ai des amis à Québec.   Je n'ai **pas d'**amis à Montréal.

➡ The negative form of **il y a** is **il n'y a pas:**

    Dans ma chambre,

il y a une radio.	**Il n'y a pas de** télé.	*There is no TV.*
il y a des affiches.	**Il n'y a pas de** photos.	*There are no photographs.*

➡ After **être,** the articles **un, une,** and **des** do NOT change.

    Philippe est un voisin.   Éric n'est **pas un** voisin.

    Ce sont des vélos.   Ce ne sont **pas des** mobylettes.

---

9 **Possessions**

Ask your classmates if they own the following.

▶ un ordinateur

Est-ce que tu as un ordinateur?

Oui, j'ai un ordinateur.

(Non, je n'ai pas d'ordinateur.)

1. un appareil-photo
2. une moto
3. une mobylette
4. une clarinette
5. des disques de jazz
6. des affiches
7. un boa
8. un alligator
9. des hamsters

10 **Oui et non**

One cannot have everything. Say that the following people do not have what is indicated in parentheses.

▶ Paul a un vélo. (un scooter)
   Il n'a pas de scooter.

1. Julien a un scooter. (une voiture).
2. J'ai une radio. (une télé)
3. Vous avez des cassettes. (des compacts)
4. Vous avez des frères. (une soeur)
5. Nous avons un chien. (des chats)
6. Tu as des copains à Bordeaux. (des copains à Lyon)
7. Marc a un oncle à Québec. (un oncle à Montréal)
8. Nathalie a des cousins à San Francisco. (des cousins à Los Angeles)

11 Le grenier *(The attic)*

Your friend is cleaning the attic. Ask if the following items are up there. Your friend (a classmate) will answer according to the illustration.

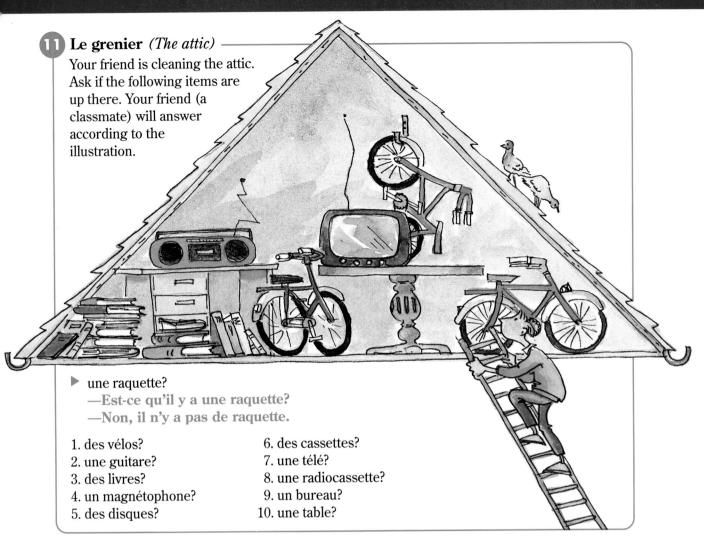

▶ une raquette?
—Est-ce qu'il y a une raquette?
—Non, il n'y a pas de raquette.

1. des vélos?
2. une guitare?
3. des livres?
4. un magnétophone?
5. des disques?

6. des cassettes?
7. une télé?
8. une radiocassette?
9. un bureau?
10. une table?

Expression pour la conversation

How to contradict a negative statement or question:

Si! *Yes!* —Tu n'as pas de chaîne stéréo?
—**Si!** J'ai une chaîne stéréo.

Tu n'as pas de chaîne stéréo?

Si! J'ai une chaîne stéréo.

12 Contradictions!

Contradict all of the following negative statements.

▶ Tu ne parles pas anglais! **Si, je parle anglais!**

1. Tu ne parles pas français!
2. Tu n'étudies pas!
3. Tu ne joues pas au basket!

4. Tu n'aimes pas les sports!
5. Tu n'aimes pas la musique!
6. Tu n'écoutes pas le professeur!

E. L'usage de l'article défini dans le sens général

In French, the definite article (le, la, les) is used more often than in English. Note its use in the following sentences.

J'aime **la musique.**	*(In general) I like **music.***
Tu préfères **le tennis** ou **le golf?**	*(Generally) do you prefer **tennis** or **golf?***
Pauline aime **les westerns.**	*(In general) Pauline likes **westerns.***
Nous aimons **la liberté.**	*(In general) we love **liberty.***

The definite article (le, la, les) is used to introduce ABSTRACT nouns, or nouns used in a GENERAL or COLLECTIVE sense.

J' ♥ le français

13 Expression personnelle

Say how you feel about the following things, using one of the suggested expressions.

Je n'aime pas . . .
J'aime un peu . . .
J'aime beaucoup . . .

▶ Je n'aime pas la violence.

la musique	le français	la violence	le théâtre
la nature	les maths	l'injustice	le cinéma
les sports	les sciences	la liberté	la danse
le camping			la photo
			(photography)

14 C'est évident! *(It's obvious!)*

Read about the following people and say what they like. Choose the appropriate item from the list. (Masculine nouns are in blue. Feminine nouns are in red.)

▶ Cécile écoute des cassettes.
   Cécile aime la musique.

art   cinéma   danse   français   musique   nature   tennis

1. Jean-Claude a une raquette.
2. Vous faites une promenade dans la forêt.
3. Les touristes visitent un musée *(museum)*.
4. Tu regardes un film.
5. Nous étudions en classe de français.
6. Véronique et Roger sont dans une discothèque.

F. L'usage de l'article défini avec les jours de la semaine

Compare the following sentences.

REPEATED EVENTS	SINGLE EVENT
Le samedi, je dîne avec des copains.	**Samedi,** je dîne avec mon cousin.
(On) Saturdays *(in general), I have dinner with friends.*	***(On) Saturday*** *(that is, this Saturday), I am having dinner with my cousin.*

To indicate a repeated or habitual event, French uses the construction:

> **le** + DAY OF THE WEEK

➡ When an event happens only once, no article is used.

15 Questions personnelles

1. Est-ce que tu étudies le samedi?
2. Est-ce que tu dînes au restaurant le dimanche? Si *(If)* oui, avec qui?
3. Est-ce que tu as une classe de français le lundi? le mercredi?
4. Est-ce que tu regardes les matchs de football américain le samedi? le dimanche?
5. Quel programme de télé est-ce que tu regardes le vendredi? le jeudi?
6. Est-ce que tu travailles? Où? *(Name of place or store)* Quand?

16 L'emploi du temps

	LUNDI	MARDI	MERCREDI	JEUDI	VENDREDI
9 h	français	physique	sciences	biologie	
10 h		histoire		maths	anglais
11 h	maths	sciences	anglais		français

The following students all have the same morning schedule. Complete the sentences accordingly.

▶ **Nous avons une classe de français le lundi . . .**

1. J'ai une classe de maths _____ .
2. Tu as une classe de sciences _____ .
3. Jacques a une classe de physique _____ .
4. Thérèse a une classe d'histoire _____ .
5. Vous avez une classe de biologie _____ .
6. Les élèves ont une classe d'anglais _____ .

Prononciation	**le** /lə/ **les** /le/

Les articles *le* et *les*

le sac   **les sacs**

Be sure to distinguish between the pronunciation of **le** and **les**. In spoken French, that is often the only way to tell the difference between a singular and a plural noun.

Répétez:	/lə/	**le**	**le sac**	**le vélo**	**le disque**	**le copain**	**le voisin**
	/le/	**les**	**les sacs**	**les vélos**	**les disques**	**les copains**	**les voisins**

À votre tour!

1 Allô!

Jean-Marc is phoning some friends. Match his questions on the left with his friends' answers on the right.

1 Quel âge a ton copain?

2 Est-ce qu'Éric a un scooter?

3 Où est l'appareil-photo?

4 Tu as des cassettes?

5 Est-ce que tu aimes étudier l'anglais?

6 Tu as soif?

a Oui, mais je n'ai pas de magnétophone.

b Il est sur la table.

c Quatorze ans.

d Oui, je voudrais une limonade.

e Oui, mais je préfère l'espagnol.

f Non, mais il a une moto.

2 Un sondage

A French consumer research group wants to know what things American teenagers own. Conduct a survey in your class asking who has the objects on the list. Count the number of students who raise their hands for each object, and report your findings on a separate piece of paper.

Qui a des cassettes?... Quinze élèves ont des cassettes.

UN SONDAGE

15

3 Créa-dialogue

Ask your classmates if they like the following things. Then ask if they own the corresponding object.

le tennis

1. la musique	2. le jogging	3. les maths	4. la photo	5. les matchs de baseball	6. l'exercice

▶ —Tu aimes le tennis?　　　　—Tu as une raquette?
　—Oui, j'aime le tennis.　　　—Oui, j'ai une raquette.
　　(Non, je n'aime pas le tennis.)　　(Non, je n'ai pas de raquette.)

4 Quelle est la différence?

Sophie went away with her family for the weekend and she took some of her belongings with her. Describe what is in her room on Friday and what is missing on Saturday.

VENDREDI　　　　SAMEDI

▶ Il y a . . .　　　　▶ Il n'y a pas de . . .

5 Inventaire (Inventory)

Write a short paragraph naming two things that may be found in each of the following places. Also indicate one thing that is usually not found in that place.

▶ Dans le salon, il y a une télé et des chaises. Il n'y a pas de lit.

- dans ma chambre
- dans mon sac
- dans le garage
- dans la rue (street)
- sur la table

6 Composition: Ma semaine

In a short paragraph, describe what you do (or do not do) regularly on various days of the week. Select three days and two different activities for each day. Use only vocabulary that you know. Perhaps you might want to exchange paragraphs with a friend by FAX or modem. ▶

Le lundi, j'ai une classe de français.
Je regarde «La roue de la fort...
(Wheel of Fort...

Le lundi, j'ai une classe de français.
Je regarde «La roue de la fortune»
(Wheel of Fortune) à la télé.

Le samedi, je n'étudie pas. Je dîne
au restaurant avec mon copain.

19

Le copain de Mireille

Nicolas and Jean-Claude are having lunch at the school cafeteria. Nicolas is looking at the students seated at the other end of their table.

NICOLAS:	Regarde la fille là-bas!	
JEAN-CLAUDE:	La fille blonde?	
NICOLAS:	Oui! Qui est-ce?	
JEAN-CLAUDE:	C'est Mireille Labé.	
NICOLAS:	Elle est <u>mignonne</u>!	*cute*
JEAN-CLAUDE:	Elle est aussi <u>amusante</u>, intelligente et <u>sympathique</u>.	*fun / nice*
NICOLAS:	Est-ce qu'elle a un copain?	
JEAN-CLAUDE:	Oui, elle a un copain.	
NICOLAS:	Il est sympathique?	
JEAN-CLAUDE:	Oui . . . Très sympathique!	
NICOLAS:	Et intelligent?	
JEAN-CLAUDE:	Aussi!	
NICOLAS:	Dommage! . . . Qui est-ce?	
JEAN-CLAUDE:	C'est moi!	
NICOLAS:	Euh . . . oh . . . Excuse-moi et <u>félicitations</u>!	*congratulations*

● Compréhension

1. Qui est-ce que Nicolas regarde?
2. Comment s'appelle la fille?
3. Est-ce qu'elle est jolie?
4. Est-ce qu'elle a d'autres *(other)* qualités?
5. Est-ce qu'elle a un copain?
6. Qui est le copain de Mireille *(Mireille's boyfriend)*?

■ NOTE ■
CULTURELLE

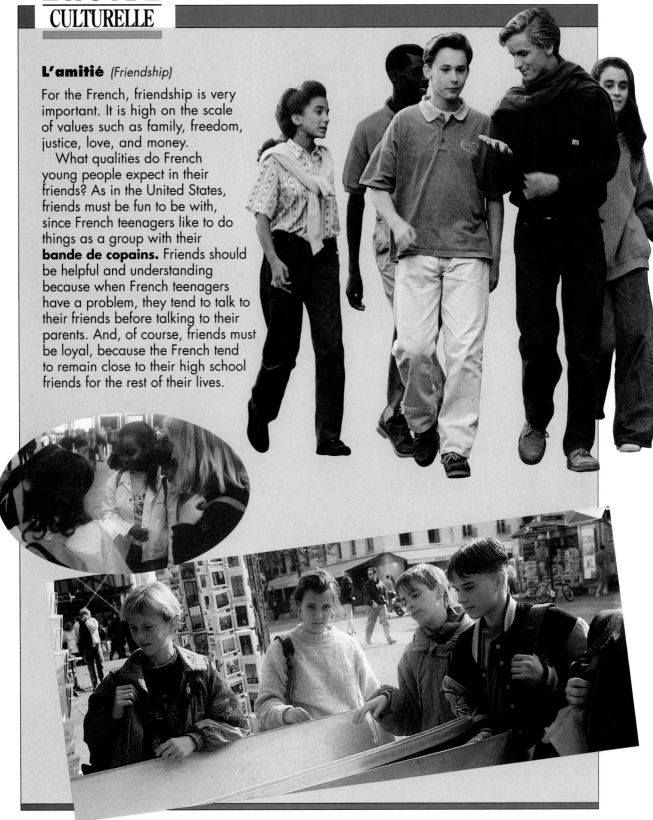

L'amitié *(Friendship)*

For the French, friendship is very important. It is high on the scale of values such as family, freedom, justice, love, and money.

What qualities do French young people expect in their friends? As in the United States, friends must be fun to be with, since French teenagers like to do things as a group with their **bande de copains.** Friends should be helpful and understanding because when French teenagers have a problem, they tend to talk to their friends before talking to their parents. And, of course, friends must be loyal, because the French tend to remain close to their high school friends for the rest of their lives.

A. Les adjectifs: masculin et féminin

Compare the forms of the adjectives in heavy print as they describe masculine and feminine nouns.

MASCULINE	FEMININE
Le scooter est **petit.**	La voiture est **petite.**
Patrick est **intelligent.**	Caroline est **intelligente.**
L'ordinateur est **moderne.**	La télé est **moderne.**

In written French, feminine adjectives are usually formed as follows:

> MASCULINE ADJECTIVE + **-e** = FEMININE ADJECTIVE

➡ If the masculine adjective ends in **-e,** there is no change in the feminine form.

Jérôme est **timide.**   Juliette est **timide.**

➡ Adjectives that follow the above patterns are called REGULAR adjectives. Those that do not are called IRREGULAR adjectives. For example:

Marc est **beau.**   Sylvie est **belle.**
Paul est **canadien.**   Marie est **canadienne.**

NOTE: French dictionaries list adjectives by their masculine forms. For irregular adjectives, the feminine form is indicated in parentheses.

NOTES DE PRONONCIATION:

- If the masculine form of an adjective ends in a silent consonant, that consonant is pronounced in the feminine form.
- If the masculine form of an adjective ends in a vowel or a pronounced consonant, the masculine and feminine forms sound the same.

DIFFERENT PRONUNCIATION		SAME PRONUNCIATION	
peti~~t~~	peti**te**	timide	timide
blon~~d~~	blon**de**	joli	jolie
françai~~s~~	françai**se**	espagnol	espagnole

1 Vive la différence!

People can be friends and yet be quite different. Describe the girls named in parentheses, indicating that they are not like their friends.

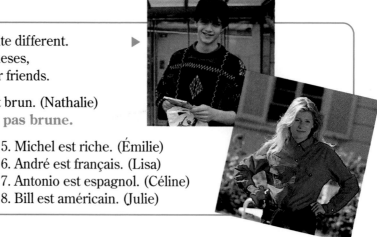

▶ Jean-Claude est brun. (Nathalie)
  Nathalie n'est pas brune.

1. Jean-Louis est blond. (Carole)
2. Paul est petit. (Mireille)
3. Éric est beau. (Marthe)
4. Jérôme est grand. (Louise)
5. Michel est riche. (Émilie)
6. André est français. (Lisa)
7. Antonio est espagnol. (Céline)
8. Bill est américain. (Julie)

Vocabulaire: La description

ADJECTIFS		**Voici Jean-Claude.**	**Voici Mireille.**
amusant	*amusing, fun*	Il est **amusant.**	Elle est **amusante.**
intelligent	*intelligent*	Il est **intelligent.**	Elle est **intelligente.**
intéressant	*interesting*	Il est **intéressant.**	Elle est **intéressante.**
méchant	*mean, nasty*	Il n'est pas **méchant.**	Elle n'est pas **méchante.**
bête	*silly, dumb*	Il n'est pas **bête.**	Elle n'est pas **bête.**
sympathique	*nice, pleasant*	Il est **sympathique.**	Elle est **sympathique.**
timide	*timid*	Il est **timide.**	Elle n'est pas **timide.**
gentil (gentille)	*nice, kind*	Il est **gentil.**	Elle est **gentille.**
mignon (mignonne)	*cute*	Il est **mignon.**	Elle est **mignonne.**
sportif (sportive)	*athletic*	Il est **sportif.**	Elle est **sportive.**

ADVERBES		
assez	*rather*	Nous sommes **assez** intelligents.
très	*very*	Vous n'êtes pas **très** sportifs!

2 Oui ou non?

In your opinion, do the following people have the suggested traits? (Note: These traits are given in the masculine form only.)

Il est intéressant.

Il n'est pas intéressant.

▶ le prince Charles / intéressant?

1. le Président / sympathique?
2. Martina Hingis / sportif?
3. ma copine / gentil?
4. Jennifer Aniston / mignon?
5. Oprah Winfrey / intelligent?
6. Einstein / bête?
7. Jay Leno / amusant?
8. le prof / méchant?

3 Descriptions

Select one of the following characters. Using words from the **Vocabulaire,** describe this character in two affirmative or negative sentences.

▶ Frankenstein
  Il est très méchant.
  Il n'est pas très mignon.

1. Tarzan	6. Wonder Woman
2. King Kong	7. Charlie Brown
3. Big Bird	8. Blanche-Neige *(Snow White)*
4. Batman	9. Garfield
5. Miss Piggy	10. Snoopy

4 L'idéal

Now you have the chance to describe your ideal people. Use two adjectives for each one.

1. Le copain idéal est . . . et . . .
2. La copine idéale est . . . et . . .
3. Le professeur idéal est . . . et . . .
4. L'étudiant idéal est . . . et . . .
5. L'étudiante idéale est . . . et . . .

B. Les adjectifs: le pluriel

Compare the forms of the adjectives in heavy print as they describe singular and plural nouns.

SINGULAR	PLURAL
Paul est **intelligent** et **timide**.	Paul et Éric sont **intelligents** et **timides**.
Alice est **intelligente** et **timide**.	Alice et Claire sont **intelligentes** et **timides**.

In written French, plural adjectives are usually formed as follows:

> SINGULAR ADJECTIVE + **-s** = PLURAL ADJECTIVE

➡ If the masculine singular adjective already ends in **-s,** there is no change in the plural form.

	Patrick est **français**.	Patrick et Daniel sont **français**.
BUT:	Anne est **française**.	Anne et Alice sont **françaises**.

NOTE DE PRONONCIATION: Because the final **-s** of plural adjectives is silent, singular and plural adjectives sound the same.

SUMMARY: Forms of regular adjectives

	MASCULINE	FEMININE	*also:*
SINGULAR	**–** **grand**	**-e** **grand<u>e</u>**	timide timide
PLURAL	**-s** **grand<u>s</u>**	**-es** **grand<u>es</u>**	français français<u>es</u>

---

5 **Une question de personnalité**

Indicate whether or not the following people exhibit the personality traits in parentheses. (These traits are given in the masculine singular form only. Make the necessary agreements.)

> Elles ne sont pas timides.

▶ Alice et Thérèse aiment parler en public. (timide?)

1. Claire et Valérie sont très populaires. (amusant?)
2. Robert et Jean-Luc n'aiment pas danser. (timide?)
3. Catherine et Martine aiment jouer au foot. (sportif?)
4. Laure et Gisèle ont un «A» en français. (intelligent?)
5. Thomas et Vincent n'aiment pas le jogging. (sportif?)
6. Les voisins n'aiment pas parler avec nous. (sympathique?)

Vocabulaire: Les adjectifs de nationalité

américain	*American*	**italien (italienne)**	*Italian*
mexicain	*Mexican*	**canadien (canadienne)**	*Canadian*
français	*French*	**japonais**	*Japanese*
anglais	*English*	**chinois**	*Chinese*
espagnol	*Spanish*		
suisse	*Swiss*		

➡ Words that describe nationality are adjectives and take adjective endings.

Monsieur Katagiri est **japonais.**

Kumi et Michiko sont **japonaises.**

Expression pour la conversation

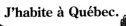

J'habite à Québec.

Alors, tu es canadien.

How to introduce a conclusion:

alors   *so, then*   —J'habite à Québec.

—**Alors,** tu es canadien!

---

6 ## Quelle nationalité?

Your classmate wants to know more about the following people: where they live and what their nationality is. Act out the dialogues.

▶ —Où habitent Janet et Barbara?
—Elles habitent à San Francisco.
—Alors, elles sont américaines?
—Mais oui, elles sont américaines.

Janet et Barbara		**1. Jim et Bob**	**2. Laure et Céline**
San Francisco		**Liverpool**	**Toulouse**
américain		**anglais**	**français**
3. Luisa et Teresa		**4. Éric et Vincent**	**5. ??**
Madrid		**Montréal**	**??**
espagnol		**??**	**??**

7 ## Les nationalités

Read the descriptions of the following people and give their nationalities.

▶ Silvia et Maria sont étudiantes à Rome.
Elles sont italiennes.

1. Lise et Nathalie étudient à Québec.
2. Michael et Dennis sont de Liverpool.
3. Luis et Paco étudient à Madrid.
4. Isabel et Carmen travaillent à Acapulco.
5. Yoko et Liliko sont étudiantes à l'université de Tokyo.
6. Monsieur et Madame Chen habitent à Beijing.
7. Jean-Pierre et Claude sont de Genève.
8. Françoise et Sylvie travaillent à Paris.

C. La place des adjectifs

Note the position of the adjectives in the sentences on the right.

Philippe a une voiture.   Il a une voiture **anglaise.**
Denise invite des copains.   Elle invite des copains **américains.**
Voici un livre.   Voici un livre **intéressant.**
J'ai des amies.   J'ai des amies **sympathiques.**

In French, adjectives usually come AFTER the noun they
modify, according to the pattern:

ARTICLE	+	NOUN	+	ADJECTIVE
une		voiture		**française**
des		copains		**intéressants**

R.S.V.P.
Le Club de Correspondance

Étudiant français, 16 ans,
brun, grand, sportif,
assez intelligent, un peu
timide, voudrait
correspondre avec
étudiante américaine
sportive et sympathique.

Envoyez votre message à :
Correspondants
13 rue de la Cerisaie
75004 Paris

---

8 Préférences personnelles

For each person or object below, choose
among the characteristics in parentheses.
Indicate your preference.

▶ avoir un copain (sympathique,
intelligent, sportif)
**Je préfère avoir un copain
intelligent.**

1. avoir une copine (amusante,
   mignonne, intelligente)
2. avoir un professeur (gentil,
   intelligent, amusant)
3. avoir des voisins (sympathiques,
   intéressants, riches)
4. avoir une voiture (moderne,
   confortable, rapide)
5. avoir une calculatrice (japonaise,
   américaine, française)
6. avoir une montre (suisse, japonaise,
   française)
7. dîner dans un restaurant (italien,
   chinois, français)
8. regarder un film (intéressant,
   amusant, intelligent)
9. travailler avec des personnes
   (gentilles, amusantes, sérieuses)
10. faire un voyage avec des gens
    (amusants, riches, sympathiques)

9 Qui se ressemble . . .
(Birds of a feather . . .)
Say that the following people have
friends, relatives, or acquaintances with
the same personality or nationality.

▶ Claire est anglaise. (un copain)
Elle a un copain anglais.

1. Jean-Pierre est sympathique.
   (des cousines)
2. La prof est intelligente. (des étudiants)
3. Madame Simon est intéressante.
   (des voisines)
4. Alice est américaine. (des copines)
5. Véronique est amusante. (un frère)
6. Michel est sportif. (une soeur)
7. Pedro est espagnol. (des camarades)
8. Antonio est mexicain. (une copine)
9. Bernard est sportif. (un voisin)

Birds of a feather flock together.

10 Préférences internationales

Choose an item from Column A and indicate
your preference as to country of origin by
choosing an adjective from Column B. Be sure to
make the necessary agreement.

Je préfère
les voitures italiennes.

	A	B
	la musique	anglais
	la cuisine	américain
	les voitures	français
Je préfère . . .	les ordinateurs	mexicain
	les appareils-photo	chinois
	les compacts	japonais
	les restaurants	italien

Prononciation

Les consonnes finales

/-/   /d/

As you know, when the last letter of a word
is a consonant, that consonant is often silent.
But when a word ends in "**e**," the consonant
before it is pronounced. As you practice the
following adjectives, be sure to distinguish
between the masculine and the feminine forms.

blond   **blonde**

MASCULINE ADJECTIVE
(no final consonant sound)

FEMININE ADJECTIVE
(final consonant sound)

Répétez:

blond		/d/	**blonde**
grand			**grande**
petit		/t/	**petite**
amusant			**amusante**
français		/z/	**française**
anglais			**anglaise**
américain		/n/	**américaine**
canadien			**canadienne**

Joli, petit et bon! Bureau 45 euros Table 60 euros **Jolie, petite et bonne!**

IKEA *Miracle économique!*

Leçon 19   167

À votre tour!

1 Allô!

Valérie is phoning some friends. Match her questions on the left with her friends' answers on the right.

1. Ton frère aime jouer au foot?

2. Cécile et Sophie sont mignonnes, n'est-ce pas?

3. Pourquoi est-ce que tu invites Olivier?

4. Tu aimes la classe?

5. Tu as des cousins?

a. Oui, et intelligentes aussi!

b. Parce qu'il est amusant et sympathique.

c. Oui, j'ai un professeur très intéressant.

d. Oui, il est très sportif.

e. Oui, mais ils ne sont pas très sympathiques.

2 Créa-dialogue

With your classmates, talk about the people of different nationalities you may know or objects you may own.

des cousins

mignon?

▸ —J'ai des <u>cousins mexicains</u>.
—<u>Ils sont mignons?</u>
—<u>Oui, ils sont très mignons.</u>

1. une voisine	2. un prof	3. des copines	4. un livre	5. une voiture
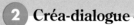			ASTÉRIX	
blond?	sympathique?	sportif?	intéressant?	grand?

3 Une invitation

Comment s'appelle ta cousine? Quel âge a-t-elle?

A French friend has invited you to go to a party with his/her cousin. You want to know as much as you can about this cousin. You may first ask your friend the cousin's name and age.

Then ask as many questions as you can about the cousin's physical appearance and personality traits. Act out your conversation with a classmate.

4 Avis de recherche

(Missing person's bulletin)

The two people in the pictures below have been reported missing. Describe each one as well as you can, using your imagination. Mention:

- the (approximate) age of the person
- the way he/she looks
- personality traits
- other features or characteristics

5 Composition: Descriptions

Describe one of the following well-known French people in a short paragraph, giving the person's name, profession, and approximate age. Also briefly describe the person's physical appearance.

Isabelle Adjani (actrice)

Surya Bonaly (athlète)

Jean-Jacques Goldman (chanteur)

Jacques Chirac (président)

6 Composition: Rencontres

Select two people whom you would like to meet (a man and a woman). These people may be famous singers, actors or actresses, sports figures, politicians, professional people, community leaders, etc. (You might even be able to contact them directly by e-mail!) Describe each person (physical traits and personality), using either affirmative or negative sentences.

```
Je voudrais
rencontrer X.
Il (Elle) est...
```

La voiture de Roger

Dans la <u>rue</u>, il y a une voiture <u>rouge</u>.   *street / red*
C'est une petite voiture. C'est une voiture
de sport.
Dans la rue, il y a aussi un café. Au café,
il y a un jeune homme.
Il s'appelle Roger.
C'est le <u>propriétaire</u> de la voiture rouge.   *owner*

Une jeune fille <u>entre dans</u> le café.   *enters*
Elle s'appelle Véronique.
C'est <u>l'amie de Roger</u>.   *Roger's friend*
Véronique parle à Roger.

VÉRONIQUE:	Tu as une <u>nouvelle</u> voiture, n'est-ce pas?	*new*
ROGER:	Oui, j'ai une nouvelle voiture.	
VÉRONIQUE:	Est-ce qu'elle est grande ou petite?	
ROGER:	C'est une petite voiture.	
VÉRONIQUE:	De quelle couleur est-elle?	
ROGER:	C'est une voiture rouge.	
VÉRONIQUE:	Est-ce que c'est une voiture italienne?	
ROGER:	Oui, c'est une voiture italienne. Mais <u>dis donc</u>, Véronique, tu es <u>vraiment</u> très curieuse!	*hey there* *really*
VÉRONIQUE:	Et toi, tu n'es pas <u>assez curieux</u>!	*curious enough*
ROGER:	Ah bon? Pourquoi?	
VÉRONIQUE:	Pourquoi?! . . . Regarde la <u>contractuelle</u> là-bas!	*meter maid*
ROGER:	Ah, zut alors!	

Compréhension

1. Qu'est-ce qu'il y a dans la rue?
2. Est-ce que la voiture est grande?
3. Comment s'appelle le jeune homme?
4. Où est-il?
5. Comment s'appelle la jeune fille?
6. De quelle couleur est la voiture?

NOTE CULTURELLE

Les Français et l'auto

France is one of the leading producers of automobiles in the world. The two automakers, **Renault** and **Peugeot-Citroën**, manufacture a variety of models ranging from sports cars to mini-vans and buses.

To obtain a driver's license in France, you must be eighteen years old and pass a very difficult driving test. French teenagers can, however, begin to drive at the age of sixteen, as long as they take lessons at an accredited driving school (**auto-école**) and are accompanied by an adult.

On the whole, because cars (even used cars) are expensive to buy and maintain, few French teenagers have cars. Instead, many get around on two-wheelers: motorcycles, scooters, and mopeds.

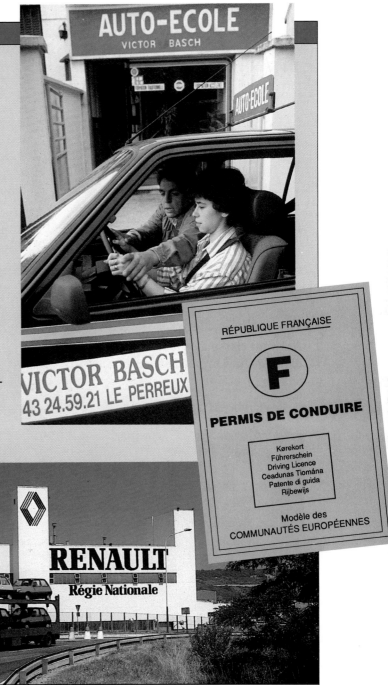

RÉPUBLIQUE FRANÇAISE

F

PERMIS DE CONDUIRE

Kørekort
Führerschein
Driving Licence
Ceadunas Tiomána
Patente di guida
Rijbewijs

Modèle des
COMMUNAUTÉS EUROPÉENNES

A. Les couleurs

Note the form and position of the color words in the following sentences:

Alice a un vélo **bleu**.   *Alice has a **blue** bicycle.*

Nous avons des chemises **bleues**.   *We have **blue** shirts.*

Names of colors are ADJECTIVES and take adjective ENDINGS. Like most descriptive adjectives, they come *after* the noun.

Vocabulaire: Les couleurs

De quelle couleur . . . ?   *What color . . . ?*   —**De quelle couleur** est la moto?

—Elle est rouge.

blanc (blanche)	**noir** (noire)	**bleu** (bleue)	**rouge** (rouge)	**jaune** (jaune)	**vert** (verte)	**gris** (grise)	**marron** (marron)	**orange** (orange)	**rose** (rose)

➡ The colors **orange** and **marron** are INVARIABLE. They do not take any endings.

    un sac **orange**   des sacs **orange**

    un tee-shirt **marron**   une chemise **marron**

---

1 De quelle couleur?

Ask your classmates to name the colors of things they own. (They may invent answers.)

▶ ta chambre?

> De quelle couleur est ta chambre?

> Elle est blanche et bleue.

1. ta bicyclette?
2. ton tee-shirt?
3. ton appareil-photo?
4. ta montre?
5. ta raquette de tennis?
6. ton livre de français?
7. ton livre d'anglais?
8. ton chien (chat)?

2 Possessions

Ask what objects or pets the following people own. A classmate will answer, giving the color.

▶ —Est-ce que Monsieur Thomas a une voiture?

—Oui, il a une voiture bleue.

M. Thomas

1. Mme Mercier

2. Marc

3. Delphine

4. Sophie

5. Éric

6. Stéphanie

3 **L'arche de Noé**

Noah's ark has just landed. Give the colors
of the animals as they get off the ship.

▶ le chien   Le chien est blanc.

1. le chat
2. l'éléphant *(m.)*
3. la panthère
4. le zèbre
5. le flamant
6. le cardinal
7. le lion
8. le perroquet

B. La place des adjectifs avant le nom

Compare the position of the adjectives in the following sentences.

Voici une voiture **française.**   Voici une **petite** voiture.
Paul est un garçon **intelligent.**   Pierre est un **beau** garçon.

▌ A few adjectives like **petit** and **beau** come BEFORE the noun they modify.

➡ The article **des** often becomes **de** before an adjective. Compare:
   des voitures   →   **de** petites voitures

Vocabulaire: Les adjectifs qui précèdent le nom		
beau (belle)	*beautiful, handsome*	Regarde la **belle** voiture!
joli	*pretty*	Qui est la **jolie** fille avec André?
grand	*big, large, tall*	Nous habitons dans un **grand** appartement.
petit	*little, small, short*	Ma soeur a un **petit** ordinateur.
bon (bonne)	*good*	Tu es un **bon** copain.
mauvais	*bad*	Patrick est un **mauvais** élève.

➡ There is a LIAISON after the above adjectives when the noun which follows begins with a
  vowel sound. Note that in liaison:
  • the "**d**" of **grand** is pronounced /t/: **un grand appartement**
  • **bon** is pronounced like **bonne: un bon élève**

4 Opinions personnelles

Give your opinion about the following people and things, using the adjectives **bon** or **mauvais**.

▶ Meryl Streep est (une) actrice *(actress)*.
   Meryl Streep est une bonne actrice (une mauvaise actrice).

1. *La Menace fantôme* est un film.
2. «Star Trek» est un programme de télé.
3. Whitney Houston est (une) chanteuse.
4. Will Smith est (un) acteur.
5. Cameron Diaz est (une) actrice.
6. Dracula est une personne.
7. McDonald's est un restaurant.
8. Les Yankees sont une équipe *(team)* de baseball.
9. Les Lakers sont une équipe de basket.
10. Je suis [un(e)] élève.

Expressions pour la conversation

How to get someone's attention:

Dis!	*Say! Hey!*	**Dis,** Éric, est-ce que tu as une voiture?
Dis donc!	*Hey there!*	**Dis donc,** est-ce que tu veux faire une promenade avec moi?

---

5 Dialogue

Christine asks her cousin Thomas if he has certain things. He responds affirmatively, describing each one. Play both roles.

▶ un ordinateur (petit)

▶ une voiture (anglaise)

1. une télé (petite)
2. une guitare (espagnole)
3. un vélo (rouge)
4. une calculatrice (petite)
5. un sac (grand)
6. des livres (intéressants)
7. une copine (amusante)
8. une mobylette (bleue)
9. une montre (belle)
10. un copain (bon)
11. une cousine (jolie)
12. une radio (japonaise)

C. *Il est* ou *c'est*?

When describing a person or thing, French speakers use two different constructions,
il est (elle est) and **c'est.**

		Il est + ADJECTIVE **Elle est** + ADJECTIVE	**C'est** + ARTICLE + NOUN (+ ADJECTIVE)
Roger	*He is . . .*	**Il est** amusant.	**C'est** un copain. **C'est** un copain amusant.
Véronique	*She is . . .*	**Elle est** sportive.	**C'est** une amie. **C'est** une bonne amie.
un scooter	*It is . . .*	**Il est** joli.	**C'est** un scooter français. **C'est** un bon scooter.
une voiture	*It is . . .*	**Elle est** petite.	**C'est** une voiture anglaise. **C'est** une petite voiture.

➡ Note the corresponding plural forms:

(Pierre et Marc)	*They are . . .*	**Ils sont** amusants.	Ce sont des copains.
(Claire et Anne)	*They are . . .*	**Elles sont** timides.	Ce sont des copines.

➡ In negative sentences, **c'est** becomes **ce n'est pas.**

Ce n'est pas un mauvais élève.   ***He's not** a bad student.*
Ce n'est pas une Peugeot.   ***It's not** a Peugeot.*

➡ **C'est** is also used with names of people
C'est Véronique.   **C'est** Madame Lamblet.

SCOOTERS PEUGEOT

6 Descriptions

Complete the following descriptions with **Il est, Elle est,** or **C'est,** as appropriate.

A. Roger
1. _____ grand.
2. _____ brun.
3. _____ un garçon sympathique.
4. _____ un mauvais élève.

B. Véronique
5. _____ une fille brune.
6. _____ une amie sympathique.
7. _____ très amusante.
8. _____ assez grande.

C. La voiture de Roger
9. _____ une voiture moderne.
10. _____ une petite voiture.
11. _____ rouge.
12. _____ très rapide.

D. Le scooter de Véronique
13. _____ bleu et blanc.
14. _____ très économique.
15. _____ un joli scooter.
16. _____ assez confortable.

D. Les expressions impersonnelles avec *c'est*

Note the use of **c'est** in the following sentences.

J'aime parler français.   **C'est** intéressant.   *It's interesting.*
Je n'aime pas travailler le weekend.   **Ce n'est pas** amusant.   *It's no(t) fun.*

To express an opinion on a general topic, the French use the construction:

> **C'est**
> **Ce n'est pas** } + MASCULINE ADJECTIVE

Vocabulaire: Opinions

C'est . . .	*It's . . . , That's . . .*
Ce n'est pas . . .	*It's not . . . , That's not . . .*

vrai	*true*	**chouette**	*neat*
faux	*false*	**super**	*great*
		extra	*terrific*
facile	*easy*	**pénible**	*a pain, annoying*
difficile	*hard, difficult*	**drôle**	*funny*

➡ To express an opinion, the French also use adverbs like **bien** and **mal.**

C'est bien.   *That's good.*   Tu étudies? **C'est bien.**
C'est mal.   *That's bad.*   Alain n'étudie pas. **C'est mal.**

---

7 **Vrai ou faux?**

Imagine that your little sister is talking about where certain cities are located. Tell her whether her statements are right or wrong.

1. Paris est en Italie.
2. Los Angeles est en Californie.
3. Genève est en Italie.
4. Dakar est en Afrique.
5. Fort-de-France est au Canada.
6. Québec est en France.

8 Opinion personnelle

Ask your classmates if they like to do the following things. They will answer, using an expression from the **Vocabulaire.**

▶ parler français

Tu aimes parler français?

Oui, c'est extra! (Non, c'est difficile!)

1. téléphoner
2. parler en public
3. nager
4. danser
5. voyager
6. dîner en ville
7. regarder «Star Trek»
8. étudier le weekend
9. écouter la musique classique

Prononciation ch /∫/

Les lettres «ch»

The letters "**ch**" are usually pronounced like the English "*sh.*"

Répétez: **chien   chat   chose   marche
chouette   chocolat   affiche
Michèle a un chat et deux chiens.**

chien

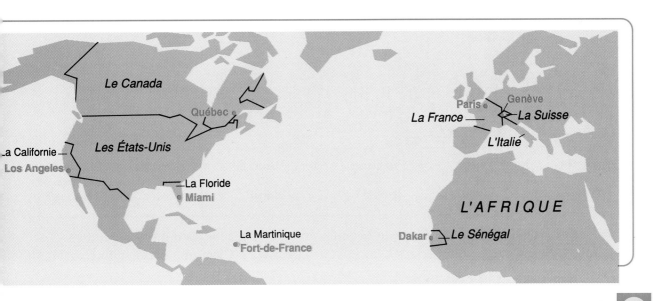

Le Canada

Québec

Les États-Unis

La Californie
Los Angeles

La Floride
Miami

La Martinique
Fort-de-France

Paris   Genève
La France   La Suisse
L'Italie

L'AFRIQUE

Dakar   Le Sénégal

À votre tour!

1 **Allô!**

Christophe is phoning some friends. Match his questions on the left with his friends' answers on the right.

1. De quelle couleur est ton vélo?

a. Non, il est canadien.

2. Ta raquette est bleue?

b. C'est vrai! Il est très timide.

3. Tu aimes regarder la télé?

c. Non, elle est blanche.

4. C'est un magazine français?

d. Oui, c'est amusant.

5. Philippe n'aime pas parler en public?

e. Il est vert.

2 **Créa-dialogue**

There has been a burglary in the rue Saint-Pierre. By walkie-talkie, two detectives are describing what they see. Play both roles.

(le)	1. (la)	2. (la)	3. (le)	4. (le)	5. (la)
CAFÉ	PHARMACIE	LIBRAIRIE	Restaurant	CINÉMA	fontaine
grande ou petite?	rouge ou bleue?	grande ou petite?	brun ou blond?	anglais ou français?	noir ou jaune?

▶ DÉTECTIVE 1: **Qu'est-ce qu'il y a devant <u>le café</u>?**   DÉTECTIVE 1: **<u>Elle</u> est <u>grande</u> ou <u>petite</u>?**
  DÉTECTIVE 2: **Il y a <u>une voiture</u>.**   DÉTECTIVE 2: **C'est <u>une petite voiture</u>.**

3 **Faisons connaissance!**

Try to find out which students have the same interests you do. Select two activities you enjoy from Column A and ask a classmate if he/she likes to do them. Your classmate will answer yes or no, using an appropriate expression from Column B.

Tu aimes voyager?

Oui, c'est amusant.

A	B
chanter	chouette
danser	super
nager	extra
téléphoner	amusant
voyager	intéressant
jouer au foot	pénible
jouer au volley	drôle
organiser des boums	difficile
parler avec les voisins	facile
parler français en classe	
dîner au restaurant	

Tu aimes parler français en classe?

Non, c'est difficile.

4 **Composition: La chambre de Véronique**

Look at the picture of Véronique's room. Write a short paragraph in which you describe five of the following items. You may want to mention color or size **(grand? petit?),** and perhaps give your opinion **(joli? beau? drôle? bon?,** etc.)

la chambre
la porte
le lit
la table
la chaise
la radiocassette
la guitare
l'affiche

▶ La chambre de Véronique est bleue et blanche. Elle a un grand lit. . . .

5 **Composition: Ma chambre**

Write a short description of your own room: real or imaginary. Use only vocabulary that you know. You may use the suggestions about Véronique's room as a guide.

Vive la différence!
Le monde personnel

Parlons° de votre monde° personnel. Répondez aux questions suivantes.° D'après° vous, quelles sont les réponses des jeunes Français en général à ces° questions?

1 Combien de télés est-ce qu'il y a chez vous?°

- zéro
- une
- deux
- trois ou plus°

Et dans une maison française typique, combien est-ce qu'il y a de télés?

2 Combien de livres est-ce qu'il y a chez vous?

- dix
- cinquante
- cent
- plus de° cent cinquante

Et dans une maison française typique, combien de livres est-ce qu'il y a?

3 Dans la classe de français, quel est le pourcentage d'élèves qui ont un walkman?

- moins de° 25% (vingt-cinq pour cent)
- entre° 26% et 50%
- entre 51% et 75%
- entre 76% et 100% (cent pour cent)

Selon° vous, quel est le pourcentage de jeunes Français qui ont un walkman?

4 En général, comment sont vos relations avec vos parents?

- très bonnes
- bonnes
- assez bonnes
- mauvaises

Et en France, comment sont les relations entre parents et enfants?°

5 Quand vous avez une chose importante à discuter° (par exemple, un problème personnel), à qui est-ce que vous préférez parler?

- à votre frère ou à votre soeur
- à votre père ou à votre mère
- à un copain ou à une copine
- à un professeur

Et les jeunes Français, à qui est-ce qu'ils préfèrent parler de leurs° problèmes?

6 En général, qu'est-ce que vous pensez° de vos professeurs?

- Ils sont «cool».
- Ils sont compréhensifs.°
- Ils sont sévères.°
- Ils sont sympathiques.

Et les élèves français, qu'est-ce qu'ils pensent de leurs professeurs?

7 Quelle est la chose la plus° importante dans votre vie?°

- l'argent°
- l'amitié°
- l'indépendance
- les études°

Et pour les jeunes Français, quelle est la chose la plus importante?

Et les Français?

1. La majorité des familles françaises ont seulement *(only)* une télé.   2. Les Français aiment lire *(to read)*. Ils ont en moyenne *(on the average)* plus de cent livres par famille.
3. 41% (quarante et un pour cent)   4. La majorité des jeunes Français ont de très bonnes relations avec leurs parents.   5. En général, ils préfèrent parler à un copain ou à une copine.   6. En général, ils pensent que leurs professeurs sont sympathiques.
7. C'est l'amitié.

Parlons *Let's talk*   **monde** *world*   **suivantes** *following*   **D'après** *According to*
ces *these*   **chez vous** *in your home*   **plus** *more*   **plus de** *more than*
moins de *less than*   **entre** *between*   **Selon** *According to*   **enfants** *children*
discuter *to discuss*   **leurs** *their*   **pensez** *think*   **compréhensifs** *understanding*
sévères *strict*   **la plus** *the most*   **vie** *life*   **argent** *money*   **amitié** *friendship*
études *studies*

EN FRANCE

La mobylette

Because mopeds or cyclomoteurs are easy and fun to drive, they are very popular with French teenagers. During the week, many students go to school on their mopeds. On weekends, they take their mopeds to go downtown or to go for a ride in the country with their friends.

Although the term mobylette is a trade name, students tend to use the term (or its shortened form mob) to refer to any type of moped. In France, you can drive a mobylette at age 14, and the only restrictions are that you must wear a helmet and cannot exceed 45 kilometers per hour.

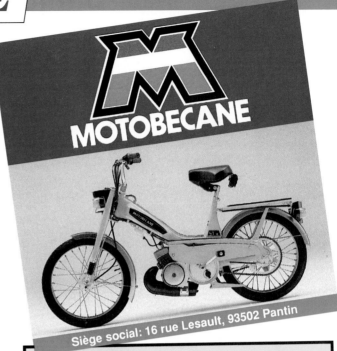

MOTOBECANE

Siège social: 16 rue Lesault, 93502 Pantin

Look at the ads on the right. Which moped would you like to have? Describe it using words that you know. (What color is it? What country is it from? Is it big or small?)

PEUGEOT
concessionnaire
Ets SOUHART

scooters • cyclos • motos
métro Bir Hakeim   5, bd. de Grenelle   75015 PARIS
01 45 79 33 01

boulmich
MOTO

129, bd St-Michel Paris 5
01 43 29 53 10

LA MOTO VERTE
**Concessionnaire Exclusif
Yamaha**
85 r Chardon Lagache
75016 Paris 01 42 24 56 56

Entre amis: Bonjour, Brigitte!

Chers° copains américains,

Je m'appelle Brigitte Lavie. J'ai quatorze ans. Voici ma photo. Je ne suis pas très grande, mais je ne suis pas petite. Je suis de taille° moyenne.° Je suis brune mais j'ai les yeux° verts. Je suis sportive. J'aime le ski, le jogging et la danse moderne.

J'habite à Toulouse avec ma famille. Mon père travaille dans l'industrie aéronautique. Il est ingénieur.° Ma mère travaille dans une banque. Elle est directrice° du personnel.

J'ai une soeur et un frère. Ma petite soeur s'appelle Ariane. Elle a cinq ans. Elle est très mignonne. Mon frère s'appelle Jérôme. Il a treize ans. Il est pénible. J'ai un chien. Il s'appelle Attila mais il est très gentil. (Il est plus gentil que° mon frère!) J'ai aussi deux poissons rouges.° Ils n'ont pas de nom.°

J'ai une chaîne stéréo et des quantités de compacts. J'ai aussi une mobylette. Le weekend, j'adore faire des promenades° à mobylette avec mes copains. J'ai beaucoup de copains, mais je n'ai pas de « petit copain ». Ça n'a pas d'importance!° Je suis heureuse° comme ça !

Amitiés,
Brigitte

Chers *Dear* **taille** *size* **moyenne** *average* **yeux** *eyes* **ingénieur** *engineer* **directrice** *director*
plus gentil que *nicer than* **poissons rouges** *goldfish* **nom** *name* **faire des promenades** *go for rides*
petit copain *boyfriend* **Ça n'a pas d'importance!** *It doesn't matter!* **heureuse** *happy* **comme ça** *like that*

■ NOTE ■
CULTURELLE

Toulouse

Toulouse, with a population of over half a million people, is the center of the French aeronautic and space industry. It is in Toulouse that the Airbus planes and the Ariane rockets are being built in cooperation with other European countries.

Comment lire
GUESSING FROM CONTEXT

- As you read French, try to guess the meanings of unfamiliar words before you look at the English equivalents. Often the context provides good hints. For example, Brigitte writes:

    Je ne suis pas très grande, mais je ne suis pas petite.
    Je suis <u>de taille moyenne</u>.

    She is neither tall nor short. She must be about average:

    de taille moyenne = *of medium height or size*

- Sometimes you know what individual words in an expression mean, but the phrase does not seem to make sense. Then you have to guess at the real meaning. For example, Brigitte writes that she has:

    deux poissons rouges *??red fish??*

    If you guessed that these are most likely *goldfish,* you are right!

Enrichissez votre vocabulaire
MORE ON COGNATES

- Some words are PARTIAL COGNATES. The English word may help you remember the regular meaning. For example:

    | **gentil** | looks like | *gentle* | but means | *nice* |
    | **grand** | looks like | *grand* | but means | *tall, big* |
    | **j'adore** | looks like | *I adore* | but means | *I love* |

- Some cognates are spelled differently in the two languages. Knowing cognate patterns makes it easier to identify new words. For example:

FRENCH	ENGLISH	FRENCH	ENGLISH
-ique	*-ic*	**aéronautique**	*aeronautic, aeronautical*
-ique	*-ical*	**typique**	*typical*
-té	*-ty*	**quantité**	*quantity*

Activité
Can you identify the English equivalents of the following French words?
    la musique classique, une personne dynamique, un film comique,
    une guitare électrique, une société, une activité, une possibilité,
    la curiosité, la beauté

Activité: Une lettre à Brigitte
Write a letter to Brigitte in which you describe yourself and your family. You may tell her:

- your name and how old you are
- if you are tall or short
- if you like sports
- if you have brothers and sisters (If so, give their names and ages.)
- if you have pets (If so, say what type and give their names.)
- a few things you own
- a few things you like to do with your friends

Comment écrire *(to write)* **une lettre**
Begin with: *(to a boy)* **Cher**   **Cher Patrick,**
            (to a girl) **Chère**   **Chère Brigitte,**
End with: **Amicalement,** *(In friendship,)*
            Amitiés, *(Best regards,)*

Variétés

Petit catalogue des compliments et des insultes

LES ANIMAUX ET LE LANGAGE

Selon° toi, est-ce que les animaux ont une personnalité? Pour les Français, les animaux ont des qualités et des défauts,° comme° nous. Devine° comment on° complète les phrases suivantes° en français.

1 Philippe n'aime pas étudier. Il préfère dormir.° Il est paresseux° comme° . . .

un tigre

un chat

un lézard

2 Charlotte adore parler. Elle est bavarde° comme . . .

une poule

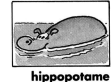
une pie

un lion

3 Isabelle est une excellente élève. Elle a une mémoire extraordinaire. Elle a une mémoire d' (de) . . .

éléphant

hippopotame

kangourou

4 Le petit frère de Christine est jeune, mais il est très intelligent. Il est malin° comme . . .

un cheval

un singe

une girafe

5 Où est Jacques? Il n'est pas prêt!° Oh là là! Il est lent° comme . . .

une tortue

un poisson

un rhinocéros

6 Nicole a très, très faim. Elle a une faim de (d') . . .

lion

ours

loup

Voici les réponses:
1. un lézard 2. une pie 3. un éléphant 4. un singe 5. une tortue 6. loup

---

Selon *According to* **défauts** *shortcomings* **comme** *like* **Devine** *Guess* **on** *one* **phrases suivantes** *following sentences* **dormir** *to sleep* **paresseux** *lazy* **comme** *as* **bavarde** *talkative* **malin** *clever* **prêt** *ready* **lent** *slow*

REFERENCE SECTION

CONTENTS

APPENDIX 1

Maps

The French-Speaking World

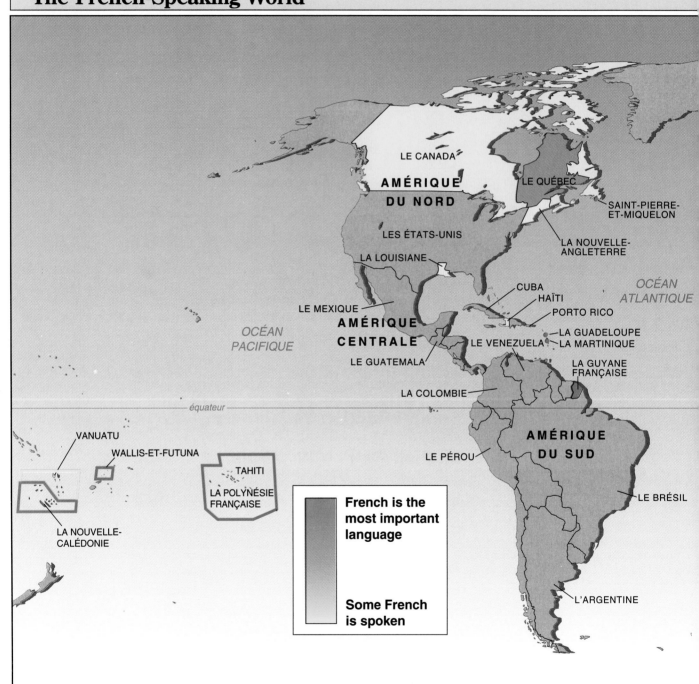

LE CANADA

AMÉRIQUE DU NORD

LE QUÉBEC

SAINT-PIERRE-ET-MIQUELON

LES ÉTATS-UNIS

LA NOUVELLE-ANGLETERRE

LA LOUISIANE

OCÉAN ATLANTIQUE

CUBA
HAÏTI
PORTO RICO

LE MEXIQUE

OCÉAN PACIFIQUE

AMÉRIQUE CENTRALE

LE VENEZUELA

LA GUADELOUPE
LA MARTINIQUE

LE GUATEMALA

LA GUYANE FRANÇAISE

LA COLOMBIE

équateur

VANUATU

WALLIS-ET-FUTUNA

AMÉRIQUE DU SUD

LE PÉROU

TAHITI
LA POLYNÉSIE FRANÇAISE

LA NOUVELLE-CALÉDONIE

LE BRÉSIL

French is the most important language

Some French is spoken

L'ARGENTINE

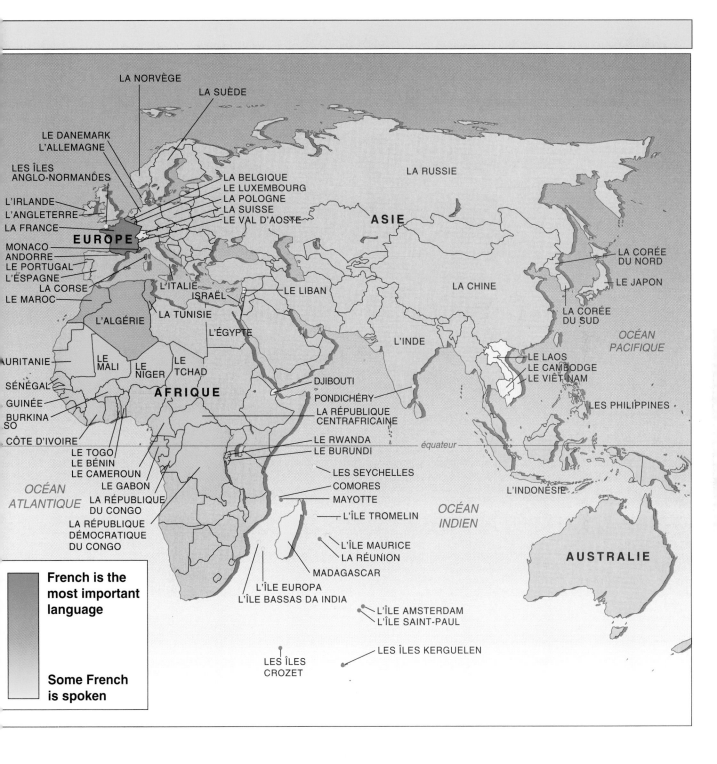

LA NORVÈGE
LA SUÈDE
LE DANEMARK
L'ALLEMAGNE
LES ÎLES
ANGLO-NORMANDES
L'IRLANDE
L'ANGLETERRE
LA FRANCE
MONACO
ANDORRE
LE PORTUGAL
L'ESPAGNE
LA CORSE
LE MAROC
L'ALGÉRIE
AURITANIE
LE MALI
LE NIGER
LE TCHAD
SÉNÉGAL
GUINÉE
BURKINA
SO
CÔTE D'IVOIRE
LE TOGO
LE BÉNIN
LE CAMEROUN
LE GABON
LA RÉPUBLIQUE
DU CONGO
LA RÉPUBLIQUE
DÉMOCRATIQUE
DU CONGO

LA BELGIQUE
LE LUXEMBOURG
LA POLOGNE
LA SUISSE
LE VAL D'AOSTE
L'ITALIE
ISRAËL
LA TUNISIE
L'ÉGYPTE
LE LIBAN

EUROPE

AFRIQUE

DJIBOUTI
PONDICHÉRY
LA RÉPUBLIQUE
CENTRAFRICAINE
LE RWANDA
LE BURUNDI
LES SEYCHELLES
COMORES
MAYOTTE
L'ÎLE TROMELIN
L'ÎLE MAURICE
LA RÉUNION
MADAGASCAR
L'ÎLE EUROPA
L'ÎLE BASSAS DA INDIA

LA RUSSIE

ASIE

LA CHINE

L'INDE

équateur

LA CORÉE
DU NORD
LE JAPON
LA CORÉE
DU SUD
OCÉAN
PACIFIQUE
LE LAOS
LE CAMBODGE
LE VIÊT-NAM
LES PHILIPPINES

L'INDONÉSIE

OCÉAN
INDIEN

AUSTRALIE

OCÉAN
ATLANTIQUE

L'ÎLE AMSTERDAM
L'ÎLE SAINT-PAUL
LES ÎLES KERGUELEN
LES ÎLES
CROZET

French is the most important language

Some French is spoken

France

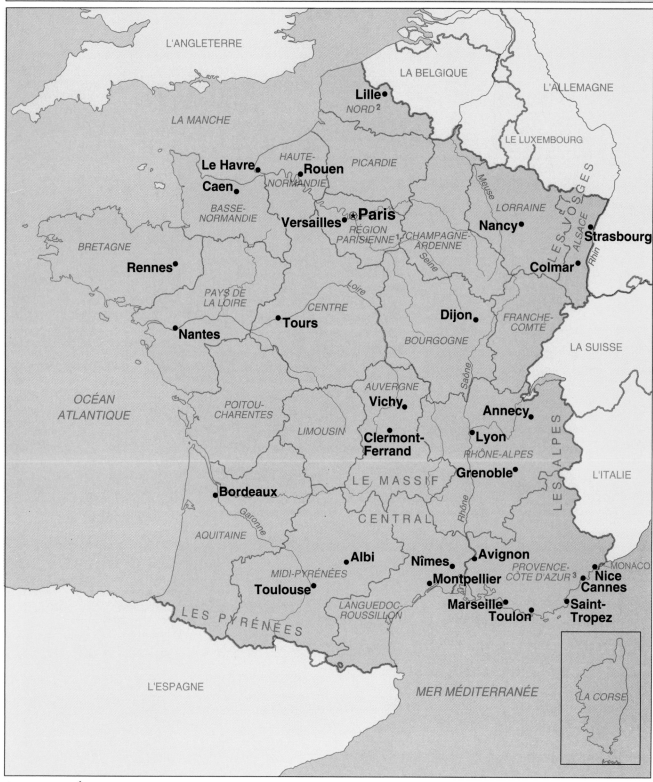

L'ANGLETERRE

LA BELGIQUE

L'ALLEMAGNE

LA MANCHE

Lille•
NORD [2]

LE LUXEMBOURG

PICARDIE

HAUTE-
NORMANDIE

Le Havre•   •**Rouen**

Caen•

LORRAINE

Nancy•

LES VOSGES

ALSACE

•**Strasbourg**

Versailles•⊛ **Paris**
RÉGION
PARISIENNE [1]

CHAMPAGNE-
ARDENNE

Seine

Meuse

Colmar•

Rhin

BASSE-
NORMANDIE

BRETAGNE

Rennes•

PAYS DE
LA LOIRE

CENTRE

Loire

Dijon•

BOURGOGNE

FRANCHE-
COMTÉ

LA SUISSE

Nantes•   •**Tours**

OCÉAN
ATLANTIQUE

POITOU-
CHARENTES

AUVERGNE

Vichy•

Saône

Annecy•

LIMOUSIN

**Clermont-
Ferrand**•

•**Lyon**

RHÔNE-ALPES

Grenoble•

LES ALPES

L'ITALIE

Bordeaux•

Garonne

LE MASSIF

CENTRAL

Rhône

AQUITAINE

Albi•

Nîmes•   **Avignon**•

PROVENCE-
CÔTE D'AZUR [3]

MONACO

•**Nice**

Toulouse•

MIDI-PYRÉNÉES

Montpellier•

Cannes

Marseille•

**Saint-
Tropez**•

LES PYRÉNÉES

LANGUEDOC-
ROUSSILLON

Toulon•

L'ESPAGNE

MER MÉDITERRANÉE

LA CORSE

[1]Also known as Île-de-France
[2]Also known as Nord-Pas-de-Calais
[3]Also known as Provence-Alpes-Côte d'Azur *(Bottin 1989)*

Vowels

Sound	Spelling	Examples
/a/	**a, à, â**	Madame, là-bas, théâtre
/i/	**i, î**	visite, Nice, dîne
	y (initial, final, or between consonants)	Yves, Guy, style
/u/	**ou, où, oû**	Toulouse, où, août
/y/	**u, û**	tu, Luc, sûr
/o/	**o** (final or before silent consonant)	piano, idiot, Margot
	au, eau	jaune, Claude, beau
	ô	hôtel, drôle, Côte-d'Ivoire
/ɔ/	**o**	Monique, Noël, jolie
	au	Paul, restaurant, Laure
/e/	**é**	Dédé, Québec, télé
	e (before silent final **z, t, r**)	chez, et, Roger
	ai (final or before final silent consonant)	j'ai, mai, japonais
/ɛ/	**è**	Michèle, Ève, père
	ei	seize, neige, tour Eiffel
	ê	tête, être, Viêt-nam
	e (before two consonants)	elle, Pierre, Annette
	e (before pronounced final consonant)	Michel, avec, cher
	ai (before pronounced final consonant)	française, aime, Maine
/ə/	**e** (final or before single consonant)	je, Denise, venir
/ø/	**eu, oeu**	deux, Mathieu, euro, oeufs
	eu (before final **se**)	nerveuse, généreuse, sérieuse
/œ/	**eu** (before final pronounced consonant except /z/)	heure, neuf, Lesieur
	oeu	soeur, coeur, oeuf
	oe	oeil

Nasal vowels

Sound	Spelling	Examples
/ɑ̃/	**an, am**	France, quand, lampe
	en, em	Henri, pendant, décembre
/ɔ̃/	**on, om**	non, Simon, bombe
/ɛ̃/	**in, im**	Martin, invite, impossible
	yn, ym	syndicat, sympathique, Olympique
	ain, aim	Alain, américain, faim
	(o) + in	loin, moins, point
	(i) + en	bien, Julien, viens
/œ̃/	**un, um**	un, Lebrun, parfum

Semi-vowels

Sound	Spelling	Examples
/j/	**i, y** (before vowel sound)	b<u>i</u>en, p<u>i</u>ano, L<u>y</u>on
	-il, -ill (after vowel sound), **-ll**	oe<u>il</u>, trava<u>ill</u>e, Marse<u>ill</u>e, f<u>ill</u>e
/ɥ/	**u** (before vowel sound)	l<u>u</u>i, S<u>u</u>isse, j<u>u</u>illet
/w/	**ou** (before vowel sound)	<u>ou</u>i, L<u>ou</u>is, j<u>ou</u>er
/wa/	**oi, oî**	v<u>oi</u>ci, Ben<u>oî</u>t
	oy (before vowel)	v<u>oy</u>age

Consonants

Sound	Spelling	Examples
/b/	**b**	<u>B</u>ar<u>b</u>ara, <u>b</u>anane, <u>B</u>elgique
/k/	**c** (before **a, o, u,** or consonant)	<u>C</u>oca-<u>C</u>ola, <u>c</u>uisine, <u>c</u>lasse
	ch(**r**)	<u>Ch</u>ristine, <u>Ch</u>ristian, <u>Ch</u>ristophe
	qu, q (final)	<u>Qu</u>ébec, <u>qu</u>'est-ce <u>qu</u>e, cin<u>q</u>
	k	<u>k</u>ilo, <u>K</u>i<u>k</u>i, <u>k</u>etchup
/ʃ/	**ch**	<u>Ch</u>arles, blan<u>ch</u>e, <u>ch</u>ez
/d/	**d**	<u>D</u>i<u>d</u>ier, <u>d</u>ans, mé<u>d</u>ecin
/f/	**f**	<u>F</u>élix, <u>f</u>ranc, neu<u>f</u>
	ph	<u>Ph</u>ilippe, télé<u>ph</u>one, <u>ph</u>oto
/g/	**g** (before **a, o, u,** or consonant)	<u>G</u>abriel, <u>g</u>orge, lé<u>g</u>umes, <u>g</u>ris
	gu (before **e, i, y**)	va<u>gu</u>e, <u>Gu</u>illaume, <u>Gu</u>y
/ɲ/	**gn**	mi<u>gn</u>on, champa<u>gn</u>e, Allema<u>gn</u>e
/ʒ/	**j**	<u>j</u>e, <u>J</u>érôme, <u>j</u>aune
	g (before **e, i, y**)	rou<u>g</u>e, <u>G</u>i<u>g</u>i, <u>g</u>ymnastique
	ge (before **a, o, u**)	oran<u>ge</u>ade, <u>G</u>eorges, na<u>ge</u>ur
/l/	**l**	<u>L</u>ise, e<u>ll</u>e, cheva<u>l</u>
/m/	**m**	<u>M</u>aman, <u>m</u>oi, to<u>m</u>ate
/n/	**n**	ba<u>n</u>a<u>n</u>e, <u>N</u>ancy, <u>n</u>ous
/p/	**p**	<u>p</u>eu, <u>P</u>a<u>p</u>a, <u>P</u>ierre
/r/	**r**	a<u>rr</u>ive, <u>r</u>ent<u>r</u>e, Pa<u>r</u>is
/s/	**c** (before **e, i, y**)	<u>c</u>e, <u>C</u>é<u>c</u>ile, Nan<u>c</u>y
	ç (before **a, o, u**)	<u>ç</u>a, gar<u>ç</u>on, dé<u>ç</u>u
	s (initial or before consonant)	<u>s</u>ac, <u>S</u>ophie, re<u>s</u>te
	ss (between vowels)	boi<u>ss</u>on, de<u>ss</u>ert, Sui<u>ss</u>e
	t (before **i** + vowel)	atten<u>t</u>ion, Na<u>t</u>ions Unies, nata<u>t</u>ion
	x	di<u>x</u>, si<u>x</u>, soi<u>x</u>ante
/t/	**t**	<u>t</u>rop, <u>t</u>élé, <u>T</u>ours
	th	<u>Th</u>érèse, <u>th</u>é, Mar<u>th</u>e
/v/	**v**	<u>V</u>iviane, <u>v</u>ous, nou<u>v</u>eau
/gz/	**x**	e<u>x</u>amen, e<u>x</u>emple, e<u>x</u>act
/ks/	**x**	Ma<u>x</u>, Me<u>x</u>ique, e<u>x</u>cellent
/z/	**s** (between vowels)	dé<u>s</u>ert, Loui<u>s</u>e, télévi<u>s</u>ion
	z	Su<u>z</u>anne, <u>z</u>ut, <u>z</u>éro

A. Cardinal numbers

0	zéro	18	dix-huit	82	quatre-vingt-deux
1	un (une)	19	dix-neuf	90	quatre-vingt-dix
2	deux	20	vingt	91	quatre-vingt-onze
3	trois	21	vingt et un (une)	100	cent
4	quatre	22	vingt-deux	101	cent un (une)
5	cinq	23	vingt-trois	102	cent deux
6	six	30	trente	200	deux cents
7	sept	31	trente et un (une)	201	deux cent un
8	huit	32	trente-deux	300	trois cents
9	neuf	40	quarante	400	quatre cents
10	dix	41	quarante et un (une)	500	cinq cents
11	onze	50	cinquante	600	six cents
12	douze	60	soixante	700	sept cents
13	treize	70	soixante-dix	800	huit cents
14	quatorze	71	soixante et onze	900	neuf cents
15	quinze	72	soixante-douze	1.000	mille
16	seize	80	quatre-vingts	2.000	deux mille
17	dix-sept	81	quatre-vingt-un (une)	1.000.000	un million

Notes:
1. The word **et** occurs only in the numbers 21, 31, 41, 51, 61, and 71: **vingt et un** / **soixante et onze**
2. **Un** becomes **une** before a feminine noun: **trente et une filles**
3. **Quatre-vingts** becomes **quatre-vingt** before another number: **quatre-vingt-cinq**
4. **Cents** becomes **cent** before another number: **trois cent vingt**
5. **Mille** never adds an **-s**: **quatre mille**

B. Ordinal numbers

1$^{er\ (ère)}$	**premier (première)**	5^e	**cinquième**	9^e	**neuvième**
2^e	**deuxième**	6^e	**sixième**	10^e	**dixième**
3^e	**troisième**	7^e	**septième**	11^e	**onzième**
4^e	**quatrième**	8^e	**huitième**	12^e	**douzième**

Note: Premier becomes **première** before a feminine noun: **la première histoire**

C. Metric equivalents

1 gramme	= 0.035 ounces		1 ounce	= **28,349 grammes**
1 kilogramme	= 2.205 pounds		1 pound	= **0,453 kilogrammes**
1 litre	= 1.057 quarts		1 quart	= **0,946 litres**
1 mètre	= 39.37 inches		1 foot	= **30,480 centimètres**
1 kilomètre	= 0.62 miles		1 mile	= **1,609 kilomètres**

APPENDIX 4
Verbs

A. Regular verbs

Infinitive	Present		Passé composé	
parler *(to talk, speak)*	je **parle** tu **parles** il **parle**	nous **parlons** vous **parlez** ils **parlent**	j'ai **parlé** tu **as parlé** il **a parlé**	nous **avons parlé** vous **avez parlé** ils **ont parlé**
	IMPERATIVE: **parle, parlons, parlez**			
finir *(to finish)*	je **finis** tu **finis** il **finit**	nous **finissons** vous **finissez** ils **finissent**	j'ai **fini** tu **as fini** il **a fini**	nous **avons fini** vous **avez fini** ils **ont fini**
	IMPERATIVE: **finis, finissons, finissez**			
vendre *(to sell)*	je **vends** tu **vends** il **vend**	nous **vendons** vous **vendez** ils **vendent**	j'ai **vendu** tu **as vendu** il **a vendu**	nous **avons vendu** vous **avez vendu** ils **ont vendu**
	IMPERATIVE: **vends, vendons, vendez**			

B. -er verbs with spelling changes

Infinitive	Present		Passé composé
acheter *(to buy)*	j'**achète** tu **achètes** il **achète**	nous **achetons** vous **achetez** ils **achètent**	j'ai **acheté**
	Verb like **acheter:** amener *(to bring, take along)*		
espérer *(to hope)*	j'**espère** tu **espères** il **espère**	nous **espérons** vous **espérez** ils **espèrent**	j'ai **espéré**
	Verbs like **espérer:** célébrer *(to celebrate)*, préférer *(to prefer)*		
commencer *(to begin, start)*	je **commence** tu **commences** il **commence**	nous **commençons** vous **commencez** ils **commencent**	j'ai **commencé**
manger *(to eat)*	je **mange** tu **manges** il **mange**	nous **mangeons** vous **mangez** ils **mangent**	j'ai **mangé**
	Verbs like **manger:** nager *(to swim)*, voyager *(to travel)*		
payer *(to pay, pay for)*	je **paie** tu **paies** il **paie**	nous **payons** vous **payez** ils **paient**	j'ai **payé**
	Verbs like **payer:** nettoyer *(to clean)*		

Infinitive	Present		Passé composé
avoir *(to have, own)*	j'**ai** tu **as** il **a**	nous **avons** vous **avez** ils **ont**	j'**ai eu**
	IMPERATIVE: **aie, ayons, ayez**		
être *(to be)*	je **suis** tu **es** il **est**	nous **sommes** vous **êtes** ils **sont**	j'**ai été**
	IMPERATIVE: **sois, soyons, soyez**		
aller *(to go)*	je **vais** tu **vas** il **va**	nous **allons** vous **allez** ils **vont**	je **suis allé(e)**
	IMPERATIVE: **va, allons, allez**		
boire *(to drink)*	je **bois** tu **bois** il **boit**	nous **buvons** vous **buvez** ils **boivent**	j'**ai bu**
connaître *(to know)*	je **connais** tu **connais** il **connaît**	nous **connaissons** vous **connaissez** ils **connaissent**	j'**ai connu**
devoir *(to have to, should, must)*	je **dois** tu **dois** il **doit**	nous **devons** vous **devez** ils **doivent**	j'**ai dû**
dire *(to say, tell)*	je **dis** tu **dis** il **dit**	nous **disons** vous **dites** ils **disent**	j'**ai dit**
dormir *(to sleep)*	je **dors** tu **dors** il **dort**	nous **dormons** vous **dormez** ils **dorment**	j' **ai dormi**
écrire *(to write)*	j' **écris** tu **écris** il **écrit**	nous **écrivons** vous **écrivez** ils **écrivent**	j'**ai écrit**
	Verb like **écrire**: décrire *(to describe)*		
faire *(to make, do)*	je **fais** tu **fais** il **fait**	nous **faisons** vous **faites** ils **font**	j'**ai fait**
lire *(to read)*	je **lis** tu **lis** il **lit**	nous **lisons** vous **lisez** ils **lisent**	j'**ai lu**
mettre *(to put, place)*	je **mets** tu **mets** il **met**	nous **mettons** vous **mettez** ils **mettent**	j'**ai mis**
	Verb like **mettre**: promettre *(to promise)*		

Infinitive	Present		Passé composé
ouvrir *(to open)*	j'**ouvre** tu **ouvres** il **ouvre**	nous **ouvrons** vous **ouvrez** ils **ouvrent**	j'ai **ouvert**

Verbs like **ouvrir**: découvrir *(to discover)*, offrir *(to offer)*

partir *(to leave)*	je **pars** tu **pars** il **part**	nous **partons** vous **partez** ils **partent**	je **suis parti(e)**
pouvoir *(to be able, can)*	je **peux** tu **peux** il **peut**	nous **pouvons** vous **pouvez** ils **peuvent**	j'ai **pu**
prendre *(to take)*	je **prends** tu **prends** il **prend**	nous **prenons** vous **prenez** ils **prennent**	j'ai **pris**

Verbs like **prendre**: apprendre *(to learn)*, comprendre *(to understand)*

savoir *(to know)*	je **sais** tu **sais** il **sait**	nous **savons** vous **savez** ils **savent**	j'ai **su**
sortir *(to go out, get out)*	je **sors** tu **sors** il **sort**	nous **sortons** vous **sortez** ils **sortent**	je **suis sorti(e)**
venir *(to come)*	je **viens** tu **viens** il **vient**	nous **venons** vous **venez** ils **viennent**	je **suis venu(e)**

Verb like **venir**: revenir *(to come back)*

voir *(to see)*	je **vois** tu **vois** il **voit**	nous **voyons** vous **voyez** ils **voient**	j'ai **vu**
vouloir *(to want)*	je **veux** tu **veux** il **veut**	nous **voulons** vous **voulez** ils **veulent**	j'ai **voulu**

D. Verbs with *être* in the *passé composé*

aller *(to go)*	je **suis allé(e)**	**passer** *(to go by, through)*	je **suis passé(e)**
arriver *(to arrive, come)*	je **suis arrivé(e)**	**rentrer** *(to go home)*	je **suis rentré(e)**
descendre *(to go down)*	je **suis descendu(e)**	**rester** *(to stay)*	je **suis resté(e)**
entrer *(to enter, go in)*	je **suis entré(e)**	**revenir** *(to come back)*	je **suis revenu(e)**
monter *(to go up)*	je **suis monté(e)**	**sortir** *(to go out, get out)*	je **suis sorti(e)**
mourir *(to die)*	Il/elle **est mort(e)**	**tomber** *(to fall)*	je **suis tombé(e)**
naître *(to be born)*	je **suis né(e)**	**venir** *(to come)*	je **suis venu(e)**
partir *(to leave)*	je **suis parti(e)**		

VOCABULARY

French-English

The French-English vocabulary contains active and passive words from the text, as well as the important words of the illustrations used within the units. Obvious passive cognates have not been listed.

The numbers following an entry indicate the lesson in which the word or phrase is activated. (**B** stands for the photo essay that precedes **Niveau B;** and **E** stands for **Entracte.**)

Nouns: If the article of a noun does not indicate gender, the noun is followed by *m. (masculine)* or *f. (feminine).* If the plural (*pl.*) is irregular, it is given in parentheses.

Adjectives: Adjectives are listed in the masculine form. If the feminine form is irregular, it is given in parentheses. Irregular plural forms (*pl.*) are also given in parentheses.

Verbs: Verbs are listed in the infinitive form. An asterisk (*) in front of an active verb means that it is irregular. (For forms, see the verb charts in Appendix 4C.) Irregular present tense forms are listed when they are used before the verb has been activated. Irregular past participle (*p.p.*) forms are listed separately.

Words beginning with an **h** are preceded by a bullet (•) if the **h** is aspirate; that is, if the word is treated as if it begins with a consonant sound.

A

a: il y a there is, there are **17**
à at, in, to **14**
  à côté next door, next to
  à demain! see you tomorrow! **8**
  à partir de as of, beginning
  à samedi! see you Saturday! **8**
abolir to abolish
abondant plentiful, copious, large
un **abricot** apricot
absolument absolutely
un **accent** accent mark, stress
accepter to accept
un **accord** agreement
  d'accord okay, all right **13**
  être d'accord to agree **14**
un **achat** purchase
un **acteur, une actrice** actor, actress
une **activité** activity
l' **addition** *f.* check
adorer to love
une **adresse** address

l'**adresse électronique** e-mail address
adroit skilled, skillful
un(e) **adulte** adult
aéronautique aeronautic, aeronautical
un **aéroport** airport
affectueusement affectionately *(at the end of a letter)*
une **affiche** poster **17**
affirmativement affirmatively
l' **Afrique** *f.* Africa
l' **âge** *m.* age
  quel âge a-t-il/elle? how old is he/she? **17**
  quel âge as-tu? how old are you? **7**
  quel âge a ton père/ta mère? how old is your father/your mother? **7**
âgé old
une **agence** agency
  une agence de tourisme tourist office
  une agence de voyages travel agency
agiter to shake
agité agitated
ah! ah!, oh!

ah bon? oh? really? **16**
ah non! ah, no!
ai (*see* **avoir**): **j'ai** I have **17**
  j'ai... ans I'm ... (years old) **7**
une **aile** wing
aimer to like **15**
  est-ce que tu aimes...? do you like ...? **13**
  j'aime... I like ... **13**
  je n'aime pas... I don't like ... **13**
  j'aimerais I would like
ainsi thus
aîné older
  un frère aîné older brother
  une soeur aînée older sister
ajouter to add
l' **Algérie** *f.* Algeria *(country in North Africa)*
algérien (algérienne) Algerian
l' **Allemagne** *f.* Germany
allemand German
* **aller** to go
allez (*see* **aller**): **allez-vous-en!** go away!
  allez-y come on!, go ahead!, do it!

comment allez-vous? how are you? 3

allô! hello! (*on the telephone*)

alors so, then 19

une **alouette** lark

les **Alpes** *f.* (the) Alps

l' **alphabet** *m.* alphabet

l' **Alsace** *f.* Alsace (*province in eastern France*)

américain American 2, 19

à l'américaine American-style

un **Américain, une Américaine** American person

l' **Amérique** *f.* America

un **ami, une amie** (*close*) friend 5

amicalement love, cordially (*at the end of a letter*)

l' **amitié** *f.* friendship

amitiés best regards (*at the end of a letter*)

amusant funny, amusing 19

amuser to amuse

s' **amuser** to have fun

on s'est bien amusé! we had a good time!

un **an** year

avoir... ans to be ... (years old) 18

il/elle a... ans he/she is ... (years old) 7

j'ai... ans I'm ... (*years old*) 7

l'an dernier last year

par an per year

un **ananas** pineapple

ancien (ancienne) former, old, ancient

un **âne** donkey

un **ange** angel

anglais English 2, 19

un **Anglais, une Anglaise** English person

un **animal** (*pl.* **animaux**) animal

une **animation** live entertainment

animé animated, lively

une **année** year 8

toute l'année all year long

un **anniversaire** birthday 8

c'est quand, ton anniversaire? when is your birthday? 8

joyeux anniversaire! happy birthday!

mon anniversaire est le (2 mars) my birthday is (March 2nd) 8

un **annuaire** telephone directory

un **anorak** ski jacket

les **antiquités** *f.* antiquities, antiques

août *m.* August 8

un **appareil-photo** (*pl.* **appareils-photo**) (*still*) camera 17

s' **appeler** to be named, called

comment s'appelle...? what's . . .'s name? 6

comment s'appelle-t-il/elle? what's his/her name? 17

comment t'appelles-tu? what's your name? 1

il/elle s'appelle... his/her name is . . . 6

je m'appelle... my name is . . . 1

apporter: apporte-moi (apportez-moi) bring me B

apprécier to appreciate

approprié appropriate

après after, afterwards

d'après according to

de l'après-midi in the afternoon, p.m. 4

l' **arabe** *m.* Arabic (*language*)

un **arbre** tree

un arbre généalogique family tree

l' **arche** *f.* **de Noé** Noah's Ark

l' **argent** *m.* money

l'argent de poche allowance, pocket money

arrêter to arrest; to stop

arriver to come, to arrive

j'arrive! I'm coming!

une **arrivée** arrival

un **arrondissement** district

un **artifice: le feu d'artifice** fireworks

un **artiste, une artiste** artist

as (*see* **avoir**): **est-ce que tu as...?** do you have . . . ? 17

un **ascenseur** elevator

un **aspirateur** vacuum cleaner

s' **asseoir: asseyez-vous!** sit down! B

assez rather, enough 19

associer to associate

l' **Atlantique** *m.* Atlantic Ocean

attention *f.*: **faire attention** to be careful, pay attention 16

attentivement carefully

au (**à + le**) to (the), at (the), in (the) 14

au revoir! good-bye! 3

une **auberge** inn

aucun: ne... aucun none, not any

aujourd'hui today 8

aujourd'hui, c'est... today is . . . 8

aussi also, too 2, 15

une **auto (automobile)** car, automobile 17

une auto-école driving school

l' **autobus** *m.* bus

l' **automne** *m.* autumn, fall

en automne in (the) autumn, fall 12

l' **autoroute** *f.* **de l'information** the information highway

autre other

d'autres others

un(e) autre another

avant before

avant-hier the day before yesterday

en avant let's begin

avantageux (avantageuse) reasonable, advantageous

avec with 14

avec moi, avec toi with me, with you 13

avec qui? with who(m)? 16

un **avis** opinion

un avis de recherche missing person's bulletin

à votre avis in your opinion

* **avoir** to have 18

avoir... ans to be ... (years old) 18

avoir faim to be hungry 18

avoir lieu to take place

avoir soif to be thirsty 18

avril *m.* April 8

le **babyfoot** tabletop soccer game

le **babysitting: faire du babysitting** to baby-sit

les **bagages** *m.* bags, baggage

la **bande de copains** group of friends

une **bande dessinée** comic strip

des bandes dessinées comics

la **Bannière étoilée** Star-Spangled Banner

une **banque** bank

une **barbe: quelle barbe!** what a pain! *(colloq.)*

le **bas** the bottom

au bas at the bottom

basé based

le **basket (basketball)** basketball

jouer au basket to play basketball **13**

un **bateau-mouche** sightseeing boat

battre to beat

bavard talkative

beau (bel, belle; *m.pl.* beaux) handsome, good-looking, beautiful **17, 20**

il est beau he is good-looking, handsome **17**

il fait beau it's beautiful (nice) out **12**

un **beau-frère** stepbrother, brother-in-law

un **beau-père** stepfather, father-in-law

beaucoup (de) much, very much, many, a lot **15**

la **beauté** beauty

un **bec** beak

la **Belgique** Belgium

belle (*see* **beau**) beautiful **17, 20**

elle est belle she is beautiful **17**

une **belle-mère** stepmother, mother-in-law

une **belle-soeur** stepsister, sister-in-law

les **Bermudes** *f.* Bermuda

le **besoin** need

des besoins d'argent money needs

bête dumb, silly **19**

une **bicyclette** bicycle **17**

bien well, very well, carefully **15**

bien sûr of course **13**

ça va bien everything's fine (going well) **3**

ça va très bien I'm (everything's) very well **3**

c'est bien that's good (fine) **20**

je veux bien (...) I'd love to (. . .), I do, I want to **13**

oui, bien sûr... yes, of course . . . **14**

très bien very well **15**

bientôt: à bientôt! see you soon!

bienvenue welcome

le **bifteck** steak

un bifteck de tortue turtle steak

bilingue bilingual

la **biologie** biology

une **bise** a kiss **1**

une **biscotte** dry toast

blaff de poisson *m.* fish stew

blanc (blanche) white **20**

Blanche-Neige Snow White

blanchir to blanch, turn white

bleu blue **20**

blond blond **17**

il/elle est blond(e) he/she is blond **17**

une **boisson** drink, beverage **10**

une **boîte** box

un **bol** deep bowl

bon (bonne) good **20**

ah bon? oh, really? **16**

de bonne humeur in a good mood

il fait bon the weather's good (pleasant) **12**

le **bonheur** happiness

bonjour hello **1, 3**

une **bouche** mouth **E3**

une **boucherie** butcher shop

le **boudin** sausage

une **boulangerie** bakery **3**

une **boum** a party **13, 15**

boxe: un match de boxe boxing match

un **bras** arm **E3**

brésilien (brésilienne) Brazilian

la **Bretagne** Brittany *(province in northwestern France)*

bricoler to do things around the house

broche: à la broche on the spit

bronzé tan

un **bruit** noise

brun brown, dark-haired **17**

il/elle est brun(e) he/she has dark hair **17**

brunir to turn brown

Bruxelles Brussels

le **bulletin de notes** report card

un **bureau** desk **B, 17**; office

un **bus** bus

un **but** goal; end

ça that, it

ça fait combien? ça fait... how much is that (it)? that (it) is . . . **11**

ça, là-bas that (one), over there **17**

ça va? how's everything? how are you? **3**

ça va everything's fine, I'm OK **3**

ça va (très) bien, ça va bien everything's going very well, everything's fine (going well) **3**

ça va comme ci, comme ça everything's (going) so-so **3**

ça va (très) mal things are going (very) badly **3**

regarde ça look at that **17**

une **cabine d'essayage** fitting room

les **cabinets** *m.* toilet

un **cadeau** (*pl.* **cadeaux**) gift, present

cadet (cadette) younger

un frère cadet (a) younger brother

une soeur cadette (a) younger sister

le **café** coffee **10**

un **café au lait** coffee with hot milk

un **café** café (French coffee shop) **14**

au café to (at) the café **14**

un **cahier** notebook **B, E3**

une **calculatrice** calculator **17**

un **calendrier** calendar

un **camarade, une camarade** classmate **17**

le **Cambodge** Cambodia (country in Asia)

un **cambriolage** burglary

un **cambrioleur** burglar

une **caméra** movie camera

la **campagne** the country(side)

une **auberge de campagne** country inn

le **Canada** Canada

canadien (canadienne) Canadian **2, 19**

un **Canadien, une Canadienne** Canadian person

un **canard** duck

un **car** touring bus

un **car scolaire** school bus

une **carotte** carrot

des **carottes râpées** grated carrots

un **carré** square

le **Vieux Carré** the French Quarter in New Orleans

une **carte** map **B**; card

une **carte postale** postcard

un **cas** case

en cas de in case of

un **casque** headphones

une **cassette** cassette tape **B, 17**

le **catch** wrestling

une **cathédrale** cathedral

une **cave** cellar

un **CD (un compact)** CD, compact disc **B**

un **CD vidéo** laserdisc, videodisc

un **lecteur de CD (vidéo)** CD player (laserdisc player)

ce (c') this, that, it

ce n'est pas that's/it's not **20**

ce que that which, what

ce sont these are, those are, they are **20**

une **cédille** cedilla

cela that

célèbre famous

cent one hundred **6**

une **centaine** about a hundred

un **centime** centime (1/100 of a euro)

un **centre** center

certain certain

certains some of them

c'est (see ce)

ce n'est pas it's (that's) not **20**

c'est it's, that's **5, 17, 20**

c'est + day of the week it's … **8**

c'est + name or noun it's … **5**

c'est bien/mal that's good/bad **20**

c'est combien? how much is that/it? **11**

c'est le (12 octobre) it's (October 12) **8**

qu'est-ce 17

qu'est-ce que c'est? what is it? what's that? **17**

qui est-ce? who's that/this? **17**

chacun each one, each person

une **chaîne** (TV) channel

une **mini-chaîne** compact stereo

une **chaîne stéréo** stereo set **17**

une **chaise** chair **B, 17**

la **chaleur** heat, warmth

un **champion, une championne** champion

la **chance** luck

une **chanson** song

chanter to sing **13, 15**

un **chanteur, une chanteuse** singer

une **chambre** bedroom

chaque each, every

charmant charming

un **chat** cat **7**

un **château** (pl. **châteaux**) castle

chaud warm, hot

il fait chaud it's warm (hot) (weather) **12**

chauffer to warm, heat up

un **chauffeur** driver

un **chef** boss; chef

un **cheval** (pl. **chevaux**) horse **E5**

chic (inv.) nice; elegant, in style

une **chic fille** a great girl

un **chien** dog **7**

la **chimie** chemistry

chinois Chinese **19**

le **chinois** Chinese (language)

le **chocolat** hot chocolate, cocoa **10**

une **glace au chocolat** chocolate ice cream

un **choix** choice

au choix choose one, your choice

une **chorale** choir

une **chose** thing **17**

les **mêmes choses** the same things

chouette great, terrific **20**

le **cidre** cider

un **cinéaste, une cinéaste** film maker

le **cinéma** the movies

au cinéma to (at) the movies, movie theater **14**

cinq five **1**

cinquante fifty **3**

une **circonstance** circumstance

cité: la Cité Interdite Forbidden City

une **classe** class

en classe in class **14**

classique classical

le **clavier** keyboard

un **client, une cliente** customer

un **clip** music video

un **cochon** pig

un **coiffeur, une coiffeuse** hairdresser

un **coin** spot

une **coïncidence** coincidence

le **Colisée** the Coliseum (a large stadium built by the Romans)

un **collège** junior high school, middle school

une **colonie** colony

une **colonne** column

combien how much

ça fait combien? how much is this (it)? **11**

c'est combien? how much is this (it)? **11**

combien coûte...? how much does . . . cost? **11**

combien de temps? how long?

combien d'heures? how many hours?

commander to order

comme like, as, for

comme ci, comme ça so-so

ça va comme ci, comme ça everything's so-so **3**

commencer to begin, start

comment? how? **16**; what?

comment allez-vous? how are you? **3**

comment est-il/elle? what's he/she like? what does he/she look like? **17**

comment lire reading hints

comment s'appelle...? what's . . .'s name? **6**

comment s'appelle-t-il/elle? what's his/her name? **17**

comment t'appelles-tu? what's your name? **1**

comment vas-tu? how are you? **3**

un **commentaire** comment, commentary

le **commérage** gossip

communiquer to communicate

un **compact disque (un CD)** compact disc **17**

compléter to complete

compréhensif understanding

* **comprendre** to understand

je (ne) comprends (pas) I (don't) understand **B**

compter to count (on); to expect, intend

concerne: en ce qui concerne as for

une **connaissance** acquaintance

faire connaissance (avec) to become acquainted (with)

* **connaître** to know, be acquainted

tu connais...? do you know . . .? are you acquainted with . . .? **6**

un **conseil** piece of advice, counsel

des conseils *m.* advice

un **conservatoire** conservatory

une **consonne** consonant

se **contenter** to limit oneself

le **contenu** contents

une **contradiction** disagreement

une **contravention** (traffic) ticket

cool cool, neat

un **copain, une copine** friend, pal **5**

un petit copain, une petite copine boyfriend, girlfriend

copier to copy

coréen (coréenne) Korean

un **corps** body

correspondant corresponding

correspondre to correspond, agree

la **Corse** Corsica *(French island off the Italian coast)*

un **costume** man's suit

la **Côte d'Azur** Riviera *(southern coast of France on the Mediterranean)*

la **Côte d'Ivoire** Ivory Coast *(French-speaking country in West Africa)*

côté: à côté (de) next door; next to

une **côtelette de porc** pork chop

le **cou** neck **E3**

une **couleur** color **20**

de quelle couleur...? what color . . .? **20**

un **couloir** hall, corridor

coup: dans le coup *(colloq.)* "with it"

courageux (courageuse) courageous

le **courrier électronique** e-mail, electronic mail

une **course** race

un **cousin, une cousine** cousin **7**

le **coût: le coût de la vie** the cost of living

coûter to cost

combien coûte...? how much does . . . cost? **11**

il (elle) coûte... it costs . . . **11**

un **couturier, une couturière** fashion designer

un **crabe** crab

des matoutou crabes stewed crabs with rice

la **craie** chalk

un morceau de craie piece of chalk **B**

un **crayon** pencil **17**

créer to create

une **crêpe** crepe *(pancake)* **9**

une **crêperie** crepe restaurant

un **crétin** idiot

une **crevaison** flat tire

une **croisade** crusade

un **croissant** crescent (roll) **9**

une **cuillère** spoon

une cuillère à soupe soup spoon

cuit cooked

culturel (culturelle) cultural

curieux (curieuse) curious, strange

la **curiosité** curiosity

le **Cyberespace** information highway, cyberspace

les **cybernautes** people who like to use the Internet

un **cyclomoteur** moped

D ▬▬▬▬▬▬▬▬▬▬

d'accord okay, all right

être d'accord to agree **14**

oui, d'accord yes, okay **13**

une **dame** lady, woman *(polite term)* **5**

dangereux (dangereuse) dangerous

dans in **17**

danser to dance **13, 15**

la **date** date **8**

quelle est la date? what's the date? **8**

de (d') of, from, about **14**

de l'après-midi in the afternoon **4**

de quelle couleur...? what color . . .? **20**

de qui? of whom? **16**

de quoi? about what?

de temps en temps from time to time

d'habitude usually
    pas de not any, no **18**

débarquer to land

décembre *m.* December **8**

décider (de) to decide (to)

une **déclaration** statement

décoré decorated

* **découvrir** to discover

un **défaut** shortcoming

un **défilé** parade

dehors outside
    en dehors de outside of

déjà already; ever

demain tomorrow **8**
    à demain! see you tomorrow! **8**
    demain, c'est... (jeudi) tomorrow is ... (Thursday) **8**

demi half
    ...heure(s) et demie half past ... **4**
    midi et demi half past twelve (noon) **4**
    minuit et demi half past midnight **4**

un **demi-frère** half-brother

une **demi-soeur** half-sister

un **démon** devil

une **dent** tooth

un **départ** departure

se **dépêcher: dépêchez-vous!** hurry up!

dépend: ça dépend (des) it depends (on)

une **dépense** expense

derrière behind, in back of **17**

des some, any **18**; of (the), from (the)

le **désert** desert

désirer to wish, want
    vous désirez? what would you like? may I help you? **10**

désolé sorry

le **dessin** art, drawing

détester to hate, detest
    un dessin animé cartoon

deux two **1**
    le deuxième étage third floor

devant in front of **17**

développer to develop

deviner to guess

les **devoirs** *m.* homework

différemment differently

différent different

difficile hard, difficult **20**

la **dignité** dignity

dimanche *m.* Sunday **8**

dîner to have dinner **15**
    dîner au restaurant to have dinner at a restaurant **13**

* **dire** to say, tell
    comment dit-on... en français? How do you say . . . in French? **B**

directement straight

un **directeur, une directrice** director, principal

dirigé directed, guided

dis! (*see* **dire**) say!, hey! **20**
    dis donc! say there!, hey there! **20**

discuter to discuss

une **dispute** quarrel, dispute

un **disque** record **17**
    un (disque) compact compact disc **17**
    le disque dur hard drive (computer)
    un disque optique CD-ROM **B**

une **disquette** floppy disc **B**

dit (*p.p. of* **dire**) said

dix ten **1, 2**

dix-huit eighteen **2**

dix-neuf nineteen **2**

dix-sept seventeen **2**

un **docteur** doctor

dois (*see* **devoir**): **je dois** I have to (must) **13**

domestique domestic
    les animaux *m.* **domestiques** pets **7**

dommage! too bad! **15**

donner to give
    donne-moi... give me . . . **9**
    donnez-moi... give me **10**
    s'il te plaît, donne-moi... please, give me . . . **10**

doré golden brown

* **dormir** to sleep

douze twelve **2**

drôle funny **20**

du (*partitive*) of the
    du matin in the morning, a.m. **4**
    du soir in the evening, p.m. **4**

dur hard
    des oeufs (*m.*) **durs** hard-boiled eggs

durer to last

dynamique dynamic

E

e-mail e-mail, electronic mail

un **échange** exchange

les **échecs** *m.* chess

une **éclosion** hatching

économiser to save money

écouter to listen to **B, 15**
    écouter la radio to listen to the radio **13**

un **écran** screen (of a computer, TV)

l' **éducation** *f.* education
    l'éducation civique civics
    l'éducation physique physical education

égyptien (égyptienne) Egyptian

électronique electronic
    une guitare électrique electric guitar

un **éléphant** elephant **E5**

élevé high

un(e) **élève** student (middle school, high school) **17**

elle she, it **11, 14, 18**
    elle coûte... it costs . . . **11**
    elle est (canadienne) she's (Canadian) **6**
    elle s'appelle... her name is . . . **6**

embrasser: je t'embrasse love and kisses (*at the end of a letter*)

un **emploi du temps** time-table (*of work*)

emprunter à to borrow from

en in, on, to, by
    en ce qui concerne as for
    en face opposite, across (*the street*)
    en fait in fact

en famille at home
en moyenne on the average
en plus in addition
en scène on stage
en solde on sale
un(e) **enfant** child
entier (entière) entire
l' **entracte** *m.* interlude
entre between
une **entrée** entry (*of a house*)
les **études** *f.* studies
un **entretien** discussion
envers toward
l' **envie** *f.* envy
envoyer to send
envoyer quelque chose par e-mail to send something via e-mail
envoyer quelque chose par la messagerie vocale to leave a voice mail message
épicé hot (spicy)
une **épicerie** grocery store
les **épinards** *m.* spinach
une **équipe** team
une **erreur** error, mistake
es (*see* **être**)
tu es + *nationality* you are . . . **2**
tu es de...? are you from . . .? **2**
un **escalier** staircase
un **escargot** snail
l' **Espagne** *f.* Spain
espagnol Spanish **19**
parler espagnol to speak Spanish **13**
un **esprit** spirit
essayer to try on, to try
l' **essentiel** *m.* the important thing
est (*see* **être**)
c'est... it's . . ., that's . . . **5, 7, 20**
c'est le + *date* it's . . . **8**
est-ce que (qu')...? phrase used to introduce a question **14**
il/elle est + *nationality* he/she is . . . **6**
n'est-ce pas...? isn't it? **14**
où est...? where is . . .? **14**

quel jour est-ce? what day is it? **8**
qui est-ce? who's that (this)? **5, 17**
l' **est** *m.* east
et and **2, 14**
et demi(e), et quart half past, quarter past **4**
et toi? and you? **1**
établir to establish
un **étage** floor of a building, story
les **États-Unis** *m.* United States
l' **été** *m.* summer
en été in (the) summer **12**
l'heure d'été daylight savings time
étendre to spread
une **étoile** star
étrange strange
étranger (étrangère) foreign
* **être** to be **14**
être à to belong to
être d'accord to agree **14**
une **étude** study
un **étudiant, une étudiant(e)** (college) student **17**
étudier to study **13, 15**
eu (*p.p.* **avoir**)
il y a eu there was
euh... er . . ., uh . . .
euh non... well, no
un **euro** monetary unit of Europe
européen (européenne) European
eux: eux-mêmes themselves
un **événement** event
un **examen** exam, test
réussir à un examen to pass an exam, a test
un **exemple** example
par exemple for instance
un **exercice** exercise
faire des exercices to exercise
exiger to insist
exprimer to express
extérieur: à l'extérieur outside
extra terrific **20**
extraordinaire extraordinary
il a fait un temps extraordinaire! the weather was great!

F ▬▬▬▬▬▬▬▬▬▬

face: en face (de) opposite, across (the street) from
facile easy **20**
faible weak
la **faim** hunger
j'ai faim I'm hungry **9**
tu as faim? are you hungry? **9**
* **faire** to do, make **16**
faire attention to pay attention, be careful **16**
faire correspondre to match
faire partie de to be a member of
faire sauter to flip
faire un match to play a game (match) **16**
faire un voyage to take a trip **16**
faire une promenade to take a walk **16**
fait (*see* **faire**): **ça fait combien?** how much is that (it)? **11**
ça fait... euros/francs that's (it's) . . . euros/francs **11**
en fait in fact
il fait (beau, etc.) it's (beautiful, etc.) (weather) **12**
quel temps fait-il? what (how) is the weather? **12**
familial with the family
une **famille** family **7**
en famille at home
un **fana, une fana** fan
un **fantôme** ghost
la **farine** flour
fatigué tired
faux (fausse) false **20**
favori (favorite) favorite
un **fax-modem** fax machine
faxer to fax
les **félicitations** *f.* congratulations
une **femme** woman **17**
une **fenêtre** window **17**
fermer to close **B**
une **fête** party; holiday
le **feu** fire
le feu d'artifice fireworks
une **feuille** sheet, leaf **B**
une feuille de papier sheet of paper **B**

un **feuilleton** series, serial story (in newspaper, TV)
février *m.* February **8**
la **fièvre** fever
une **fille** girl **5**
un **film policier** detective movie
la **fin** end
flamand Flemish
un **flamant** flamingo
une **fleur** flower
un **fleuve** river
un **flic** cop (*colloq.*)
une **fois** time
à la fois at the same time
la **folie: à la folie** madly
folklorique: une chanson folklorique folksong
fonctionner to work, function
fondé founded
le **foot(ball)** soccer
jouer au foot to play soccer **13**
le **football américain** football
une **forêt** forest
formidable great!
fort strong
un **fouet** whisk
la **fourrure** fur
un manteau de fourrure fur coat
frais: il fait frais it's cool (weather) **12**
un **franc** franc (*former monetary unit of France*) **11**
ça fait... francs that's (it's) ... francs **11**
le **français** French (language) **2, 9**
un **Français, une Française** French person
la **France** France **14**
en France in France **14**
francophone French-speaking
parler français to speak French **13**
un **frère** brother **7**
un steak-frites steak and French fries **9**
froid cold
il fait froid it's cold out (weather) **12**

le **fromage** cheese
un sandwich au fromage cheese sandwich
furieux (furieuse) furious
une **fusée** rocket

G

un **garçon** boy **5**; waiter
une **gare** train station
une **garniture** side dish
gauche left
une **gelée** jelly
généralement generally
généreux (généreuse) generous
la **générosité** generosity
génial brilliant
des **gens** *m.* people **18**
gentil (gentille) nice, kind **19**; sweet
la **géographie** geography
une **glace** ice cream **9**; mirror, ice
glacé iced
un **goûter** afternoon snack
une **goyave** guava
grand tall **17**; big, large **20**; big
une grande surface big store, self-service store
une **grand-mère** grandmother **7**
un **grand-père** grandfather **7**
grandir to get tall; to grow up
grec (grecque) Greek
un **grenier** attic
une **grillade** grilled meat
une **grille** grid
grillé: le pain grillé toast
une tartine de pain grillé buttered toast
la **grippe** flu
gris gray **20**
gros (grosse) fat, big
la **Guadeloupe** Guadeloupe (*French island in the West Indies*)
une **guerre** war
une **guitare** guitar **17**
un **gymnase** gym

H

habillé dressed
habiter to live **15**
Haïti Haiti (*French island in the West Indies*)

un **hamburger** hamburger **9**
la•**hâte** haste
en hâte quickly
•**haut** high
plus haut above
•**hélas!** too bad
hésiter to hesitate
l' **heure** *f.* time, hour; o'clock **4**
...heure(s) (dix) (ten) past ... **4**
...heure(s) et demie half past ... **4**
...heure(s) et quart quarter past ... **4**
...heure(s) moins (dix) (ten) of ... **4**
...heure(s) moins le quart quarter to ... **4**
à... heures at ... o'clock **14**
à quelle heure (est)...? at what time (is) ...? **4, 16**
combien d'heures? how many hours?
il est... heure(s) it's ... o'clock **4**
par heure per hour, an hour
quelle heure est-il? what time is it? **4**
heureux (heureuse) happy
hier yesterday
avant hier the day before yesterday
une **histoire** story, history
l' **hiver** *m.* winter **12**
en hiver in (the) winter **12**
•**hollandais** Dutch
un **homme** man **17**
honnête honest
une **horreur** horror
quelle horreur! what a scandal! how awful!
un•**hot dog** hot dog **9**
l' **huile** *f.* oil
•**huit** eight **1**
l' **humeur** *f.* mood
de bonne humeur in a good mood
un **hypermarché** shopping center

I

ici here **14**
ignorer to be unaware of
il he, it **11, 14, 18**
  est-ce qu'il y a...? is there, are there . . . ? **17**
  il est it (he) is **20**
  il/elle est + *nationality* he/she is . . . **6**
  il y a there is, there are **17**
  il n'y a pas de... there is/are no . . . **18**
  il y a eu there was
  qu'est-ce qu'il y a...? what is there . . .? **17**
une **île** island
illustré illustrated
l' **impératif** *m.* imperative (command) mood
impoli impolite
l' **importance** *f.* importance
  ça n'a pas d'importance it doesn't matter
importé imported
impressionnant impressive
une **imprimante** printer
inactif (inactive) inactive
inclure to include
l' **indicatif** *m.* area code
les **informations** *f.* news
l' **informatique** *f.* computer science
s' **informer (de)** to find out about
l' **Inforoute** *f.* the information highway
un **ingénieur** engineer
un **inspecteur, une inspectrice** police detective
intelligent intelligent **19**
interactif (interactive) interactive
intéressant interesting **19**
l' **intérieur** *m.* interior, inside
les **internautes** people who like to use the Internet
Internet the Internet
interroger to question
interviewer to interview
inutilement uselessly
un **inventaire** inventory
un **invité, une invitée** guest
inviter to invite **15**

israélien (israélienne) Israeli
italien (italienne) Italian **19**
un **Italien, une Italienne** Italian person

J

j' (*see* **je**)
jamais ever; never
  jamais le dimanche! never on Sunday!
la **Jamaïque** Jamaica
janvier *m.* January **8**
japonais Japanese **19**
jaune yellow **20**
jaunir to turn yellow
je I **14**
je ne sais pas I don't know **B, 17**
j'ai un rendez-vous I have an appointment **4**
un **jeu** (*pl.* **jeux**) game
  les jeux électroniques computer games
  les jeux télévisés TV game shows
jeudi *m.* Thursday **8**
jeune young **17**
les **jeunes** *m.* young people
un **job** (part-time) job
joli pretty (*for girls, women*) **17**
  plus joli(e) que prettier than
jouer to play **15**
  jouer au tennis (volley, basket, foot) to play tennis (volleyball, basketball, soccer) **13**
un **jour** day **8**
  le jour de l'an New Year's Day
  par jour per day, a day
  quel jour est-ce? what day is it? **8**
un **journal** (*pl.* **journaux**) newspaper
une **journée** day, whole day
  bonne journée! have a nice day!
joyeux (joyeuse) happy
  joyeux anniversaire! happy birthday! **17**
juillet *m.* July **8**

le quatorze juillet Bastille Day (French national holiday)
juin *m.* June **8**
un **jumeau** (*pl.* **jumeaux**), une **jumelle** twin
le **jus** juice
  le jus d'orange orange juice **10**
  le jus de pomme apple juice **10**
  le jus de raisin grape juice **10**
  le jus de tomate tomato juice **10**
jusqu'à until
juste right, fair
  le mot juste the right word

K

un **kangourou** kangaroo **E5**
un **kilo** kilogram

L

l' (see **le, la**)
la the **6, 18**; her, it
là here, there **14**
  là-bas over there **14**
  ça, là-bas that (one), over there **17**
  oh là là! uh, oh!; oh, dear!; wow!; oh, yes!
laid ugly
une **langue** language
large wide
se **laver** to wash (oneself), wash up
le the **6, 18**
  le + *number* + *month* the . . . **8**
  le (lundi) on (Mondays) **18**
une **leçon** lesson
un **lecteur** reader, player
  un lecteur de CD vidéo, de (disque) compact laserdisc player, compact disc player
  un lecteur optique interne/ de CD-ROM internal CD-ROM drive **B**
lent slow

les (*pl.*) the **18**
une **lettre** letter
se **lever** to get up, stand
  lève-toi! (levez-vous!)
    stand up! **B**
un **lézard** lizard **E5**
le **Liban** Lebanon (*country in the Middle East*)
  libanais Lebanese
  libéré liberated
une **librairie** bookstore
  libre free
un **lieu** place, area
  avoir lieu to take place
une **ligne** line
  limité limited
la **limonade** lemon soda **10**
* **lire** to read
  comment lire reading hints
une **liste** list
  une liste des courses shopping list
un **lit** bed **17**
un **living** living room (*informal*)
un **livre** book **17**
  local (*m.pl.* **locaux**) local
une **location** rental
un **logiciel** software
  logique logical
  logiquement logically
  loin: loin d'ici far (from here)
le **loisir** leisure, free time
un **loisir** leisure-time activity
  Londres London
  longtemps (for) a long time
    moins longtemps que for a shorter time
le **loto** lotto, lottery, bingo
  lui-même: en lui-même to himself
  lundi *m.* Monday **8**
le **Luxembourg** Luxembourg
un **lycée** high school

M ▬▬▬▬▬▬▬▬▬▬

m' (*see* **me**)
M. (monsieur) Mr. (Mister) **3**
ma my **7**
  et voici ma mère and this is my mother **7**

ma chambre my bedroom **17**
une **machine** machine
  une machine à coudre sewing machine
Madagascar Madagascar (*French-speaking island off of East Africa*)
Madame (Mme) Mrs., ma'am **3**
Mademoiselle (Mlle) Miss **3**
un **magasin** (department) store
  faire les magasins to go shopping (*browsing from store to store*)
  magnétique magnetic
un **magnétophone** tape recorder **17**
un **magnétoscope** VCR **B**
  magnifique magnificent
mai *m.* May **8**
  maigre thin, skinny
une **main** hand **E3**
  maintenant now **15**
  mais but **14**
    j'aime..., mais je préfère... I like . . ., but I prefer . . . **13**
    je regrette, mais je ne peux pas... I'm sorry, but I can't . . . **13**
    mais oui! sure! **14**
    mais non! of course not! **14**
une **maison** house
  à la maison at home **14**
mal badly, poorly **3, 15**
  ça va mal things are going badly **3**
  ça va très mal things are going very badly **3**
  c'est mal that's bad **20**
malade sick
malheureusement unfortunately
malin clever
manger to eat **13**
  j'aime manger I like to eat **13**
un **manteau** long coat
  un manteau de fourrure fur coat
un **marchand, une marchande** merchant, shopkeeper, dealer

un **marché** open-air market
  un marché aux puces flea market
marcher to work, to run (*for objects*) **17**; to walk (*for people*) **17**
  il/elle (ne) marche (pas) bien it (doesn't) work(s) well **17**
  est-ce que la radio marche? does the radio work? **17**
mardi *m.* Tuesday **8**
  le Mardi gras Shrove Tuesday
le **mariage** wedding, marriage
  marié married
une **marmite** covered stew pot
le **Maroc** Morocco (*country in North Africa*)
une **marque** brand (name)
une **marraine** godmother
  marrant fun
  marron (*inv.*) brown **20**
  mars *m.* March **8**
  martiniquais (person) from Martinique
la **Martinique** Martinique (*French island in the West Indies*)
un **match** game, (sports) match
  faire un match to play a game, (sports) match **16**
les **maths** *f.* math
le **matin** in the morning
  du matin in the morning, a.m. **4**
des **matoutou crabes** *m.* stewed crabs with rice
  mauvais bad **20**
  c'est une mauvaise idée that's a bad idea
  il fait mauvais it's bad (weather) **12**
  méchant mean, nasty **19**
un **médecin** doctor
  un médecin de nuit doctor on night duty
la **Méditerranée** Mediterranean Sea
  mélanger to mix, stir
  même same; even
    eux-mêmes themselves
    les mêmes choses the same things

une **mémoire** memory
mentionner to mention
merci thank you **3**
  oui, merci yes, thank you **13**
mercredi *m.* Wednesday **8**
une **mère** mother **7**
mériter to deserve
la **messagerie vocale** voice mail
le **métro** subway
mexicain Mexican **19**
midi *m.* noon **4**
mieux better
mignon (mignonne) cute **19**
militaire military
mille one thousand **6, 25**
une **mini-chaîne** compact stereo
minuit *m.* midnight **4**
mixte mixed
Mlle Miss **3**
Mme Mrs. **3**
une **mob (mobylette)** motorbike, moped **17**
la **mode** fashion
moi me **1**
  avec moi with me **13**
  donne-moi give me **9**
  donnez-moi give me **10**
  moi, je m'appelle (Marc) myself, my name is (Marc) **1**
  prête-moi... lend me . . . **11**
  s'il te plaît, donne-moi... please give me . . . **10**
un **moine** monk
moins less
  ...heure(s) moins (dix) (ten) of . . . **4**
  ...heure(s) moins le quart quarter of . . . **4**
  moins de less than
un **mois** month **8**
  par mois per month, a month
mon (ma; mes) my **7**
  mon anniversaire est le... my birthday is the . . . **8**
  voici mon père this is my father **7**
le **monde** world
  du monde in the world
  tout le monde everyone
la **monnaie** money; change
Monsieur (M.) Mr., sir **3**

un **monsieur** (*pl.* **messieurs**) gentleman, man (polite term) **5**
une **montre** watch **17**
un **morceau** piece
un **mot** word
une **moto** motorcycle **17**
la **moutarde** mustard
un **mouton** sheep
moyen (moyenne) average, medium
  en moyenne on the average
un **moyen** means
muet (muette) silent
le **multimédia** multimedia

N

n' (*see* **ne**)
nager to swim **15**
  j'aime nager I like to swim **13**
une **nationalité** nationality **2**
naviguer to navigate
ne (n')
  ne... aucun none, not any
  ne... pas not **14**
  ne... plus no longer
  n'est-ce pas? right?, no?, isn't it (so)?, don't you?, aren't you? **14**
né(e) born
nécessaire necessary
négatif (négative) negative
négativement negatively
la **neige** snow
neiger to snow
  il neige it's snowing **12**
le **Net** the Internet
netsurfer/surfer sur le Net to "surf the Net"
neuf nine **1**
un **neveu** (*pl.* **neveux**) nephew
une **nièce** niece
un **niveau** (*pl.* **niveaux**) level
Noël *m.* Christmas
noir black **20**
un **nom** name; noun
un **nombre** number
nombreux (nombreuses) numerous
nommé named
non no **2, 14**

non plus neither
mais non! of course not! **14**
le **nord** north
  le nord-est northeast
normalement normally
une **note** grade
nous we **14**
la **Nouvelle-Angleterre** New England
la **Nouvelle-Calédonie** New Caledonia (*French island in the South Pacific*)
novembre *m.* November **8**
  le onze novembre Armistice Day
la **nuit** night
un **numéro** number

O

objectif (objective) objective
un **objet** object **17**
une **occasion** occasion; opportunity
occupé occupied
un **océan** ocean
octobre *m.* October **8**
une **odeur** odor
un **office: office de tourisme** tourist office
officiel (officielle) official
offert (*p.p. of* **offrir**) offered
* **offrir** to offer, to give
oh là là! uh,oh!, oh, dear!, wow!, oh, yes!
un **oiseau** (*pl.* **oiseaux**) bird
une **omelette** omelet **9**
on one, they, you
  comment dit-on... en français? how do you say . . . in French?
  on est... today is . . .
  on va dans un café? shall we go to a café?
  on y va let's go
un **oncle** uncle **7**
onze eleven **2**
opérer to operate
l' **or** *m.* gold
orange (*inv.*) orange (color) **20**
une **orange** orange (fruit)
  le jus d'orange orange juice **10**

un **ordinateur** computer **17**
une **oreille** ear **E3**
organiser to organize **15**
originairement originally
l' **origine** *f.* origin, beginning
d'origine bretonne from Brittany
l' **orthographe: les signes** *m.* **orthographiques** spelling marks
ou or **2, 14**
où where **14, 16**
où est...? where is . . .? **14**
oublier to forget
l' **ouest** *m.* west
oui yes **2, 14**
oui, bien sûr... yes, of course . . . **13**
oui, d'accord... yes, okay . . . **13**
oui, j'ai... yes, I have . . . **17**
oui, merci... yes, thank you . . . **13**
mais, oui! sure! **14**
un **ouragan** hurricane
ouvert open
* **ouvrir** to open
ouvre... (ouvrez...) open . . . **B**

P ▬▬▬▬▬▬▬▬

pâle pale
une **panne** breakdown
une panne d'électricité power failure
une **panthère** panther
une **papaye** papaya
le **papier** paper
par per
par exemple for example
par jour per day
un **parc** park
un parc public city park
parce que (parce qu') because **16**
paresseux (paresseuse) lazy
parfait perfect
rien n'est parfait nothing is perfect
parfois sometimes
parisien (parisienne) Parisian

parler to speak, talk **15**
parler (français, anglais, espagnol) to speak (French, English, Spanish) **13**
parlons (de)... let's talk (about) . . .
un **parrain** godfather
une **partie** part
* **partir** to leave
à partir de as of, beginning
partitif (partitive) partitive
pas not
ne... pas not **14**
pas de not a, no, not any **18**
pas possible not possible
pas toujours not always **13**
pas très bien not very well
le **passé composé** compound past tense
passionnément passionately
une **pâte** dough
patient patient
le **patinage** ice skating, roller skating
une **patinoire** skating rink
une **pâtisserie** pastry, pastry shop
une **patte** foot, paw *(of bird or animal)*
un **pays** country
la **peau** skin, hide
* **peindre** to paint
peint painted
une **pellicule** film *(camera)*
pendant during
pénétrer to enter
pénible bothersome, a pain **20**
une **pension** inn, boarding house
Pentecôte *(f.)* Pentecost
perdu *(p.p. of* **perdre***)* lost
un **père** father **7**
* **permettre** to permit
un **perroquet** parrot
une **personne** person **5, 17**
personnel (personnelle) personal
personnellement personally
péruvien (péruvienne) Peruvian
petit small, short **17, 20**
il/elle est petit(e) he/she is short **17**

un **petit copain, une petite copine** boyfriend, girlfriend
plus petit(e) smaller
le **petit-fils, la petite-fille** grandson, granddaughter
peu little, not much
un peu a little, a little bit **15**
peut (*see* **pouvoir**)
peut-être perhaps, maybe **14**
peux (*see* **pouvoir**)
est-ce que tu peux...? can you . . .? **13**
je regrette, mais je ne peux pas... I'm sorry, but I can't . . . **13**
la **photo** photography
la **physique** physics
piloter to pilot (a plane)
une **pincée** pinch
une **pizza** pizza **9**
un **placard** closet
plaît: s'il te plaît please *(informal)* **9**; excuse me (please)
s'il te plaît, donne-moi... please, give me . . . **10**
s'il vous plaît please *(formal)* **10**; excuse me (please)
un **plan** map
une **plante** plant
le **plat principal** main course
un **plateau** tray
pleut: il pleut it's raining **12**
plier to fold
plumer to pluck
plus more
en plus in addition
le plus the most
ne... plus no longer, no more
non plus neither
plus de more than
plus joli que prettier than
plusieurs several
une **poche** pocket
l'argent *m.* **de poche** allowance, pocket money
une **poêle** frying pan
un **point de vue** point of view

un **poisson**
    un poisson rouge
    goldfish
    blaff de poisson fish stew
la **poli** polite
un **politicien, une politicienne**
    politician
une **pomme** apple
    le jus de pomme apple
    juice **10**
    **une purée de pommes
    de terre** mashed
    potatoes
le **porc: une côtelette de porc**
    pork chop
une **porte** door **17**
un **porte-monnaie** change
    purse, wallet
    portugais Portuguese
    poser: poser une question
    to ask a question
une **possibilité** possibility
la **poste** post office
    pouah! yuck! yech!
une **poule** hen **E5**
    pour for **14**; in order to
    pour que so that
    pour qui? for whom? **16**
le **pourcentage** percentage
    pourquoi why **16**
    pratique practical
    pratiquer to participate in
des **précisions** f. details
    préférer
    je préfère I prefer **13**
    préféré favorite
    tu préférerais? would you
    prefer?
    premier (première)
    c'est le premier juin it's
    June first **8**
    le premier de l'an New
    Year's Day
    le premier étage second
    floor *(in US)*
    le premier mai Labor
    Day *(in France)*
un **prénom** first name
    près near
    près d'ici nearby, near
    here
    tout près very close
une **présentation** appearance

la **présentation
    extérieure** outward
    appearance
des **présentations** f.
    introductions
    pressé in a hurry
    prêt ready
un **prêt** loan
    prêter à to lend to, to loan
    prête-moi... lend me . . .
    11
    principalement mainly
le **printemps** spring **12**
    au printemps in the
    spring **12**
un **prix** price
un **problème** problem
un **produit** product
un **prof, une prof** teacher
    (informal) **5, 17**
un **professeur** teacher **17**
    **professionnel
    (professionnelle)**
    professional
un **programme** program
un **projet** plan
une **promenade** walk
    **faire une promenade à
    pied** to go for a walk
    16
* **promettre** to promise
une **promo** special sale
    proposer to suggest
    propre (one's) own
un **propriétaire, une
    propriétaire**
    landlord/landlady, owner
la **Provence** Provence *(province
    in southern France)*
    pu *(p.p.* **pouvoir)** **n'a pas pu**
    was not able to
    public: un parc public city
    park
    un jardin public public
    garden
la **publicité** commercials,
    advertising, publicity
une **puce** flea
    un marché aux puces
    flea market
    puis then, also
    puisque since

les **Pyrénées** (the) Pyrenees
    *(mountains between
    France and Spain)*

Q ━━━━━━━━━━━━

    qu' *(see* **que)**
une **qualité** quality
    quand when **16**
    **c'est quand, ton
    anniversaire?** when is
    your birthday? **8**
    quarante forty **3**
un **quart** one quarter
    ...heure(s) et quart
    quarter past . . . **4**
    **...heure(s) moins le
    quart** quarter of . . . **4**
    quatorze fourteen **2**
    quatre four **1**
    quatre-vingt-dix ninety **6**
    quatre-vingts eighty **6**
    que that, which
    ce que that which, what
    qu'est-ce que (qu') what
    *(phrase used to introduce
    a question)* **16**
    qu'est-ce qu'il y a? what
    is there? **17**; what's the
    matter?
    qu'est-ce que c'est? what
    is it? what's that? **17**
    qu'est-ce que tu veux?
    what do you want? **9**
    qu'est-ce qui ne va pas?
    what's wrong?
un **Québécois, une Québécoise**
    person from Quebec
    québécois from Quebec
    quel (quelle)...! what a . . .!
    **quel âge a ta mère/ton
    père?** how old is your
    mother/your father? **7**
    quel âge a-t-il/elle? how
    old is he/she? **17**
    quel âge as-tu? how old
    are you? **7**
    quel jour est-ce? what
    day is it? **8**
    quel temps fait-il? what's
    (how's) the weather? **12**
    quelle est la date? what's
    the date? **8**

quelle heure est-il? what time is it? **4**

à quelle heure (est)...? at what time (is) . . .? **4**

de quelle couleur...? what color is . . .? **20**

quelques some, a few **17**

une **question** question

une **queue** tail

qui who, whom **16**

à qui? to whom? **16**

avec qui? with who(m)? **16**

c'est qui? who's that? (casual speech)

de qui? about who(m)? **16**

pour qui? for who(m)? **16**

qui est-ce? who's that (this)? **5, 17**

qui se ressemble... birds of a feather . . .

quinze fifteen **2**

quoi? what? **17**

quotidien (quotidienne) daily

la vie quotidienne daily life

R

raconter to tell about

une **radio** radio **17**

écouter la radio to listen to the radio **13**

une **radiocassette** boom box **17**

un **raisin** grape

le jus de raisin grape juice **10**

une **raison** reason

rapidement rapidly

un **rapport** relationship

une **raquette** racket **17**

rarement rarely, seldom **15**

un **rayon** department (in a store)

réalisé made

récemment recently

une **recette** recipe

recherche: un avis de recherche missing person's bulletin

un **récital** (pl. **récitals**) (musical) recital

reconstituer to reconstruct

un **réfrigérateur** refrigerator

refuser to refuse

regarder to look at, watch **15**

regarde ça look at that **17**

regarder la télé to watch TV **13**

un **régime** diet

être au régime to be on a diet

régional (m.pl. **régionaux**) regional

regretter to be sorry

je regrette, mais... I'm sorry, but . . . **13**

régulier (régulière) regular

une **reine** queen

une **rencontre** meeting, encounter

rencontrer to meet

un **rendez-vous**

j'ai un rendez-vous à... I have a date, appointment at . . . **4**

rendre visite à to visit, come to visit (a person)

la **rentrée** first day back at school in fall

rentrer to go back, come back; to return

réparer to fix, repair

un **repas** meal

* **repeindre** to repaint

le **répondeur** answering machine

répondre (à) to answer, respond (to) **B**

répondez-lui (moi) answer him (me)

répondre que oui to answer yes

une **réponse** answer

un **reportage** documentary

représenter to represent

un **réseau** network

réservé reserved

une **résolution** resolution

un **restaurant** restaurant

au restaurant to (at) the restaurant **14**

dîner au restaurant to have dinner at a restaurant **13**

un restaurant trois étoiles three star restaurant

rose pink

rester to stay

retard: un jour de retard one day behind

en retard late

retourner to return; to turn over

réussir to succeed

réussir à un examen to pass an exam

* **revenir** to come back

revoir: au revoir! good-bye! **3**

le **rez-de-chaussée** ground floor

un **rhinocéros** rhinoceros

riche rich

rien (de) nothing

rien n'est parfait nothing is perfect

ne... rien nothing

une **rive** (river) bank

une **rivière** river, stream

le **riz** rice

une **robe** dress

le **roller** rollerblading

romain Roman

le **rosbif** roast beef

rose pink

rosse nasty (colloq.)

une **rôtie** toast (Canadian)

rôtir to roast

une **roue** wheel

rouge red **20**

rougir to turn red

rouler to roll

roux (rousse) red-head

une **rue** street

dans la rue (Victor Hugo) on (Victor Hugo) street

russe Russian

S

sa his, her

un **sac** bag, handbag **17**

sais (see **savoir**)

je sais I know **B, 17**

je ne sais pas I don't know **B, 17**

tu sais you know

une **saison** season **12**

en toute saison all year round (in every season)

une **salade** salad **9**; lettuce

un **salaire** salary
une **salle** hall, large room
  une salle à manger
    dining room
  une salle de bains
    bathroom
  une salle de séjour
    informal living room
un **salon** formal living room
  salut hi!, good-bye! **3**
une **salutation** greeting
  samedi *m.* Saturday **8**
  à samedi! see you
    Saturday! **8**
  le samedi on Saturdays
    18
  samedi soir Saturday night
une **sandale** sandal
un **sandwich** sandwich **9**
  sans without
des **saucisses** *f.* sausages
le **saucisson** salami
* **savoir** to know (information)
  je sais I know **17**
  je ne sais pas I don't
    know **17**
  tu sais you know
un **saxo (saxophone)**
    saxophone
une **scène** scene, stage
les **sciences** *f.* **économiques**
    economics
les **sciences** *f.* **naturelles**
    natural science
un **scooter** motorscooter **17**
  second second
  seize sixteen **2**
un **séjour** stay; informal living
    room
le **sel** salt
  selon according to
  selon toi in your opinion
une **semaine** week **8**
  cette semaine this week
  la semaine dernière last
    week
  la semaine prochaine
    next week
  par semaine per week, a
    week
  semblable similar
le **Sénégal** Senegal *(French-speaking country in Africa)*

  sensationnel
    (sensationnelle)
    sensational
  séparer to separate
  sept seven **1**
  septembre *m.* September
    8
  septième seventh
une **série** series
  sérieux (sérieuse) serious
un **serveur, une serveuse**
    waiter, waitress
  servi served
une **serviette** napkin
  ses his, her **24**
  seul alone, only; by oneself
  seulement only, just
  sévère strict, severe
un **short** shorts
  si if, whether **C**
  si! so, yes! *(to a negative question)* **18**
un **signal** (*pl.* **signaux**) signal
un **signe** sign
  un signe orthographique
    spelling mark
un **singe** monkey
  situé situated
  six six **1**
  sixième sixth
un **skate** skateboard
le **ski** skiing
  le ski nautique
    waterskiing
  faire du ski to ski
  faire du ski nautique to
    go water-skiing
  skier to ski
  snob snobbish
la **Société Nationale des**
    Chemins de Fer
    (SNCF) French railroad
    system
une **société** society
un **soda** soda **10**
une **soeur** sister **7**
la **soie** silk
la **soif** thirst
  avoir soif to be thirsty
  j'ai soif I'm thirsty **10**
  tu as soif? are you thirsty?
    10
un **soir** evening, night(time)
  ce soir this evening,
    tonight

  demain soir tomorrow
    night (evening)
  du soir in the evening,
    p.m. **4**
  hier soir last night
  le soir in the evening
une **soirée** (whole) evening;
    (evening) party
  soixante sixty **3, 5**
  soixante-dix seventy **5**
un **soldat** soldier
un **solde** (clearance) sale
  en solde on sale
la **sole** sole (fish)
le **soleil** sun
  les lunettes *f.* **de soleil**
    sunglasses
  sommes (*see* **être**)
  nous sommes... it is,
    today is . . . *(date)*
  son (sa; ses) his, her
un **sondage** poll
une **sorte** sort, type, kind
* **sortir** to leave, come out
un **souhait** wish
la **soupe** soup
une **souris** mouse (computer)
  un tapis de souris
    mousepad
  sous under **17**
le **sous-sol** basement
  souvent often **15**
  soyez (*see* **être**)**: soyez**
    logique be logical
les **spaghetti** *m.* spaghetti
  spécialement especially
  spécialisé specialized
une **spécialité** specialty
le **sport** sports
  faire du sport to play
    sports
  des vêtements *m.* **de**
    sport sports clothing
  une voiture de sport
    sports car
  sportif (sportive) athletic **19**
un **stade** stadium
un **stage** sports training camp;
    internship
une **station-service** gas station
un **steak** steak **9**
un **steak-frites** steak and French
    fries **9**
un **stylo** pen **B, 17**
le **sucre** sugar

le **sud** south
suggérer to suggest
suis (*see* être) (I) am . . . **2**
je suis + *nationality* I'm (*nationality*)
je suis de... I'm from . . . **2**
suisse Swiss **19**
la **Suisse** Switzerland
suivant following
suivi followed
un **sujet** subject, topic
super terrific **15**; great **20**
un **supermarché** supermarket
supersonique supersonic
supérieur superior
supplémentaire supplementary, extra
sur on **17**; about
sûr sure, certain
bien sûr! of course! **14**
oui, bien sûr... yes, of course . . .! **13**
tu es sûr(e)? are you sure?
sûrement surely
la **surface: une grande surface** big store, self-service store
surtout especially, above all
un **survêtement** jogging or track suit
un **sweat** sweatshirt
une **sweaterie** shop specializing in sweatshirts and sportswear
sympa nice, pleasant (*colloq.*)
sympathique nice, pleasant **19**
une **synagogue** Jewish temple or synagogue
un **synthétiseur** electronic keyboard, synthesizer

T ▬▬▬▬▬

t' (*see* te)
ta your **7**
une **table** table **B, 17**
mettre la table to set the table
un **tableau** (*pl.* **tableaux**) chalkboard **B**

Tahiti Tahiti (*French island in the South Pacific*)
la **taille** size
de taille moyenne of medium height or size
un **tailleur** woman's suit
se **taire: tais-toi!** be quiet!
une **tante** aunt **7**
un **tapis de souris** mousepad (for computer)
la **tarte** pie
une **tasse** cup
un **taxi** taxi
en taxi by taxi
te (to) you
un **tee-shirt** T-shirt
un **temple** Protestant church
le **temps** time; weather
combien de temps? how long?
de temps en temps from time to time
quel temps fait-il? what's (how's) the weather? **12**
tout le temps all the time
le **tennis** tennis
jouer au tennis to play tennis **13**
des **tennis** *m.* tennis shoes, sneakers **25**
la **télé** TV **B, 17**
à la télé on TV
regarder la télé to watch TV **13**
un **téléphone** telephone **17**
téléphoner (à) to call, phone **13, 15**
télévisé: des jeux *m.* **télévisés** TV game shows
un **terrain de sport** (playing) field
une **terrasse** outdoor section of a café, terrace
la **terre** earth
une pomme de terre potato
terrifiant terrifying
tes your
la **tête** head
le **thé** tea **10**
un thé glacé iced tea
un **théâtre** theater
le **thon** tuna
tiens! look!, hey! **5, 18**

un **tigre** tiger
timide timid, shy **19**
le **tissu** fabric
un **titre** title
toi you (*fam.*)
avec toi with you **13**
et toi? and you? **1**
les **toilettes** bathroom, toilet **21**
un **toit** roof
une **tomate** tomato
le jus de tomate tomato juice **10**
un **tombeau** tomb
ton (ta; tes) your **7**
c'est quand, ton anniversaire? when's your birthday? **8**
tort: avoir tort to be wrong
une **tortue** turtle
un bifteck de tortue turtle steak
toujours always **15**
je n'aime pas toujours... I don't always like . . . **13**
un **tour** turn
à votre tour it's your turn
la **Touraine** Touraine (*province in central France*)
le **tourisme: office de tourisme** tourist office
tourner to turn
la **Toussaint** All Saint's Day (*November 1*)
tout (toute; tous, toutes) all, every, the whole; completely, very
pas du tout not at all
tous les jours every day
tout ça all that
tout de suite right away
tout droit straight
tout le monde everyone
tout le temps all the time
tout près very close
toutes sortes all sorts, kinds
un **train** train
tranquille quiet
laisse-moi tranquille! leave me alone!
un **transistor** transistor radio
un **travail** (*pl.* **travaux**) job

travailler to work **13, 15**
une **traversée** crossing
treize thirteen **2**
trente thirty **3**
un **tréma** diaeresis
très very **19**
  ça va très bien things are going very well **3**
  ça va très mal things are going very badly **3**
  très bien very well **15**
trois three **1**
troisième third
  en troisième ninth grade *(in France)*
trop too, too much
trouver to find, to think of
  comment trouves-tu…? what do you think of …? how do you find …?
  s'y trouve is there
tu you **14**
la **Tunisie** Tunisia *(country in North Africa)*

U

un, une one **1**; a, an **5, 18**
unique only
uniquement only
une **université** university, college
l' **usage** *m.* use
un **ustensile** utensil
utile useful
utiliser to use **C**
  en utilisant (by) using
  utilisez… use … **C**

V

va *(see* **aller)**
  ça va? how are you? how's everything? **3**
  ça va! everything's fine (going well); fine, I'm OK **3**
  comment vas-tu? how are you? **3**
  on va dans un café? shall we go to a café?
  on y va! let's go!
  va-t'en! go away!

les **vacances** *f.* vacation
  bonnes vacances! have a nice vacation!
  en vacances on vacation **14**
  les grandes vacances summer vacation
une **vache** cow
vais *(see* **aller): je vais** I'm going
la **vaisselle** dishes
  faire la vaisselle to do the dishes
valable valid
une **valise** suitcase
vanille: une glace à la vanille vanilla ice cream
varié varied
les **variétés** *f.* variety show
vas *(see* **aller)**
  comment vas-tu? how are you? **3**
  vas-y! come on!, go ahead!, do it!
le **veau** veal
une **vedette** star
un **vélo** bicycle **17**
  à vélo by bicycle
  faire une promenade à vélo to go for a bicycle ride
un **vendeur, une vendeuse** salesperson
vendre to sell
vendredi *m.* Friday **8**
vendu *(p.p. of* **vendre)** sold
* **venir** to come
le **vent** wind
une **vente** sale
le **ventre** stomach
venu *(p.p. of* **venir)** came, come
vérifier to check
la **vérité** truth
un **verre** glass
verser to pour
vert green **20**
  les • haricots *m.* **verts** green beans
une **veste** jacket
des **vêtements** *m.* clothing
  des vêtements de sport sports clothing
veut *(see* **vouloir): que veut dire…?** What does … mean? **B**

veux *(see* **vouloir)**
  est-ce que tu veux…? do you want …? **13**
  je ne veux pas… I don't want … **13**
  je veux… I want … **13**
  je veux bien… I'd love to, I do, I want to … **13**
  qu'est-ce que tu veux? what do you want? **9**
  tu veux…? do you want …? **9**
la **viande** meat
une **vidéocassette** videocassette **B**
la **vie** life
  la vie quotidienne daily life
viens *(see* **venir)**
  viens… come … **B**
  oui, je viens yes, I'm coming along with you
vieux (vieil, vieille; *m.pl.* **vieux)** old
  le Vieux Carré the French Quarter in New Orleans
le **Viêt-nam** Vietnam *(country in Southeast Asia)*
vietnamien (vietnamienne) Vietnamese
une **vigne** vineyard
un **village** town, village
  un petit village small town
une **ville** city, town **6**
  en ville downtown, in town, in the city **14**
  une grande ville big city, town
le **vin** wine
vingt twenty **2, 3**
un **violon** violin
une **visite** visit
  rendre visite à to visit (a person)
visiter to visit (places) **15**
vite quickly
vite! fast!, quick!
vive: vive les vacances! three cheers for vacation!
* **vivre** to live
le **vocabulaire** vocabulary
voici… here is, this is …, here come(s) … **5**

voici + du, de la *(partitive)* here's some

voici mon père/ma mère here's my father/my mother **7**

voilà... there is . . ., there come(s) . . . **5**

voilà + du, de la *(partitive)* there's some

la **voile** sailing

faire de la voile to sail

la planche à voile windsurfing

* **voir** to see

voir un film to see a movie

un **voisin, une voisine** neighbor **17**

une **voiture** car **17**

une voiture de sport sports car

en voiture by car

faire une promenade en voiture to go for a drive by car

une **voix** voice

le **volley (volleyball)** volleyball

jouer au volley to play volleyball **13**

un **volontaire, une volontaire** volunteer

comme volontaire as a volunteer

vos your

votre *(pl.* **vos***)* your

voudrais *(see* **vouloir***)*: **je voudrais** I'd like **9, 10, 13**

* **vouloir** to want

vouloir + du, de la *(partitive)* to want some *(some of something)*

vouloir dire to mean

voulu *(p.p. of* **vouloir***)* wanted

vous you **14**; (to) you

vous désirez? what would you like? may I help you? **10**

s'il vous plaît please **10**

un **voyage** trip

bon voyage! have a nice trip!

faire un voyage to take a trip **16**

voyager to travel **13, 15**

vrai true, right, real **20**

c'est vrai! that's true! **16**

vraiment really

vu *(p.p. of* **voir***)* saw, seen

une **vue** view

un point de vue point of view

W

un **walkman** walkman **17**

les **WC** *m.* toilet

le **Web ("la toile d'araignée")** the World Wide Web

un **weekend** weekend

bon weekend! have a nice weekend!

ce weekend this weekend

le weekend on weekends

le weekend dernier last weekend

le weekend prochain next weekend

Y

y there

allons-y! let's go!

est-ce qu'il y a...? is there . . .?, are there . . .? **17**

il y a there is, there are **17**

qu'est-ce qu'il y a? what is there? **17**

vas-y! come on!, go ahead!, do it!

le **yaourt** yogurt

les **yeux** *m.* (*sg.* **oeil**) eyes

Z

un **zèbre** zebra

zéro zero **1**

zut! darn! **3**

VOCABULARY
English-French

The English-French vocabulary contains active and passive words from the text, as well as the important words of the illustrations used within the units. Obvious passive cognates have not been listed.

The numbers following an entry indicate the lesson in which the word or phrase is activated. (**B** stands for the photo essay that precedes **Niveau B;** and **E** stands for **Entracte.**)

Nouns: If the article of a noun does not indicate gender, the noun is followed by *m.* (*masculine*) or *f.* (*feminine*). If the plural (*pl.*) is irregular, it is given in parentheses.

Verbs: Verbs are listed in the infinitive form. An asterisk (*) in front of an active verb means that it is irregular. (For forms, see the verb charts in Appendix 4C.)

Words beginning with an **h** are preceded by a bullet (•) if the **h** is aspirate; that is, if the word is treated as if it begins with a consonant sound.

A

a, an un, une **5, 18**
  a few quelques **17**
  a little (bit) un peu **15**
  a lot beaucoup **15**
about whom? de qui? **16**
according to après: d'après; selon
address l'adresse *f.*
  e-mail address l'adresse électronique
afternoon: in the afternoon de l'après-midi **4**
to **agree** *être d'accord **14**
all tout
  all right d'accord **13**
  all the time tout le temps
  all year round en toute saison
also aussi **2, 15**
always toujours **15**
  not always pas toujours **13**
a.m. du matin **4**
am (*see* **to be**)
  I am + nationality . . . je suis + *nationality* **2**
American américain **2, 19**
  I'm American je suis américain(e) **2**
amusing amusant **19**

an un, une **5, 18**
and et **2, 14**
  and you? et toi? **1**
annoying pénible **20**
another un(e) autre
to **answer** répondre
answering machine un répondeur
any des; du, de la, de l', de
  not any pas de **18**
apple une pomme
  apple juice le jus de pomme **10**
April avril *m.* **8**
are (*see* **to be**)
  are there . . .? est-ce qu'il y a...? **17**
  are you . . .? tu es...? **2**
  are you acquainted with...? tu connais...? **6**
  there are il y a **17**
  these/those/they are ce sont **20**
at à **14**
  at . . . o'clock à... heure(s) **14**
  at home à la maison **14**
  at the restaurant au restaurant **14**
  at what time (is) . . .? à quelle heure (est)...? **4**

  I have an appointment at . . . j'ai un rendez-vous à... **4**
athletic sportif (sportive) **19**
attention: to pay attention *faire attention **16**
August août *m.* **8**
aunt une tante **7**
automobile une auto, une voiture **17**
autumn l'automne *m.*
  in (the) autumn en automne **12**
average: on the average en moyenne

B

back: in back of derrière **17**
bad mauvais **20**
  I'm/everything's (very) bad ça va (très) mal **3**
  it's bad (weather) il fait mauvais **12**
  that's bad c'est mal **20**
  too bad! dommage! **15**
badly mal **3**
  things are going (very) badly ça va (très) mal **3**
bag un sac **17**

to be *être 14
> to be . . . years old *avoir... ans 18
>
> to be careful *faire attention 16
>
> to be cold out (weather) il fait froid 12
>
> to be hungry *avoir faim 18
>
> to be thirsty *avoir soif 18

beautiful beau (bel, belle; *m.pl.* beaux) 17
> it's beautiful (nice) weather il fait beau 12

because parce que (qu') 16

bed un lit 17

bedroom une chambre 17

behind derrière 17

between entre

beverage une boisson 10

bicycle un vélo, une bicyclette 17

big grand 17, 20

birthday un anniversaire 8
> my birthday is (March 2) mon anniversaire est (le 2 mars) 8
>
> when is your birthday? c'est quand, ton anniversaire? 8

bit: a little bit un peu 15

black noir 20

blond blond 17

blue bleu 20

book un livre B, 17

boom box une radiocassette 17

bothersome pénible 20

boy le garçon 5, 6

boyfriend un petit copain

brother un frère 7

brown brun 17; marron (*inv.*) 20

bus un bus; l'autobus *m.*

but mais 13

C

café un café 14
> at (to) the café au café 14

calculator une calculatrice 17

to call téléphoner 15

camera un appareil-photo (*pl.* appareils-photo) 17

can pouvoir
> can you . . .? est-ce que tu peux...? 13
>
> I can't je ne peux pas 13

Canada le Canada

Canadian canadien (canadienne) 2, 19
> he's/she's (Canadian) il/elle est (canadien/ canadienne) 6

cannot: I cannot je ne peux pas 13
> I'm sorry, but I cannot je regrette, mais je ne peux pas 13

car une auto, une voiture 17

card une carte

careful: to be careful *faire attention 16

cassette tape une cassette B, 17
> cassette recorder un magnétophone 17

cat un chat 7

CD (audio) un CD, un (disque) compact B

CD player un lecteur de CD (compact, (disque) compact)

CD-ROM un disque optique, un CD-ROM B
> internal CD-ROM drive un lecteur optique interne

chair une chaise B, 17

chalk la craie B
> piece of chalk un morceau de craie B
>
> chalkboard un tableau (*pl.* tableaux) B

child un(e) enfant

Chinese chinois 19

chocolate: hot chocolate un chocolat 10

cinema le cinéma 14
> to the cinema au cinéma 14

city: in the city en ville 14

class une classe 14
> in class en classe 14
>
> classmate un (une) camarade 17

coffee le café 10

cold le froid
> it's cold (weather) il fait froid 12

college student un étudiant, une étudiante 17

color une couleur 20
> what color? de quelle couleur? 20

come: here comes . . . voici... 5

compact disc un (disque) compact (un CD, un compact) 17
> compact disc player un lecteur de compact disque

computer un ordinateur B, 17
> computer games (on CD-ROM) les jeux *m.* électroniques (sur CD-ROM)

cool: it's cool (weather) il fait frais 12

cordially (in friendship) amicalement

to cost coûter
> how much does . . . cost? combien coûte...? 11
>
> it costs . . . il/elle coûte... 11

course: of course! bien sûr! 13; mais oui! 14
> of course not! mais non! 14

cousin un cousin, une cousine 7

crepe une crêpe 9

croissant un croissant 9

cute mignon (mignonne) 19

D

to dance danser 13, 15

dark-haired brun 17

darn! zut! 3

date la date 8
> I have a date at . . . j'ai un rendez-vous à... 4
>
> what's the date? quelle est la date? 8

day un jour 8
> per day par jour
>
> what day is it? quel jour est-ce? 8
>
> whole day une journée

December décembre *m.* 8

depend: it depends (on) dépend: ça dépend (des)

desk un bureau B, 17

differently différemment

difficult difficile 20

dinner le dîner
> to have (eat) dinner dîner 15
>
> to have dinner at a restaurant dîner au restaurant 13

director une directrice (un directeur)

disc (computer) une disquette **B**
to **discuss** discuter
to **do** *faire **16**
   dog un chien **7**
   door une porte **B, 17**
   downtown en ville **14**
   drink une boisson **10**
   dumb bête **19**
   during pendant

E

   e-mail, electronic mail e-mail, le courrier électronique
      e-mail address l'adresse *f.* électronique
   easy facile **20**
to **eat** manger **15**
      I like to eat j'aime manger **13**
      to eat dinner dîner **15**
   eight •huit **1**
   eighteen dix-huit **2**
   eighty quatre-vingts **6**
   eleven onze **2, 11**
   eleventh onzième
   engineer un ingénieur
   England l'Angleterre *f.*
   English anglais(e) **2, 19**
   especially, above all surtout
   euro un euro
   evening: in the evening du soir **4**
   everything tout
      everything's going (very) well ça va (très) bien **3**
      everything's (going) so-so ça va comme ci, comme ça **3**
      how's everything? ça va? **3**
   exam un examen

F

   fall l'automne *m.* **12**
      in (the) fall en automne **12**
   false faux (fausse) **20**
   family une famille **7**
   fashion la mode
   father un père
      this is my father voici mon père **7**
to **fax** faxer
      fax machine un fax-modem, télécopieur
   February février *m.* **8**

few: a few quelques **17**
fifteen quinze **2**
fifty cinquante **3**
filmmaker un(e) cinéaste
fine ça va **3**
   fine! d'accord! **13**
   everything's fine ça va bien **3**
   that's fine c'est bien **20**
first le premier (la première)
   it's (June) first c'est le premier (juin) **8**
five cinq **1**
floppy disc une disquette **B**
following suivant(es)
for pour **14**
   for whom? pour qui? **16**
forty quarante **3**
four quatre **1**
fourteen quatorze **2**
franc un franc **11**
   that's (it's) . . . francs ça fait... francs **11**
France la France **14**
   in France en France **14**
French français(e) **2, 19**
   how do you say . . . in French? comment dit-on... en français? **B**
French fries les frites
   steak and French fries un steak-frites **9**
Friday vendredi *m.* **8**
friend un ami, une amie **5**; un copain, une copine **5**
   boyfriend, girlfriend un petit copain, une petite copine
   school friend un (une) camarade **17**
friendship l'amitié *f.*
from de **14**
   are you from . . .? tu es de...? **2**
   I'm from . . . je suis de... **2**
front: in front of devant **17**
funny amusant **19**; drôle **20**

G

game un match **16**
   computer games les jeux électroniques
   to play a game (match) *faire un match **16**
gentleman un monsieur (*pl.* messieurs) **5**

German allemand
girl une fille **15**
girlfriend une petite copine
to **give** donner
   give me . . . donne-moi, donnez-moi... **9, 10**
   please give me . . . s'il te plaît, donne-moi... **10**
good bon (bonne) **20**
   good morning (afternoon) bonjour **1**
   that's good c'est bien **20**
   the weather's good (pleasant) il fait bon **12**
good-bye! au revoir!, salut! **3**
good-looking beau (bel, belle; *m.pl.* beaux) **17, 20**
grandfather un grand-père **7**
grandmother une grand-mère **7**
grape juice le jus de raisin **10**
gray gris **20**
great chouette, super **20**
green vert **20**
guitar une guitare **17**

H

hair les cheveux *m.* **E3**
   he/she has dark hair il/elle est brun(e) **17**
half demi(e)
   half past . . . ...heure(s) et demie **4**
   half past midnight minuit et demi **4**
   half past noon midi et demi **4**
hamburger un hamburger **9**
handbag un sac **17**
handsome beau (bel, belle; *m.pl.* beaux) **17, 20**
hard difficile **20**
hard drive (computer) le disque dur
to **have** *avoir **18**
   do you have . . .? est-ce que tu as...? **17**
   I have j'ai **17**
   I have to (must) je dois **13**
   to have dinner at a restaurant dîner au restaurant **13**
he il **11, 14, 18**
   he/she is . . . il/elle est + *nationality* **6**

headphones un casque
hello bonjour **1, 3**
help: may I help you? vous désirez? **10**
her: her name is . . . elle s'appelle... **6**
  what's her name? comment s'appelle-t-elle? **17**
here ici **14**
  here comes, here is voici **5**
  here's my mother/father voici ma mère/mon père **7**
hey! dis! **20**; tiens! **5, 18**
  hey there! dis donc! **20**
hi! salut! **3**
high school student un (une) élève **17**
his: his name is . . . il s'appelle... **6**
  what's his name? comment s'appelle-t-il? **17**
home, at home à la maison **14**; chez (moi, toi...)
homework assignment un devoir **B**
hot chaud **12**
  it's hot (weather) il fait chaud **12**
hot chocolate un chocolat **10**
hot dog un •hot dog **9**
how? comment? **16**
  how are you? comment allez-vous?, comment vas-tu?, ça va? **3**
  how do you say . . . in French? comment dit-on... en français? **B**
  how many hours . . .? combien d'heures...?
  how much does . . . cost? combien coûte...? **11**
  how much is that/this/it? c'est combien?, ça fait combien? **11**
  how old are you? quel âge as-tu? **7**
  how old is he/she? quel âge a-t-il/elle? **17**
  how old is your father/mother? quel âge a ton père/ta mère? **7**
  how's everything? ça va? **3**
  how's the weather? quel temps fait-il? **12**
  hundred cent **6**

hungry avoir faim **9**
  are you hungry? tu as faim? **9**
  I'm hungry j'ai faim **9**
  to be hungry *avoir faim **18**

I

I je **14**
  I don't know je ne sais pas **B, 17**
  I have a date/appointment at . . . j'ai un rendez-vous à... **4**
  I know je sais **B, 17**
  I'm fine/okay ça va **3**
  I'm (very) well/so-so/(very) bad ça va (très) bien/comme ci, comme ça/(très) mal **3**
ice la glace **9**
  ice cream une glace **9**
in à **14**; dans **17**
  in (Boston) à (Boston) **14**
  in class en classe **14**
  in front of devant **17**
  in the afternoon de l'après-midi **4**
  in the morning/evening du matin/soir **4**
  in town en ville **14**
information highway l'autoroute de l'information, l'Inforoute, le Cyberespace
interactive interactif (interactive)
interesting intéressant **19**
internal CD-ROM drive un lecteur optique interne **B**
Internet Internet, le Net
to **invite** inviter **15**
is (*see* **to be**)
  is there? est-ce qu'il y a? **17**
  isn't it (so)? n'est-ce pas? **14**
  there is il y a **17**
it il, elle **14, 18**
  what time is it? quelle heure est-il? **4**
  who is it? qui est-ce? **5, 17**
it's . . . c'est... **5**
  it's . . . (o'clock) il est... heure(s) **4**
  it's . . . francs ça fait... francs **11**
  it's fine/nice/hot/cool/ cold/bad (weather) il fait

beau/bon/chaud/frais/froid/ mauvais **12**
  it's (June) first c'est le premier (juin) **8**
  it's not . . . ce n'est pas... **20**
  it's raining il pleut **12**
  it's snowing il neige **12**
Italian italien, italienne **19**

J

January janvier *m.* **8**
Japanese japonais(e) **19**
juice le jus
  apple juice le jus de pomme **10**
  grape juice le jus de raisin **10**
  orange juice le jus d'orange **10**
  tomato juice le jus de tomate **10**
July juillet *m.* **8**
June juin *m.* **8**

K

keyboard le clavier
kind gentil (gentille) **19**
know connaître *(people)*; savoir *(facts)*
  do you know . . .? tu connais...? **6**
  I (don't) know je (ne) sais (pas) **B, 17**

L

lady une dame **5**
large grand **17, 20**
laserdisc un CD vidéo, un vidéodisque **B**
  laserdisc player un lecteur de CD vidéo
left gauche
lemon soda la limonade **10**
to **lend** prêter à
  lend me prête-moi **11**
less : less than moins de
let's talk parlons
to **like** aimer **15**
  do you like? est-ce que tu aimes? **13**

I (also) like j'aime (aussi) 13

I don't (always) like je n'aime pas (toujours) 13

I like . . ., but I prefer . . . j'aime..., mais je préfère... 13

I'd like je voudrais 9, 10, 13

what does he/she look like? comment est-il/elle? 17

what's he/she like? comment est-il/elle? 17

what would you like? vous désirez? 10

to **listen** écouter 15

to listen to the radio écouter la radio 13

little petit 17, 20

a little (bit) un peu 15

to **live** habiter 15

living room (formal) un salon

to **look (at)** regarder 15

look! tiens! 5, 18

look at that regarde ça 17

what does he/she look like? comment est-il/elle? 17

lot: a lot beaucoup 15

love: I'd love to je veux bien 13

more than plus: plus de

morning le matin

good morning bonjour 1

in the morning du matin 4

mother une mère 7

this is my mother voici ma mère 7

motorbike une mob (mobylette) 17

motorcycle une moto 17

motorscooter un scooter 17

mouse (computer) une souris B

mousepad un tapis de souris

movie theater un cinéma 14

at (to) the movies au cinéma 14

Mr. Monsieur (M.) 3

Mrs. Madame (Mme) 3

multimedia le multimédia

much: very much beaucoup 15

how much does . . . cost? combien coûte...? 11

how much is it? ça fait combien?, c'est combien? 11

I must je dois 13

my mon, ma; mes 7

my birthday is (March 2) mon anniversaire est (le 2 mars) 8

my name is . . . je m'appelle... 1

night: tomorrow night demain soir 4

nine neuf 1

nineteen dix-neuf 2

ninety quatre-vingt-dix 6

ninth: ninth grade troisième: en troisième

no non 2,14

no . . . pas de... 18

no? n'est-ce pas? 14

noon midi *m.* 4

not ne... pas 14

not a, not any pas de 18

not always pas toujours 13

it's (that's) not ce n'est pas 20

of course not! mais non! 14

notebook un cahier B

November novembre *m.* 8

now maintenant 15

on the average en moyenne
on vacation en vacances **14**
one un, une **1**
open *ouvrir
    open . . . ouvre... (ouvrez...)
    B
or ou **2, 14**
orange (color) orange (*inv.*) **20**
    orange juice le jus d'orange
    10
to **organize** organiser **15**
over there là-bas **14**
    that (one), over there ça, là-
    bas **17**
to **own** *avoir **18**

P

p.m. du soir **4**
pain: a pain pénible **20**
paper le papier **B**
    sheet of paper une feuille de
    papier **B**
party une boum, une fête, une
    soirée
past: half past . . . ...heure(s)
    et demie **4**
    quarter past . . . ...heure(s)
    et quart **4**
to **pay: pay attention** *faire
    attention **16**
pen un stylo **B, 17**
pencil un crayon **B, 17**
people des gens *m.* **18**; on
    people who like to use the
    Internet les internautes, les
    cybernautes
per: per day par jour
perhaps peut-être **14**
person une personne **5, 17**
pet un animal (*pl.* animaux)
    domestique **7**
to **phone** téléphoner **15**
piece: piece of chalk un
    morceau de craie **B**
pink rose **20**
pizza une pizza **9**
to **play** jouer **15**
    to play a game (match)
    *faire un match **16**
    to play basketball (soccer,
    tennis, volleyball) jouer au
    basket (au foot, au tennis, au
    volley) **13**
pleasant sympathique **19**

it's pleasant (good) weather
    il fait bon **12**
please s'il vous plaît (formal)
    10; s'il te plaît (informal) **9**
    please give me . . . s'il te
    plaît, donne-moi... **10**
poorly mal **3**
poster une affiche **17**
to **prefer** préférer
    I prefer je préfère **13**
    I like . . ., but I prefer . . .
    j'aime..., mais je préfère... **13**
pretty joli **17**
printer une imprimante
pupil un (une) élève **17**

Q

quarter un quart
    quarter of . . . ... heure(s)
    moins le quart **4**
    quarter past . . . ... heure(s)
    et quart **4**
quickly vite

R

racket une raquette **17**
radio une radio **17**
    to listen to the radio
    écouter la radio **13**
rain: it's raining il pleut **12**
rarely rarement **15**
rather assez **19**
to **read** lire
really: oh, really? ah bon? **16**
record un disque **17**
red rouge **20**
restaurant: at (to) the
    restaurant au restaurant **14**
    to have dinner at a
    restaurant dîner au
    restaurant **13**
right vrai **20**; droite
    right? n'est-ce pas? **14**
    all right d'accord **13**
room une chambre **17**; une salle
to **run** (referring to objects)
    marcher **17**

S

salad une salade **9**
same: the same things les
    mêmes choses

sandwich un sandwich **9**
Saturday samedi *m.* **8**
    see you Saturday! à samedi! **8**
to **say** *dire
    say! dis (donc)! **20**
    how do you say . . . in
    French? comment dit-on...
    en français? **B**
school friend un (une)
    camarade **17**
screen (computer, TV) un
    écran
season une saison **12**
    in every season en toute
    saison
    see: see you tomorrow! à
    demain! **8**
seldom rarement **15**
to **send** envoyer
    to send an e-mail message
    envoyer un message par
    e-mail
    to send a voice mail
    message envoyer un
    message par messagerie
    vocale
September septembre *m.* **8**
seven sept **1**
seventeen dix-sept **2**
seventy soixante-dix **5**
she elle **14, 18**
sheet of paper une feuille de
    papier **B**
shoe une chaussure
short court; petit **17, 20**
    he/she is short il/elle est
    petit(e) **17**
to **shut** fermer **B**
shy timide **19**
silly bête **19**
to **sing** chanter **13, 15**
sir Monsieur (M.) **3**
sister une soeur **7**
six six **1**
sixteen seize **2**
sixty soixante **3, 5**
small petit **17, 20**
snow: it's snowing il neige **12**
so alors **19**
so-so comme ci, comme ça **3**
    everything's (going) so-so
    ça va comme ci, comme ça **3**
soda un soda **10**
    lemon soda une limonade **10**
software un logiciel

some des **18**; quelques **17**; du, de la, de l'

sorry: to be sorry regretter
I'm sorry, but (I cannot) je regrette, mais (je ne peux pas) **13**

Spanish espagnol(e) **19**

to speak parler **15**
to speak French (English, Spanish) parler français (anglais, espagnol) **13**

spring le printemps **12**
in the spring au printemps **12**

steak un steak **9**
steak and French fries un steak-frites **9**

stereo set une chaîne stéréo **17**

student (high school) un (une) élève **17**; **(college)** un étudiant, une étudiante **17**

studies les études *f.*

to study étudier **13, 15**

stupid bête **19**

summer l'été *m.* **12**
in the summer en été **12**

Sunday dimanche *m.* **8**

supper: to have (eat) supper dîner **15**

sure bien sûr **13**
sure! mais oui! **14**

to swim nager **15**
I like to swim j'aime nager **13**

Swiss suisse **19**

T

table une table **B, 17**

to take *prendre **B**
to take a trip *faire un voyage **16**

to talk parler **15**
let's talk parlons

tall grand **17, 20**

tape: tape recorder un magnétophone **17**
cassette tape une cassette **B, 17**

tea le thé **10**

teacher un (une) prof **5, 17**; un professeur **17**

telephone un téléphone **17**

to telephone téléphoner **15**

television la télé **B, 17**
to watch television regarder la télé **13**

ten dix **1, 2**

tennis le tennis
to play tennis jouer au tennis **13**

tenth dixième

terrific chouette **20**; extra **20**; super **20**

test un examen
to pass a test réussir à un examen **27**

than que

thank you merci **3**

that que; ce, cet, cette
that is . . . c'est... **17, 20**
that (one), over there ça, là-bas **17**
that which, what ce que
what's that? qu'est-ce que c'est? **17**

that's . . . c'est... **5, 17, 20**; voilà **5**
that's . . . francs ça fait... francs **11**
that's bad c'est mal **20**
that's a good idea! c'est une bonne idée!
that's good (fine) c'est bien **20**
that's not . . . ce n'est pas... **20**

the le, la, l' **6, 18**; les **18**

theater un théâtre
movie theater un cinéma

their leur, leurs

them eux, elles; les
(to) them leur
themselves eux-mêmes

then alors **19**; ensuite

there là **14**
there is (are) il y a **17**
there is (here comes someone) voilà **5**
there is (some) il y a + du, de la; voilà + du, de la *(partitive)*
over there là-bas **14**
that (one), over there ça, là-bas **17**; ce...-là
what is there? qu'est-ce qu'il y a? **17**

these ces
these are ce sont **20**

they ils, elles **14**; eux; on
they are ce sont **20**

thin: to get thin maigrir

thing une chose
things are going (very) badly ça va (très) mal **3**
the same things les mêmes choses

to think penser
to think of penser de, trouver
to think that penser que
what do you think of . . .? comment trouves-tu...?, qu'est-ce que tu penses de...?

third troisième

thirsty: to be thirsty *avoir soif
are you thirsty? tu as soif? **10**
I'm thirsty j'ai soif **10**

thirteen treize **2**

thirty trente **3**

trois three **1**
trois heures et demie 4

this ce, cet, cette
this is . . . voici... **5**

those ces
those are ce sont **20**

thousand mille **6, 25**

Thursday jeudi *m.* **8**

tie une cravate

tights des collants *m.*

time: at what time is . . .? à quelle heure est...? **4**
at what time? à quelle heure? **4**
what time is it? quelle heure est-il? **4**

title un titre

to à **14**; chez
to (the) au, à la, à l', aux
in order to pour
to class en classe **14**
to someone's house chez + person
to whom à qui **16**

today aujourd'hui **8**
today is (Wednesday) aujourd'hui, c'est (mercredi) **8**

toilet les toilettes *f.*

tomato une tomate
tomato juice le jus de tomate **10**

tomorrow demain **8**
   tomorrow afternoon demain après-midi
   tomorrow is (Thursday) demain, c'est (jeudi) **8**
   tomorrow morning demain matin
   tomorrow night (evening) demain soir
   see you tomorrow! à demain! **8**
tonight ce soir
too aussi **2, 15**; trop
   too bad! dommage! **15**
touring bus un autocar, un car
tourist: tourist office office (*m.*) de tourisme
town un village
   in town en ville **14**
track suit un survêtement
train un train
   by train en train
to travel voyager **13, 15**
   trip: to take a trip *faire un voyage **16**
trousers un pantalon
true vrai **20**
T-shirt un tee-shirt
Tuesday mardi *m.* **8**
tuna le thon
to turn tourner
   to turn on *mettre
TV la télé **B, 17**
   to watch TV regarder la télé **13**
twelfth douzième
twelve douze **2**
twenty vingt **2, 3**
two deux **1**

us nous
   (to) us nous
to use utiliser

V ────────────────

vacation les vacances *f.*
   on vacation en vacances **14**
   summer vacation les grandes vacances
VCR (videocassette recorder) un magnétoscope **B**
veal le veau
vegetable un légume
very très **19**
   very well très bien **15**
   very much beaucoup **15**
videocassette une vidéocassette **B**
videodisc un CD vidéo **B**
   videodisc player un lecteur de CD/vidéo
violin un violon
to visit (place) visiter **15**; (people) rendre visite à
voicemail la messagerie vocale
volleyball le volley (volleyball)

W ────────────────

to wait (for) attendre
walk une promenade
to take (go for) a walk *faire une promenade à pied **16**
to walk *aller à pied; marcher **17**
walkman un walkman **17**
to want *avoir envie de; *vouloir
   do you want . . .? tu veux...? **9**
   do you want to . . .? est-ce que tu veux...? **13**
   I don't want . . . je ne veux pas... **13**
   I want . . . je veux... **13**
   I want to je veux bien
   what do you want? qu'est-ce que tu veux? **9**; vous désirez? **10**
wanted voulu (*p.p. of* *vouloir)
warm chaud **12**
   to be warm (people) *avoir chaud
   it's warm (weather) il fait chaud **12**
was été (*p.p. of* *être)

to wash laver
to waste perdre
   watch une montre **17**
to watch regarder **15**
   to watch TV regarder la télé **13**
water l'eau *f.*
   mineral water l'eau minérale
to waterski *faire du ski nautique
waterskiing le ski nautique
we nous **14**; on
to wear *mettre; porter
weather: how's (what's) the weather? quel temps fait-il? **12**
   it's . . . weather il fait... **12**
Wednesday mercredi *m.* **8**
week une semaine **8**
   last week la semaine dernière
   next week la semaine prochaine
   this week cette semaine
weekend un weekend
   last weekend le weekend dernier
   next weekend le weekend prochain
   this weekend ce weekend
weight: to gain weight grossir
well bien **15**
   everything's going (very) well ça va (très) bien **3**
well! eh bien!
   well then alors **19**
went allé (*p.p. of* *aller)
what comment? quoi? **17**; qu'est-ce que **16**
   what color? de quelle couleur? **20**
   what day is it? quel jour est-ce? **8**
   what do you think of . . .? comment trouves-tu...?, qu'est-ce que tu penses de...?
   what do you want? qu'est-ce que tu veux? **9**; vous désirez? **10**
   what does . . . mean? que veut dire...? **B**
   what does he/she look like? comment est-il/elle? **17**
   what is it? qu'est-ce que c'est? **17**

what is there? qu'est-ce qu'il y a? **17**

what time is it? quelle heure est-il? **4**

what would you like? vous désirez? **10**

what's . . .'s name? comment s'appelle...? **6**

what's he/she like? comment est-il/elle? **17**

what's his/her name? comment s'appelle-t-il/elle? **17**

what's that? qu'est-ce que c'est? **17**

what's the date? quelle est la date? **8**

what's the price? quel est le prix?

what's the weather? quel temps fait-il? **12**

what's your address? quelle est ton adresse? **21**

what's your name? comment t'appelles-tu? **1**

at what time is . . .? à quelle heure est...? **4**

at what time? à quelle heure? **4, 16**

when quand **16**

when is your birthday? c'est quand, ton anniversaire? **8**

where où **14, 16**

where is . . .? où est...? **14**

where is it? où est-ce?

from where? d'où?

whether si

which quel (quelle)

that which, what ce que

white blanc (blanche) **20**

who qui **16**

who's that/this? qui est-ce? **5, 17**

whom: about whom? de qui? **16**

for whom? pour qui? **16**

of whom? de qui? **16**

to whom? à qui? **16**

with whom? avec qui? **16**

why pourquoi **16**

wife une femme

to win gagner

window une fenêtre **B, 17**

to windsurf *faire de la planche à voile

windsurfing la planche à voile

winter l'hiver *m.* **12**

in the winter en hiver **12**

with avec **14**

with me avec moi **13**

with you avec toi **13**

with whom? avec qui? **16**

"with it" dans le coup

woman une dame (polite term) **5**; une femme **17**

to work travailler **13, 15**; *(referring to objects)* marcher **17**

does the radio work? est-ce que la radio marche? **17**

it (doesn't) work(s) well il/elle (ne) marche (pas) bien **17**

world le monde

World Wide Web le Web ("la toile d'araignée")

would: I'd like je voudrais **9, 10, 13**; j'aimerais

to write *écrire

wrong faux (fausse) **20**

to be wrong *avoir tort

Y

year un an, une année **8**

he/she is . . . (years old) il/elle a... ans **7**

I'm . . . (years old) j'ai... ans **7**

to be . . . (years old) *avoir... ans **18**

yellow jaune **20**

yes oui **2, 14**; *(to a negative question)* si! **18**

yes, of course oui, bien sûr **13**

yes, okay (all right) oui, d'accord **13**

yes, thank you oui, merci **13**

yesterday hier

yesterday afternoon hier après-midi

yesterday morning hier matin

yogurt le yaourt

you tu, vous **14**; on

you are . . . tu es + *nationality* **2**

and you? et toi? **1**

(to) you te, vous

your ton, ta; tes **7**; votre; vos

what's your name? comment t'appelles-tu? **1**

young jeune **17**

Z

zero zéro **1**

Photo Credits

Cover: photo: Owen Franken © D. C. Heath; cover design, Elliot Kreloff.

All text photos by Owen Franken, © D. C. Heath, except the following: 1: *t*, Bruno Joachim/Liaison Agency; 2: *mr*, Palmer-Brilliant © D.C. Heath; 2: *bl*, Jack Elness/Miller-Comstock; 3: *tl*, P.W. Holzgraf/ Monkmeyer Press; 3: *tr*, Kennon Cooke/Valan Photos; 3: *ml*, VPG/Woods; 3: *mr*, Susan Doheny; 3: *bl*, Jack Mitchell/ Boston Ballet Co.; 3: *br*, Andrew Brilliant; 6: *b* David Ball/The Picture Cube; 7: *m*, Brian Robb; 7: *b*, G. Barone /Monkmeyer Press; 12, 13 Adine Sagalyn; 16: *t*, Yves Levy; 19: *t*, Ann Purcell; 19: *b*, Carl Purcell; 20: *l*, Mark Antman/The Image Works; 23: *bl*, 24: br, Patrick Pipard, Adine Sagalyn; 26: VPG/Woods; 28: *b*, Yves Levy; 30: *br*, Palmer-Brilliant © D.C. Heath; 32: Peter Menzel/Stock Boston; 34: Yves Levy; 36: *t*, VPG/Woods; 37: *t*, Patrick Pipard; 38: *tm*, Nancy Sheehan; 38: *bm*, Patrick Pipard; 41: *m*, Ken Kaminsky/Nawrocki Stock Photo; 41: *b*, G. Zimbel/Monkmeyer Press; 45: *t*, Adine Sagalyn; 47: Patrick Pipard; 52: *m*, Palmer-Brilliant © D.C. Heath; 53: *tl, tm*, Patrick Pipard; 53: *tr*, Palmer-Brilliant © D.C. Heath; 53: *bl*, Adine Sagalyn; 53: *bm*, Henebry Photography © D.C. Heath; 54: *tl*, J. A. Wilkinson/Valan Photos; 54: *tm*, Kevin Galvin/Stock Boston; 54: *tr*, H. Mark Weidman; 54: *ml*, © Horii/-International Stock Photo; 54: *mm*, Ed Carlin/The Picture Cube; 54: *mr*, Mike Malyszko/Stock Boston; 54: *b*, Lynn McLaren/The Picture Cube; 57: *t*, J. Charlas; 57: *b*, Sophie Reiter; 58: J. Charlas; 61: Yves Levy; 63: *t*, 64b, 65 Adine Sagalyn; 66: *b*, 67 m, *b* Susan Doheny; 69, 71: *t*, 72: *b*, 73: br, Adine Sagalyn; 76–77: Sophie Reiter; 77: *t, mr, br*, 78: *tl*, *bl, br*, Patrick Pipard; 78: *mr*, Sophie Reiter; 78: *tr, ml, ml*, Yves Levy; 78: *tm*, VPG/Woods; 79: Yves Levy; 80: *tl*, "The Bridge at Mantes," Musée de Louvre; 80: *tr*, Scala Art Resource; 80: *b*, Yves Levy; 84–85: Patrick Pipard; 86: Yves Levy; 86–87: Adine Sagalyn; 87: *t*, Patrick Pipard; 87, 89: *mr*, 90: Yves Levy; 92: Adine Sagalyn; 83: Yves Levy; 94: Sophie Reiter; 96, 97 *t*, *mr* Patrick Pipard; 97: *ml*, Yves Levy; 101, 104: *tr, bm, br*, Patrick Pipard; 110: Yves Levy; 118: *t, b*, Carl Purcell; 118: *m*, J. Pavlovsky/ Sygma; 119: *t*, Yves Levy; 119: *b*, UNESCO/ Français-Hamell/Interphot; 130: *b*, Richard Lucas/The Image Works; 133: #4, Carl Purcell; 134: *l*, Yves Levy; 135: *t*, © D.C. Heath; 134–135: Yves Levy; 138: Adine Sagalyn; 139: *t*, D. Logan/H. Armstrong Roberts; 139: *l-r* Richard Pasley/Stock Boston, Jocelyn Boutin/The Picture Cube, Ann Purcell, Bob Daemmrich/Stock Boston, Carl Purcell, Fujihara-Ivamur/ Monkmeyer Press; 140, 143: Patrick Pipard; 144: Adine Sagalyn; 146: Palmer-Brilliant © D.C. Heath; 147: Adine Sagalyn; 148: *l*, Mike Mazzaschi/Stock Boston; 148: *r*, Robert Fried/Stock Boston; 149: *t*, Dallas & John Heaton/Stock Boston; 149: *b*, © Tabuteau/The Image Works; 154: Patrick Pipard; 160: *r*, Yves Levy; 162: *l*, Adine Sagalyn; 162: *r*, Patrick Pipard; 163: *l*, Yves Levy; 163: *r*, Sophie Reiter; 167: Patrick Pipard; 169: *tl*, Sipa Press; 169: *tr*, Paul J. Sutton/Duomo; 169; *bl*, Claude Gassian; 169: *br*, Pool Passation de Pouvoir/ Mitterand-Chirac/Gamma; 170: Patrick Pipard; 171: *t*, Philippe Gontier/The Image Works; 171: *b*, Palmer-Brilliant © D.C. Heath; 175: Patrick Pipard; 176: Adine Sagalyn; 177: Andrew Brilliant; 181: Sophie Reiter; 182: *b*, Meauxsoone/Sygma.